A Soldier's Race for Gold in the Shadow of War

Kortney Clemons
with Bill Briggs

WILEY

John Wiley & Sons, Inc.

Photo Credits: Photographs on pages 101 through 110 courtesy of the Clemons family. Photographs on pages 111 through 113 © Steve G. Manuel.

Published by John Wiley & Sons, Inc., Hoboken, New Jersey
Published simultaneously in Canada

For general information about our other products and services, please contact our Customer Care Department within the United States at (800) 762-2974, outside the United States at (317) 572-3993 or fax (317) 572-4002.

Wiley also publishes its books in a variety of electronic formats. Some content that appears in print may not be available in electronic books. For more information about Wiley products, visit our web site at www.wiley.com.

Library of Congress Cataloging-in-Publication Data:

Clemons, Kortney, date.
    Amped: a soldier's race for gold in the shadow of war / Kortney Clemons with Bill Briggs.
        p.   cm.
    Includes index.
    ISBN 978-0-470-28137-6 (cloth)
        1. Clemons, Kortney, 1980–   2. Runners (sports)—United States—Biography.
3. Athletes with disabilities—United States—Biography.   I. Briggs, Bill, 1963–   II. Title
    GV1061.15.C54C54   2008
    796.42092—dc22
    [B]
                                                                              2008003760

Printed in the United States of America

10 9 8 7 6 5 4 3 2 1

This is dedicated to my mom, Lois, my pops, Mitch, my brother, Maurice, my daughter, Daytriona, and all the people who are close to me. Without you, I wouldn't have gotten as far as I've made it today.

—Kortney Clemons

For Nancy. She believed. Always.

—Bill Briggs

Contents

Acknowledgments

This memoir could not have been fully told without the help of many other soldiers, prosthetists, therapists, coaches, and, of course, my family. There are many to thank: my parents, Mitch and Lois Clemons; my cousin, Debbie Poe; my fellow soldiers Jonathan Hart, John Shatto, Bryce Rigby, Dan Perseke, Chad Turner, Evan Morgan, Connie (Spinks) Ross, and Mario Rodas; historian Harold Graham; John Fergason, chief of prosthetics at Brooke Army Medical Center; Matt Parker, my physical therapist at BAMC; John Register, Associate Director of Outreach and Development for U.S. Paralympics; Beth Bourgeois, communications manager for the Paralympic Division of the U.S. Olympic Committee; Peter Harsch, prosthetist at the Naval Medical Center in San Diego; U.S. Paralympic powerlifting coach Mary Hodge; Teri Jordan, disability recreation programs coordinator for Penn State; Tim Rayer, prosthetist and owner of Prosthetic Innovations; my fellow sprinter Wardell Swann; Dave Johnson, director of the Penn Relays; Troy Engle, U.S. Paralympics Track & Field National Team Head Coach; my literary agents, Frank Scatoni and Greg Dinkin; and Jerry Kerr, president and founder of Disability Rights Advocates for Technology. I must also acknowledge the eternal sacrifices made by Jason Timmerman, David Day, Jesse Lhotka, and their families.

I also want to thank everybody at all the military hospitals who are helping our wounded soldiers. I've been inspired by so many injured men and women who are simply fighting to be good fathers and mothers again, who are battling to restore the quality of their lives. Their comeback stories are equally important.

I have learned from people like John Register, a top figure at U.S. Paralympics, that amputees can thrive and accomplish important things in this world. He and others have taught me that pursuing an athletic dream can be fulfilling, but that there's also more to life than winning and losing in sports.

Finally, and mainly, I want to acknowledge all the wounded soldiers I have met and seen during my visits to military hospitals. When I watch a man without any legs or a soldier without a leg and an arm sweating through another day of physical therapy, it makes me want to work even harder in my life. With this book, I hope to properly represent those veterans and honor their mentality, their defiance, their toughness, and their bravery.

Author's Note

In writing this book, I've also told the stories of other people who are important to me. Many interviews with family, friends, doctors, therapists, prosthetists, coaches, and fellow soldiers were conducted to gather their recollections of the events described in this book, to hear what they were seeing, feeling, or thinking during the moments I have shared in these pages. In some instances, I learned details of my own story for the very first time. In other cases, hearing their vivid accounts triggered new symptoms of PTSD. Still, I realized that writing this book was just another part of my journey and a chance to better understand the wounds I sustained, to celebrate the accomplishments of all wounded vets who are fighting to restore their lives.

PART I

BLOOD AND TEARS

1

Medic Down

My last minutes in Iraq—my final seconds as a two-legged man—were spent helping a wounded soldier I had never met before and would never meet again. I was a combat medic. And this was my job. But on that morning, two weeks before I was scheduled to come home, I just happened to be working twenty feet from a huge, hidden bomb.

I was crouching in the dirt beside a four-lane Baghdad highway, bandaging the man. As I inserted an IV drip into his arm, jabbed a morphine pin into his thigh, and checked the deep gashes on his left leg, somebody was watching me from the window of a nearby building. He also had a job—to flash a signal light to another insurgent who stood ready to trigger the bomb with a simple call from his cell phone.

"Everything is going to be all right, man," I told the injured soldier, a military police officer from Minnesota. He was my age, twenty-four. "The chopper is coming to get you. Everything is going to be fine."

I also was saying those words for myself. For eleven and three-quarter months, I had survived numerous street patrols, raids on suspected insurgent houses, and middle-of-the-night mortar attacks on our base. I had seen an innocent Iraqi man shot to pieces, and I had been deeply shaken by the bombing death of a good friend. In about fourteen days, though, I expected to be safely back on American soil, wrapping my arms around my family, my friends, and my daughter. Everything was going to be fine.

"I've made it through this," I had told my mom, Lois, early that same morning, February 21, 2005, speaking on an army satellite phone. I was so excited for my upcoming trip home that I'd bolted awake at three in the morning, long before anyone else in the barracks. I'd strolled alone in the darkness across the base to use the phone. Then, for better reception, I had walked up and out to the roof of the command building at Camp Falcon—our walled-in foothold in southwestern Baghdad. On some nights, insurgents would launch mortar shells into the compound from surrounding neighborhoods. A few had exploded in the rocky ground next to our barracks, shaking the walls, breaking windows, and jarring us awake. During those blitzes, I worried that I'd have to rush out into the darkness to patch up wounded friends. Getting back to sleep was always tough. Those attacks would leave me on edge for years. But up on the roof early that Monday morning, the skies were quiet. I knew that anything could still happen to me, but I couldn't help counting down the days.

"I can't wait to see you all," I'd told my mom.

"Well, the Lord brought you this far," she had replied. Back in Mississippi, Mom and Dad had just finished their Sunday dinner. "Just be careful. . . . Two more weeks."

Soon after my call home, at about four o'clock, I began my workday—a routine patrol of the streets near Camp Falcon. Our task was to break in a fresh group of soldiers who were preparing to take our place. We needed to teach them how to maneuver through the neighborhoods, how to quickly and safely raid a house, how to best navigate Baghdad. My job classification was a 91-Whiskey or 91W, army shorthand for combat medic. I was attached to a platoon in the Bravo Company of 1st Battalion, 8th Cavalry Regiment—a heavy-armored regiment based at Ford Hood, Texas, yet with historic roots that coil back to the days of horse-mounted soldiers fighting in the Indian Wars of the Old West. A little ironic, since I'm part Native American.

Although I had been specially trained to treat wounds, I was a soldier first. Along with my medical kit, I carried an M-16—an air-cooled, magazine-fed rifle capable of firing up to thirty rounds per clip. I carried seven clips. During our occasional raids on insurgent houses, I often used that rifle to guard rooms full of Iraqi civilians while other U.S. soldiers scoured the rest of the dwellings for the bad guys.

Our convoy—eventually headed toward that wounded MP—consisted of three armored Humvees. Inside the rear truck, I rode in the backseat just behind my platoon sergeant, John Shatto, a bass-fishing fanatic with a slight Southern twang who had become a friend while in Iraq. I was wearing my usual field gear: desert combat boots, sand-colored fatigues, Kevlar helmet, and a green outer vest lined with bulletproof ceramic plates covering my chest and back—twenty-five pounds of body armor. Also on board was my aid bag that held intravenous needles, tubing and fluid, a tool for opening airways, two morphine pins, antibacterial cream, aspirin tablets, and lots of gauze. In a few hours, I would count on some of those items to save not only another soldier but also myself.

As we turned off an asphalt highway and bounced onto the streets of a residential neighborhood in south Baghdad, I felt the small notebook pressing against the back right pocket of my pants. This was the only noncombat item I carried, but it was as important to me as all the body armor I wore. The durable *All-Weather Field Book* was used by soldiers to jot down critical information about their daily missions—routes through the city, seat assignments inside the convoy vehicles, who had the job of blocking traffic during raids, any bad guys we thought to be in the area. Mine contained tactical notations like "Stay behind equipment/vehicle," "no wandering around," and "Kevlar on if engine on." But in addition to all those battlefield reminders, my little book was packed with personal writings. During my eleven-plus months in Iraq, I had used quiet moments before bed or spare minutes during the trips to other bases to sit and record my spiritual journey in a time of war. I would write down my thoughts about, say, the previous Sunday's Scripture reading, how the base chaplain had interpreted it, and how that message applied to my life in Baghdad.

"'I know what I am planning for you,' says the Lord. 'I have good plans for you, not plans to hurt you. I will give you hope and a good future,'" I wrote in one passage. Then I gave my interpretation. "God reveals that there is no reason to worry about tomorrow because He plans to bless us with an expected end, not a disaster."

"In the Bible, the words 'servant' and 'minister' have the same meaning just as well as 'service' and 'ministry.' My life is my ministry," I wrote on another page. "God intentionally allows me to go through things so that I can comfort the next person."

When I encountered a rough situation in camp or in the civilian areas, I described how those same biblical lessons had applied to those real-world moments. I felt the Lord was showing me important things about life and people during my time in Iraq. On the light brown cover of the notebook, even my doodles spoke to my time at war: "Perfect love cast out fear!!!" I scrawled one day. He was showing me my purpose. Sometimes, I pulled out my spiritual journal and just skimmed old passages to reflect on how my faith was holding up—or maybe growing—during the most brutal year I had ever faced.

Back in Mississippi, I had attended a Baptist church every Sunday morning, so I was intrigued that a bloody, modern war was being waged against a timeworn backdrop common to the Bible, in places I had often read about in the Scriptures. I was patrolling roads, raiding houses, and treating wounded people in an area once called Mesopotamia, the land between the Euphrates and Tigris rivers. Less than fifty miles to the south of my bunk at Camp Falcon sat the ancient ruins of Babylon and the tomb of the prophet Ezekiel. This was a sacred place. Thinking about that kept me grounded. I didn't feel like the little book in my back pocket offered me any protection against the bombs and bullets. It was just tangible proof to me that I was trying to live my life properly in Iraq, making the right choices, and hopefully becoming a better person. But soon my iron-clad faith would be invaded by anger and confusion. In time, I'd be asking God some hard questions.

One of my final entries, written hastily, seemed to foreshadow what was looming.

"Spirit of God led Jesus into wilderness to be tempted," I wrote. "God will take you to the fight."

In the neighborhood south of Baghdad, we rolled past clusters of palm trees—a tropical looking scene but far from laidback. To emphasize that point, many of the houses sat behind concrete walls and thick metal gates. I always felt most vulnerable while riding through Baghdad in a vehicle. I much preferred being on foot with my guys around me. Roadside bombs were a common and cowardly weapon of choice among the insurgents. I saw whole streets dented with craters from past IEDs—improvised explosive devices—which were nothing more than old battlefield munitions like mortars, commercial explosives, or homemade bombs buried next to highways and often triggered remotely, timed for big body counts. As of March 24, 2008, 47 percent of the four thousand U.S. soldiers killed in Iraq were the victims of roadside bombs.

Death by car is an unofficial theme of this war: our Humvees hitting their IEDs; their truck bombs wiping out entire Sunni markets or ripping through Shia shrines. The first death I ever witnessed—the first body I ever saw at home or at war—involved a car. One week after I was deployed to Iraq in March 2004, our unit was ordered to guard an Iraqi police station to ward off a threatened Al Qaeda attack. In the middle of the night, a civilian vehicle rolled quietly down the road and stopped dead near the police station entrance. From the oil refinery just next door to us, Iraqi civilian security guards—also poised for the rumored Al Qaeda assault—suddenly opened fire on the car. Then our soldiers started shooting at the car. In the shower of bullets, the Iraqi man behind the wheel was killed, but he hadn't come to do any damage. As it turned out, his car had just stalled and he had the awful luck of coming to rest in the wrong place at the wrong time. I understood that in the bizarre commotion of war, mistakes happen. Still, while I was shaking off the moment, my mind raced: *That was crazy! Oh my God, is this what it's going to be like the whole time I'm here?* The worst was yet to come.

At about six o'clock that morning, our Humvee driver abruptly hit the brakes and stopped outside a small Iraqi house protected by a six-foot metal gate and a concrete wall. It was time to show the rookies how to do a raid. The idea was to quickly burst through the gate and the front door, gaining entry and launching a search before anyone inside even realized what was happening. I showed the new guys how and where to kick the gate down, ignoring the loud, metallic crash as it fell. From there, without breaking stride, our platoon sprinted up to and through the front door, then into the house. The people inside all were asleep and the raid turned out to be a quiet one. We found no evidence of insurgent activity and left the house as quickly as we had come.

Our final task before returning to Camp Falcon was to show the replacements the best route to the Green Zone—a six-square-mile fortification of government, military, and diplomatic compounds in central Baghdad, all protected by blast walls, barbed-wire checkpoints, and Abrams tanks. (Today, that sector has been designated as the International Zone.) The Green Zone also was home to one trauma center, the 86th Combat Support Hospital or CSH. Making a word out of that army acronym as we always did, we just called it the "cash." Formerly Ibn Sina Hospital and once favored by Saddam Hussein's supporters, the bustling facility had gained some fame in a powerful TV documentary called "Baghdad ER." With its elite medical staff, the CSH helped boost the survival rate for wounded U.S. troops to 90 percent, the highest war survival rate in history.

Any soldier who is new to Baghdad needs to know how to get to the CSH, and get there fast. I had learned that lesson firsthand. One night early in my tour, not long after I watched the innocent Iraqi man get shot dead, we were back at that same Iraqi police station, guarding against another possible attack. On the horizon, we could see a battle raging. Amber-colored bullet tracers cut back and forth across the dark skyline. Not long after that, we spotted a lone Humvee rolling up to our front door. In Baghdad, U.S. Army trucks always travel in convoys for better protection. When we saw that single Hummer approach, we thought insurgents had possibly hijacked one of our vehicles during the firefight and now were trying to escape. But then I heard one of the soldiers in the truck screaming in English. They were in trouble.

I raced from the police station to the back of the Humvee, in the process leaving my weapon behind. Not a smart move, but I figured these guys had to get to the hospital fast, and I could show them the way. Inside the Humvee, one soldier was cradling the bloody thigh of another. I instantly recognized the soldier holding the leg as Specialist Taylor Burk, a fellow medic and a guy I had served with at Fort Hood. As I helped navigate their driver through the dark streets and toward the CSH, Burk told me that their convoy had been strafed by gunfire during a night patrol. Their Humvee, not yet fitted with protective armor, had been pierced several times. Two bullets had struck their gunner, Specialist Joseph Bridges, as he stood in the turret, one hitting him in the jaw and the other in the thigh, which was now hemorrhaging from an artery that Burk had wrapped with a tourniquet. Every minute mattered. As we barreled toward the Green Zone, Bridges was screaming in pain. About that time, Burk confided to me that he also had taken a bullet in the heel. They had been trying to reach the CSH when they got lost and found us.

Minutes later, we pulled into the Green Zone and arrived at the hospital. Someone had radioed ahead that were we en route. Several doctors met us at the door and took Bridges and Burk inside for treatment. Burk later received the Bronze Star and a Purple Heart for his actions that night. But in war, there is often a sad ending to these heroic stories. After six months of physical therapy back in the States, Burk convinced his superiors to let him return to Iraq and, later, to replace another combat medic who had been hurt in action. In January 2005—about one month to the day before my morning mission—a chunk of shrapnel from a roadside bomb sliced into Burk's neck and killed him. He was twenty-one. Among the people at his funeral was Joseph Bridges. Burk will always remain an inspiration to me, a prime example of the dangerous work performed by combat medics in Iraq and a reminder that we came there to serve, to help one an other and the people we encountered. Burk's life was truly about service. I was trying to live that way, too.

As we rolled past the armed checkpoints of the Green Zone, en route to the CSH, it was approaching eight o'clock. Our sector had seemed calm but it was a small relief to be inside the blast walls. When we stopped and piled out of our trucks at the three-story hospital, I peeled away from the guys to jog across the street to the Tactical Operations Center, a communications hub. My first cousin, Sgt. Debbie Poe, worked at the TOC and also in the emergency room at the hospital next door. When she wasn't compiling paperwork for the Pentagon on casualties who came through the ER doors, Debbie had several other duties, including finding additional bed space at other hospitals in Baghdad. The CSH accepted anyone wounded in battle—Americans, Brits, Iraqis who fought side-by-side with coalition troops, even insurgents. There were days when an injured U.S. soldier lay in one ER bed while an insurgent who had just tried to kill him rested in a bed across the aisle. After a "mass-cal"—army talk for a massive casualty event like a hotel bombing—the hospital would be flooded with fresh wounded. It was Debbie's job to call her medical contact at an Iraqi hospital in the unsecured neighborhood nearby and arrange for some Iraqi patients to be moved to that facility. During other medical scrambles, Debbie was pulled into the fray and asked by the ER docs to clean patient wounds, take vital signs, or tag bodies.

At the TOC, I gave Debbie a hug and a smile. She is fifteen years older than me. My mom and her dad were sister and brother. We each had been raised amid the same thick pine groves, had ridden our bikes on the same dirt road that cuts through our remote little pocket of family homes in rural east Mississippi. I still have a fuzzy photo of a teenage Debbie; my brother, Maurice; a few other cousins; and me, all wearing fancy Sunday clothes and glum faces, all gathered for the funeral of my dog, Blackie. Seeing her at the TOC stoked my excitement about my pending trip home.

"So this is where you work?" I asked.

"Yeah, this is where I work at," Debbie answered.

"This is really nice. Y'all got it made here," I said.

"So I've been thinking about what I'm going to do when my tour is over," Debbie said. "What are *you* going to do?"

"I don't know," I replied. Really, my only plans for the moment were to laugh with my loved ones, to taste some good Southern cooking, and hopefully to get back into college and play some football again. I still had this burning dream of playing in the NFL someday.

"Well, think about it: maybe we should come back over here after our tours and work as contractors because they get paid a lot of money," Debbie said.

That was true. Compared to what we earned, civilian contractors were raking in thousands of dollars. Maybe, if college didn't work out, I could come back and work as a Baghdad firefighter for big bucks. Maybe.

"Well, I am going home next," I said. "I'll be there for a bit and then I report back to Fort Hood."

"Okay, well I'll be home in September," Debbie said. "We're definitely going to have to get together and do something."

It was time for me to rejoin my unit and make our way back to Camp Falcon. We hugged good-bye. I would indeed be seeing Debbie again, but our reunion would come much sooner than I thought.

I climbed back into the Humvee, and our convoy began its trip out of the Green Zone, moving southwest through the city. I was hungry and ready for a meal. About fifteen minutes after we left the hospital, we entered the increasingly lawless Dora neighborhood. Staff Sgt. Bryce Rigby, a twenty-two-year-old outdoorsman from Utah, made a decision. Riding shotgun—the command seat—in the lead Humvee, Rigby told his driver to steer the convoy onto 60th Street, a notorious stretch of murder and mayhem.

"Let's take these new guys down there and show them what it is," Rigby said.

Six weeks earlier, on that same road, Baghdad's deputy police chief and his son had been ambushed as they drove to work. Gunmen had raked their car with bullets, killing both. It was a political assassination with a cold purpose. In areas populated by the Sunni Muslim minority, insurgents had stepped up attacks in early 2005. They intended to scare people from registering to vote for the January 30, 2005, elections that would create the new 275-member National Assembly. Then again, the sound of gunfire was nothing new on 60th Street and in the surrounding Dora neighborhood. Once a high-energy swath of mom-and-pop shops and white villas filled with a mix of Sunnis, Christians, and Shiite Muslims, Dora had steadily degenerated into chaos. During my time in Iraq, Dora's police stations and public infrastructure had been routinely bombed. Kidnappings were rampant, and its bustling market and legendary nightlife had been choked off. As a civil war brewed in late 2004, two Christian churches in Dora were bombed, driving out the small cluster of Christian residents. As 2005 began, Sunni militants increased their assaults on Shiite pilgrims who passed through Dora on their way to shrines in Najaf and Karbala. In late February, it was still a lethal place, and the new guys needed to get a look.

As we drove west on a frontage road that paralleled a major four-lane highway, we noticed that traffic on the highway had backed up, starting below an approaching overpass. Rigby was the first to spot the wreck, just ahead of us on the left. A sand-colored U.S. Army Humvee had rolled off the highway and flipped upside down onto a dirt shoulder that edged the frontage road, coming to rest against a utility pole. Its doors all hung open, and we saw a couple of American soldiers huddled over a man on the ground. More soldiers had cordoned off the immediate area, parking their remaining three Humvees in a pattern to create a 360-degree protective perimeter. This was Dora, after all. The frontage road and the far side of the highway were each bordered by rows of residential buildings, some with balconies. A crowd of Iraqis was standing and watching. Some were taking photos. The situation seemed tense. We skidded to a stop and jumped out to help.

I snatched my aid bag and sprinted to the injured soldier, Tijtong Vang, who lay face up, ten feet from his flipped Humvee. He was bleeding from a deep gash on the inside of his right leg, and he appeared to have a broken back.

Vang's platoon—there were about twelve on the ground that day—was a tight band of military policemen from the Minnesota National Guard, and many hailed from the small towns that dot western Minnesota's pine woods. Three were natives of Appleton, which has only about 2,800 people. Two of them were childhood friends. Their unit, part of the 151st Field Artillery, had been in Iraq for less than two months. That morning, their convoy had been bound for another army base where the MPs planned to do some target practice with their new rifles. Shortly after eight, just as we were leaving the Green Zone, their four trucks zoomed westbound toward this spot. When they neared a bridge that stretched atop the four-lane highway, the Humvees each began a zigzag maneuver—standard practice when approaching an overpass and a possible sniper's nest.

Inside Humvee No. 3, Vang had the wheel, gunner Corey Fennell stood in the turret with his head exposed, and team leader Sgt. Jesse Lhotka rode in the passenger seat. In mid-zag, their top-heavy truck suddenly lost traction on a patch of loose gravel, spun sideways, tipped, and began to roll onto its side, crumpling a metal guardrail along the dirt shoulder. A split second before the vehicle crashed onto its top, Lhotka yanked Fennell inside, saving him from possible decapitation. But in the tumble, Vang had been ejected. When the truck came to rest, Lhotka—"Lottie" to his friends—guided Fennell through the Humvee's rear hatch. Fennell had a bruised shoulder and could stand. Lhotka then darted over to the downed Vang and began applying hand pressure on his leg lacerations to control the bleeding. Our convoy had arrived about ten minutes later. The drama was just beginning.

Kneeling next to Vang, I bandaged the leg wound, inserted an IV drip into his arm, and injected him with one of my two morphine pins to ease the pain. I placed the other pin in one of my vest pockets.

"Hang in there," I said, trying to reassure him as I worked.

The other guys in my platoon parked our three Humvees in positions to help shore up the 360-degree perimeter. Our gunners stood in their turrets, rifles in hand, watching the crowd. Other soldiers from both units were in kneeling positions, rifles aimed, taking cover behind the guardrail—some crouching atop the buried bomb.

When I think about that IED now, tucked under the asphalt and armed for remote detonation maybe weeks or months before we got there, I can't help but shake my head. What are the odds that the MP's Humvee would crash there, so close to that deadly device? What are the chances that we would all be working next to it? During the seven minutes I spent stabilizing Vang, several soldiers stepped back and forth over the center guardrail, exactly above the bomb. And we would soon be carrying Vang's stretcher in a straight line to that IED. When I roll it all around in my head, I come up with the basic thought that it simply wasn't my time to die, and that I had more to do in this life.

No one had spotted the bomb, of course. After the truck accident, the Minnesota MPs had conducted an IED sweep, carefully inspecting the roadway, its gravel shoulders and center guardrail for any signs of man-made danger. The device—probably a 61-millimeter or 81-millimeter mortar shell—was in a covered hole next to the center guardrail between the two eastbound and westbound lanes. If it was typical of other IEDs, the insurgents who planted it would have dug a shallow trench in the soft soil next to the guardrail and then tunneled six to twelve inches under the asphalt edge of the westbound lanes, the side where the Humvee crashed. They would have positioned the base of the shell in the tunnel below the hardened tar because these rounds are "base-ejecting," meaning the tail explodes and forces hot chunks of asphalt—along with a spray of razor-sharp shrapnel—up and out of the hole. This makes the blast even more lethal: bystanders a hundred feet away can be knocked down and struck by flying shards of metal and rock. The insurgents would have placed the front end of the shell in the open part of the trench, packing the nose with a plastic explosive like C-4. They would have then attached a wire to the C-4 and pushed dirt and gravel back over the trench, leaving only part of the wire above ground—ready to be triggered later with a simple cell phone call. This end of the wire would have been carefully concealed as well, maybe with an empty soda can, plastic water bottle, or crumpled sandwich wrapper, or maybe just placed directly against a guard-rail post. However the insurgents did the deed, their bomb had been expertly camouflaged. And in a nearby building, someone watched and waited for the perfect moment to set it off.

Sure, it was implausibly bad luck to wind up next to an undetected IED that morning. But I soon would benefit from an incredible stroke of good fortune. Shatto—my platoon sergeant with the Southern drawl—asked one of the Minnesota MPs if they had already radioed for a Medivac helicopter to come and pick up Vang for transport to the CSH. In fact, the Minnesota soldiers already had called for a chopper, but the MP who spoke to Shatto told him he wasn't positive that a Blackhawk was on the way. So Shatto walked to his Humvee and radioed the Tactical Operations Center (where Debbie was working) and asked them to dispatch a Medivac to the crash site. Now, two were in the air, essentially to rescue one badly injured soldier. On a day when numerous battlefield heroes would emerge, that tiny miscommunication would help save the lives of Shatto and me.

We heard the first Blackhawk's thumping blades just a minute later. One of the Minnesota MPs, Staff Sgt. Chad Turner, laid down a one-by-three-foot marker on the highway as a suggested landing spot and then popped a red-smoke canister to help the pilot gauge the wind. With the chopper on the asphalt—sitting in the far eastbound lanes, maybe ten to twenty feet from the guardrail—Minnesota Staff Sgt. Dan Perseke walked Fennell to the Blackhawk and helped him through the side door where an air medic waited. Shatto also grabbed a backboard and a stretcher from the helicopter and carried them across the highway to me.

We carefully maneuvered Vang onto the backboard to make sure we didn't worsen his back injury during our eventual walk to the chopper. Then we eased him up onto the stretcher. I momentarily stepped away to pack up my aid bag because I planned to fly with Vang to the CSH. But when I returned to the stretcher, four guys were already standing at the corners, ready to hoist Vang and tote him across the highway. According to army protocol, litters are to be carried in a feet-first direction and the combat medic is supposed to hold the back right corner, next to the soldier's head, where he can give commands. Because one of the Minnesota MPs was already positioned at the back right corner, I stepped to the other side, intending to grab the back left corner. That's where my staff sergeant, Rigby, stood. Rigby, the young outdoorsman from Utah, figured he could just take that spot.

"No," I told him, "this is my job. I got it, Sergeant."

Rigby backed away. For years, this decision would haunt him. A number of soldiers would carry scars from that day—deep physical defects and invisible mental demons. Both are real, I would come to learn. Among many of the soldiers present that morning, many have been dogged ever since by a single, awful feeling: guilt. Like Rigby, they question decisions they made or didn't make, actions they took or didn't take, each blaming themselves. Of course, they were not responsible for what happened. And in this case, I had demanded to be on that stretcher because that was my job. Still, I also understand that Rigby, a leader and a good friend, wishes to this day that he had kept that corner. This is how professional soldiers are wired—to jump on the grenade and save our pals. Survivor's guilt is misplaced, quietly destructive, and, unfortunately, common in war.

"One, two, three, lift," I instructed.

Carrying the front left corner, about seven feet ahead of me, was Shatto, an army veteran of sixteen years who had attended church with me at Camp Falcon. The right side of the stretcher was all Minnesota National Guard guys. On the back right corner, across from me, was Lhotka. The twenty-four-year-old financial adviser had grown up in Appleton, a place that honors its war dead by naming streets after them. According to his sister, Lhotka had a "comforting smile that could warm the freezing rain." Walking three feet ahead of Lhotka was Staff Sgt. Dave Day, twenty-five, who had joined the National Guard to pay for his training to become a police officer. Prior to his deployment, Day had worked at the St. Louis Park police department in the Minneapolis suburbs. He had also married his high school sweetheart just five days before leaving home. In front of Day, on the right foot corner, was 1st Lt. Jason Timmerman, who had worked as a high school math and computer teacher in Lake Benton, a town of 703 people in southwestern Minnesota. Timmerman was known to write jokes at the top of every exam to help his students relax.

Up on our protective 360-degree perimeter, two more Appleton natives—Turner and Perseke—watched me and the other stretcher-bearers approach the guardrail. Turner, the staff sergeant who had laid down the ground marker for the chopper, had known Lhotka since childhood when Lhotka's grandmother was his babysitter. On the opposite side of the guardrail, the air medic from the Blackhawk stood and waited for our handoff.

Just behind him, the chopper's rotors spun and kicked up a breeze. It was ready for takeoff.

We reached the median and rested the foot-end of the stretcher on the top rail. That's when the man who had been watching me all along went to work. One of the Minnesota soldiers manning the perimeter noticed a bright flash in the window of a roadside building: the signal. Another insurgent in a nearby location saw the light, dialed a predetermined cell phone number, and triggered the bomb. At that moment, it was literally right beneath us. Here's the odd thing: I never heard the bang. But my father did.

Asleep in his bed back in Mississippi, Dad bolted awake and flung off his covers at the sound of a sharp explosion in his head. He shook it off as a nightmare but remained uneasy.

I hope Kortney is okay, he thought before fading back to sleep.

When I opened my eyes, the world looked blurry. I saw the blue, late morning sky on the horizon over Baghdad. I saw the brown dust and black smoke from the bomb, swirling around me. And I smelled something I will never forget—burnt flesh. I didn't know where that was coming from, but the air seemed filled with it.

The blast had knocked me on to my stomach with my face turned to my side. I knew I'd been hit although, strangely, I felt no pain. Instinctively, I began to pull myself across the pavement in an arm crawl, working back toward our Humvee on the frontage road, away from that guardrail. Shatto, also lying on the highway about fifteen feet from me, watched me wriggle about two body lengths, leaving a red trail in my wake. Shatto later would describe to me his ghastly list of injuries: he had shrapnel in his face, right arm, right upper chest cavity, and left leg; one sliver of metal had penetrated through one eye and into his brain; his left hand looked like hamburger; his right leg was laced with twenty-nine separate entry wounds and two exit wounds; and the bone in that same leg was so badly shattered, part of it was poking through the skin. In that state, he managed to make one and a half full-body rolls away from the guardrail because he expected a second IED to blow. When he looked up and saw me, he knew I was in far worse shape.

Both of my femoral arteries—the main blood supply for each leg—had been torn by shards of flying hot metal. I was gushing blood. My life was draining away in the asphalt. I also had chunks of shrapnel imbedded in my left heel, in my left big toe, and in my groin. But because I hadn't had a chance to examine myself, I didn't know the worst of it: my right leg was nearly amputated, hanging only by a few strands of tissue below my knee. My dangling right foot also had lost several toes. It was about then that I decided to try and stand up.

I owe my survival that day to a lot of heroic people, a couple of lucky breaks, and my state of mind. I was calm. Had I known the full scope of the human devastation nearby, had I understood the severity of my own wounds, I probably would have given up, lapsed into shock, and died. The scene around me was tragic. The horrific results showed that the stretcher had been directly over the bomb, although Shatto and I—carrying on the left side—were actually three to six inches closer to it than the guys on the right. I was the closest of all, standing basically on top of the unseen hole in the highway's edge. But the tail of the base-ejecting device had apparently been tilted to the right, releasing most of its deadly energy in that direction.

Turner—Lhotka's buddy since childhood—had been on the perimeter, watching our progress toward the guardrail and also keeping a sharp eye on the crowd of Iraqis that gathered after the accident. When the bomb detonated, his back was turned to the fireball, but he instantly whirled to see the carnage. The three Minnesota soldiers on the right side were blown into the air. From the foot of the stretcher to the head, Timmerman was hurled eight feet away, Day was thrown fifteen feet back, and Lhotka was sent skidding twenty feet across the pavement, landing in the middle of the inside, westbound lane. But Turner wouldn't know their exact identities until he reached the three men.

The second Minnesota staff sergeant, Perseke, had started walking toward the overturned Humvee when the blast erupted. Standing forty feet away, he took some small pieces of shrapnel in his triceps—something he never reported. From their respective positions, Perseke and Turner each bolted toward the badly injured MPs. Turner, a star high school running back, beat Perseke to the spot. First, he reached Timmerman, whose legs had been blown off, one at the thigh, the other at the knee. Turner saw that Timmerman's skin tone was already gray. He knew the math teacher was dead. Turner next checked on Day, the cop. Day had tumbled into a half-seated position with one of Timmerman's legs jammed beneath him. Turner could see that Day's right leg was attached only by fleshy fibers and that the back of his left thigh was gone. Worse, Day also had that grayish color of death. Finally, Turner raced to the third soldier who lay motionless face down but was otherwise intact. Turner couldn't find a pulse. Then he noticed the tape on the soldier's helmet. It read "Lhotka." A tiny piece of shrapnel had ripped into his friend's head, near the temple. Later, doctors would also find a fist-size hole in Lhotka's shoulder.

Perseke, who had been Lhotka's sergeant for five years, was now approaching, having just checked for any signs of a pulse in Timmerman and Day. Turner stood to deliver the news.

"Our three guys are gone," Turner said. "Lottie's dead."

Perseke started to lean down toward Lhotka. Turner tried to grab his arm to stop him.

"Dan, just don't," Turner said.

Perseke ignored him and knelt over his friend, crouching to avoid further explosions and possible bullets, not knowing if the attack would continue. He began trying to revive Lhotka with mouth-to-mouth resuscitation and chest compressions. When dark red blood oozed from Lhotka's mouth, Perseke stopped.

One week after Lhotka died, Perseke's pregnant wife, Lori, was helping decorate the church back in Appleton where Lhotka's funeral was about to be held. As she prepared for the event, Lori's water broke and hours later she gave birth to a daughter, Whitney. That single bomb sent emotional shock waves rumbling through many small towns in Minnesota. It marked the deadliest day for Minnesota soldiers since May 5, 1968, when nine died in Vietnam. At Timmerman's funeral in Marshall, the thousand-seat church couldn't accommodate the arriving crowd. Dozens had to be turned away at the door. At Day's funeral, a two-by-two procession of 110 squad cars with lights flashing drove silently through the town of Morris as a Blackhawk hovered overhead. In the streets, people laid down a carpet of pink, red, and peach roses.

Perseke couldn't linger over Lhotka for long. He scrambled to Vang, who was lying on his side, still strapped to the backboard. Perseke cut the webbing and eased Vang onto his back. Already dealing with deep leg lacerations and a broken back from the Humvee crash, Vang's body now was full of shrapnel. He would survive but, I'm told, he still has nightmares about that day. A lot of us do.

At the center guardrail, the air medic who had been waiting for the handoff now leaned limply over the top rail. He had a large chunk of shrapnel lodged in his bulletproof vest and a laceration on his right calf. Later, doctors would find that his stomach also had been hit with shrapnel. The air medic pushed himself upright and hobbled back toward the Blackhawk. He could see that the chopper's windshield had been blown out in the blast.

On the highway, about a hundred feet from me, my staff sergeant, Rigby, had been knocked on his backside. Some small bits of shrapnel had sailed into his face and arm, and his left eardrum had been blown out. From my stomach, I looked at him and we made eye contact. Still not knowing how badly I was injured, I used my arms to do a half push-up. Beneath me, I could see blood on the highway. The air around me was filled with the odor of burned hair, skin, and flesh. Later, I would find out this scent was coming from me. I also would learn that those burns to the massive wounds in my legs had helped save my life. I had been so close to the bomb, the fireball had partially cauterized my bleeding legs and slowed the flow, buying me a few extra minutes—precious time to get from the battlefield to the hospital before I bled out. But Rigby soon would play an even bigger role in my survival.

Before wobbling to his feet, Rigby saw me push myself up and then stand on my left foot. I began hopping in place. But in a matter of three or four seconds, Rigby had sprinted over and ordered me back to the ground.

"Sit down! Sit down! Sit down!" he yelled.

I did.

"You're going to be all right. You're going to be all right," Rigby said, trying to keep me calm as I had done for Vang minutes before. "Just relax."

As Rigby stuck his right hand into my badly damaged right leg in an attempt to fully control the bleeding, we heard the Blackhawk's engine roar to life. The banged-up chopper slowly began to lift into the air and evacuate—proper protocol when there has been an attack, but still hard to take when you're left lying on the ground.

Nearby, Perseke covered Vang's eyes to shield them from the dust and pebbles that were kicked up by the helicopter's blades. And from his back, Shatto watched the Blackhawk elevate into the blue sky and then disappear, leaving three severely injured soldiers behind.

"That sucks," Shatto said to himself.

We didn't know that a second Blackhawk was only a couple of minutes away, thanks our inadvertent earlier request. But in the sudden silence, Shatto wondered how much time we had before he and I bled to death.

As I lay on the pavement, blood continued to pool beneath me from my two ruptured arteries. Some of that blood slowly began seeping into my uniform pants, soaking my back pocket. Eventually, it reached the little book that held all my writings on faith, staining those pages red.

2

Southern Roots

The morning I lost my leg, I lost my identity. For as long as I could remember, I had been a football player. As a little boy, I practiced open-field jukes alone in my yard, a ball tucked in my arm. I had stretched that love of the game to a brief stint in the talent-rich junior college leagues of Mississippi. While in Iraq, I hit the weight room almost daily—sometimes twice a day—just so I could be physically ready to resume my college football career once I returned home. For fun, a few soldiers and I even played flag football on the grounds of Saddam Hussein's former home—a plush palace that, after the invasion, was turned into a recreation camp for coalition troops. I can still picture it: I'm wearing a black T-shirt and black shorts, cradling the football in both hands to protect it from defenders on my left and right, darting happily through Saddam's old backyard. Even in that strange place, football was my game. I had the skills, I believed, to play on a Division

I team and to someday make an NFL club. This is how I saw my future. This is how I defined myself. At our gym in Baghdad, I kept that football dream alive.

Located in the center of our Camp Falcon compound next to the chow hall, our weight room was bigger and nicer than some of the ritziest health clubs back in the States. The massive gym was jammed with weight racks, weight benches, resistance machines, elliptical trainers, treadmills, and stationary bikes. The walls were lined with floor-to-ceiling mirrors, small windows, and elevated televisions that aired music videos. We had speakers in the ceilings that boomed up-tempo tunes. We had an equipment desk where civilians handed out towels, footballs, basketballs, and jump ropes. We had a juice bar where we could order strawberry or banana smoothies. Probably the only difference between that fitness center and the ones back home: we leaned our rifles near the front door.

I hit the gym at least six times a week, usually in the mornings. My workouts alternated between lifting routines to strengthen my chest and back muscles and sets designed to target my biceps and triceps. I always mixed in some sweat-drenched cardio minutes on the stationary bike or the elliptical machine. If I had a mission scheduled the following day that would keep me on patrol until late, I often put in a second gym session the night before, focusing on my abs and legs. Most days, I exercised with a few soldiers from my platoon, but as we inched closer to the day we were scheduled to fly home, the gym got more crowded. Guys were bulking up for planned beach vacations with their wives, or because they were buying motorcycles and wanted to look good on their new bikes. For me, it was always about getting back on the football field. Five years earlier, barely out of my teens, I'd been cut by two different college programs because I had been considered a bit too small. As a 145-pound cornerback, I was as quick as a water bug with the ability to cover anybody on pass routes. But coaches felt

I didn't have the size to consistently make big hits. Truthfully, this was a big reason I entered the army and, eventually, found myself in a war zone.

While in the military, I fully committed myself to the weight room. I never wavered. Even when my platoon was ordered to guard a power plant in Baghdad for a few weeks, I found a flat, padded bench, a bar, and a stack of weight plates at the industrial complex—just enough to crank out some bench-press sets. The workouts reminded me of sunny days back home when my college teammates and I hardened our bodies for the long season ahead. I loved the camaraderie and jokes that flew around the gym. We did the same trash-talking at Camp Falcon. One day while we ate lunch and watched CNN in the dining hall, talk turned to bench-press stats.

"You know, Clemons can lift a lot of weight," one of my friends said to another well-muscled soldier.

"Yeah, I can," I agreed. I wasn't being cocky. That's not my style.

"Well," the big guy said, "I bet you can't do three hundred pounds."

We all stood and walked from our table to the gym next door. I lay on the bench as the other soldiers slid 300 pounds of steel plates onto the bar. Now, I wasn't the heftiest guy in the room. I had packed on 20 pounds since enlisting in the army. But I still only tipped the scales at 165. This lift was almost double my body weight.

A few deep breaths later, I grabbed the bar, hoisted it off the rack, and held it above my head, arms locked. Slowly I lowered it to my chest. Then, with a small grunt, I snapped it back toward the ceiling. Done. After a few laughs and backslaps, we all went back to work. It was a sweet, momentary taste of our worlds back home, and really, that's what time in the gym represented—a little lifeline to normalcy.

I had made one other weight-room wager while in Baghdad, that one with a close buddy. Specialist Charles Odums II, three years younger than me, was one of the medics under my supervision at Camp Falcon. As his sergeant, I couldn't hang out with him socially. Due to my higher rank, we had to keep things professional. But we had become friends while training at Fort Hood. We were a lot alike: Odums also had played high school football and, every chance he had, he called his parents and wife back in Ohio. "Odie," as some folks called him, was always trying to make people laugh. Early in our tour, we had bet that we could outlift each other on the bench—290 pounds would win the challenge. If I won, he would buy me lunch at Whataburger. If he put up more weight, I would buy him a meal at Red Lobster. Neither of us got a chance to collect.

The Sunday night before Memorial Day 2004, I walked into the communications hub at our base, and froze when I heard his name being shouted on the radio. His unit had been on patrol in Baghdad. A roadside bomb had exploded right under his Humvee. Now, from another vehicle at the confused scene, one of the soldiers in his platoon was trying to reach him by radio. It was all being broadcast back to Camp Falcon.

"Yo, Odums! . . . Odums!!" the soldier yelled.

I held my breath and listened. Silence. They kept calling his name. But Odums had been killed in the blast.

Days later, on a concrete basketball court just outside our gym, I stood at a podium beneath the backboard and read a Bible verse for my friend: "To be absent of the body is to be present with the Lord." As I spoke, my M-16 hung over my right shoulder. Privately, his death terrified me. I knew that on any random patrol, the same thing could happen to me.

When I enlisted in the army in October 2000, America was not at war, but I fully understood the risks. Hostile fire could be in my future. After I reached Iraq, I was often scared that I might lose my life. I personally knew at least ten other soldiers who were killed in battle. At night, the mortar attacks on our base intensified the feeling that we were constantly vulnerable. But beyond the fear, I always felt that joining the military was the right move for me. The decision reflected my deep desire to live life on my own terms. To better understand, I have to tell you about the little place that shaped me.

Little Rock, Mississippi, is just a friendly bend in State Highway 494, boasting a small grocery store, six churches, and 1,636 people. The nearest movie theater is twenty-two miles to the north. The nearest mall is thirty-four miles to the east. The houses—mainly one-story ranches and mobile homes—are widely scattered among thick pine groves and lime-green meadows that, in late summer, are filled with bales of rolled yellow hay. Rural and remote, the town is nestled near Mississippi's eastern edge, about forty-five minutes from the Alabama border. It's the kind of place where driveways are adorned with wagon wheels, red pickup trucks kick up dust plumes, and dogs run toward passing cars to try to get a sniff.

I grew up in a ranch-style house with yellow trim and blue shutters that sits next to a hilly gravel road named after my mother's side of the family. Davis Road is sort of like a winding driveway that connects kinfolk—my aunts and uncles, grandparents, cousins, nieces, and nephews have lived up and down this woodsy stretch for generations. It is a peaceful, down-home place. The red clay soil is some of the poorest and least-productive anywhere, but people there still get their hands dirty. Side gardens full of butterbeans, okra, and collard greens have been tenderly raised in the clumpy ground for years, reminiscent of the old cotton fields that once blanketed the area. Because folks stayed cozy with the land, it helped instill a traditional brand of values that seems almost frozen in time compared to other parts of the country, a code of conduct more suited to the 1940s. In this area of Mississippi, for example, if a person falls into financial trouble, family and church step in to help with food and cash long before that person ever would seek government aid. The place has a true community feel. At my mom's house, family drops by at all hours to eat, chat, or just watch TV.

While people in that area are close to the land, they are even closer to the Bible. At our church, Mount Pleasant Baptist, my mom sings in the small choir and my dad is an usher. The pastor preaches in that spirited Southern style, his most important words punctuated by a small musical ensemble that includes a keyboardist and drummer. The room is filled with prayer, song, clapping, and shouts to the Lord. After Sunday services, folks linger for almost an hour, sitting in the pews, talking, and laughing.

Mount Pleasant Baptist Church sits on Battlefield Road. It got that name in the 1800s when white settlers discovered the ground there was strewn with arrowheads, and they presumed great Indian wars had been waged in the area. Indeed, the Choctaw Indians have for centuries called that part of Mississippi home, but one Civil War campaign added to the region's battlefield lore. In February 1864, Union general William Tecumseh Sherman drove his twenty-thousand-man force east from Vicksburg and eventually captured a vital railroad center in Meridian, Mississippi, thirty-four miles east of Little Rock. Sherman's army marched right through the meadows and forests of my hometown but did not trade gunfire there.

The Civil War eventually brought an end to slavery, but it didn't soften the racial hostilities in the South. In the 1960s, those raw feelings still tormented my dad's hometown, Philadelphia, twenty minutes north of Little Rock. One day in the late sixties my dad's brother, Red Clemons, got into an argument with a white man at a little country store in Philadelphia. Uncle Red was then assaulted by several men—"one of those good old country woopins'," is how my dad describes it. Red was then thrown in a jail cell, and my grandmother had to go to the jailhouse and beg the authorities not to kill her son. Red was spared and later released.

The older generations of my family have told me similar tales of racial beatings or hangings in Mississippi during that era, but two events in particular have gone beyond family talk. They are part of our nation's history. Both were fueled when Mississippi became a battleground state in the civil rights movement. In 1962, Medgar Evers helped lead a boycott against white merchants that eventually forced the University of Mississippi to accept black students. One year later, Evers was returning from an NAACP meeting to his house in Jackson, Mississippi, when a gunman shot him in the back. Evers died less than an hour later. Earlier that same day, President John Kennedy had appealed for calm amid the rising racial unease. Fertilizer salesman and Ku Klux Klan member Byron De La Beckwith eventually was convicted of that crime. In 1964, civil rights workers decided to launch a voter registration drive among African Americans in Mississippi. At the time, elections in the state almost totally excluded black voters. The strategy was dubbed Freedom Summer. In Philadelphia, three men drove into town on June 20, 1964, ready to knock on doors. They were James Chaney, twenty-one, a black man from Meridian; Michael Schwerner, a twenty-four-year-old Jewish social worker from New York; and Andrew Goodman, a twenty-year-old Jewish anthropology student, also from New York.

The day after the trio arrived, a sheriff's deputy pulled over their blue Ford station wagon for a speeding violation and the men were all jailed. According to the sheriff's department, Chaney was fined twenty dollars, and the three civil rights workers were ordered to leave the county. The same deputy then reportedly followed them to the eastern edge of town, but police later found the trio's empty, charred station wagon on the opposite side of Philadelphia. In August, FBI agents discovered their bodies on a farm six miles southwest of town. Autopsies showed that Schwerner and Goodman were each shot once in the heart, and Chaney had been severely beaten and then shot three times.

In 2005, an investigation by the *Jackson Clarion-Ledger* led to an arrest in the case and the eventual murder conviction of Edgar Ray Killen, a sawmill operator and former KKK organizer. The killings and the FBI probe inspired the 1988 film *Mississippi Burning.*

As someone who has risked his life and sacrificed his limb for the United States, I am sometimes asked how my patriotism took root in a part of the country that historically has treated African Americans so poorly. In the simplest terms, I choose to see the good in people today, not wonder if there is anything unfriendly lurking in their lineage. You can't hold people accountable for what their ancestors possibly did. It's also worth noting that I haven't bumped into too many Americans who were out to hurt me. This attitude has helped give me an inner peace and the knowledge that as long as I try to do the right thing, as long as I surround myself with positive people, life will be good. This has helped me build true friendships with folks of all colors.

You simply can't go looking for the negative side in people because that approach can poison your mind and leave you bitter. Here's a real-world example: let's say I go to a Wal-Mart store and a white person cuts ahead of me in the checkout line. If I'm someone who routinely thinks I've been mistreated due to my race, that moment will probably anger me, will lead me to see this person's rudeness as racism. But if I'm looking at the sunny side, I assume that the line-cutter has kids out in the car and is simply in a rush to return to them. I don't jump to the conclusion that someone's behavior has something to do with my skin color. My philosophy has always been to pick off a little bit of the good from the people around me and then carry those positive traits with me in life. I can't say I have always been like that, but my mom and dad have been teaching me these lessons since I was a boy.

My folks were stern disciplinarians with warm hearts. For my brother, Maurice, and me, what Mom and Dad said in our house was law. My mother, Lois, has been an auditor for Peavey Electronics in nearby Decatur for twenty-eight years. My father, Mitch, spent years in factory and industrial-line jobs. They always have worked extremely hard, and I think that's why they were so strict. They didn't want Maurice and me to have to go that same exhausting route. But in the end, both sons inherited their work ethic.

My parents' dark-paneled living room is a testament to everything that's important to them. One wall is affixed with a large gold eagle that clutches an American flag in its claws. Near that hangs a crucifix, and next to that, a picture of Jesus. God and country. This room has been family central since the time I was four. Out back, the sloped basketball court has grown a layer of grass over the hard dirt surface where we used to play our pickup games. Out front, the gravel road remains unchanged from the days when I used to ride my bike up and down the shady slopes. Whenever our bikes broke, we walked them around the bend and down the hill to my granddad, Luvette Davis, for mending. He continues to live in that same house. At the foot of a large oak tree in his yard, a rusting pile of kid's bikes still waits for repair.

Sports were an essential part of my youth and my teen years, too. At Newton County High School in Decatur, I played baseball, basketball, and, of course, football. My position was cornerback. Some defensive backs like to hit. Some enjoy picking off passes. I loved the accountability that came with playing cornerback. I was the last line of defense. You got by me, you scored. I never wanted to let my friends down. I liked having people depend on me, and it inspired me to be better.

Not that I was perfect. During my sophomore year in high school, I got my girlfriend pregnant. She wanted to have the baby. As a sixteen-year-old boy, I knew that I needed to stand by her, and I did. But at school, my girlfriend frequently and loudly accused me of infidelity, causing her to get suspended. During finals week, we got into another major fight, and this time I snapped back at her in a vicious way, publicly taunting her about a sex act she had performed. The words were so vulgar that I would be uncomfortable repeating them here. But the principal overheard them and suspended me. My mom stepped in immediately.

"I know you have a child with her, but if you want to continue to do well in school, you're going to have to leave," Mom said. "It's up to you. If you want to stay there, you can. But if you do, I think you're going to get pulled down," she said.

It was good advice. I would keep my daughter in my life, but I would change schools. I transferred to West Lauderdale High in nearby Collinsville, Mississippi. As my senior year was drawing to its final months, I lacked half a social studies credit that I had lost as a result of the suspension. I could find only one school—a private institution—that offered that same class during the spring semester, so I transferred once more. In 1999, I graduated from the King's Academy in Meridian. Today, my daughter, Daytriona, is twelve and remains a vital part of my life. She is a prime reason why I continue to move forward in this world. Often she cheers for me. Sometimes she teases me with a sarcastic smile. As I accomplish things, I feel like I'm showing her how to keep pushing and keep living in spite of the setbacks we all face.

Chasing my football ambitions, I enrolled at East Mississippi Community College in Scooba, about ninety minutes northwest of my hometown. With a roster comprised mainly of Mississippians and sprinkled with players from surrounding southeastern states, EMCC plays games against nearby junior colleges such as the Coahoma Tigers, the Holmes Bulldogs, and the Itawamba Indians. This was a solid starting point for me. Juco talent runs thick in Mississippi. These little schools are a breeding ground for Division I programs, and over the years they've sent dozens of players to the NFL, including big names like Javon Walker of Oakland, Joe Horn of Atlanta, and Duce Staley who played for Philadelphia. Even better, EMCC had a poignant football tradition that only later would I fully appreciate: the black-and-red uniforms worn by the EMCC Lions carry five stars on the front and back. These unique jerseys were designed in the 1960s by the school's legendary coach, Bob "Bull" Sullivan. Each star represents a fallen soldier who had served with Sullivan in Okinawa during World War II. After Sullivan died, a sixth star was added.

The way I saw it, I could use a couple of seasons with the Lions as a springboard to a Division I program like the University of Southern Mississippi. From there, I hoped to get a look in the NFL. But as a freshman walk-on player at EMCC, my small size kept me buried on the depth chart. I immediately went to work in the weight room to bulk up. When conventional gym hours didn't feel adequate in my quest to gain muscle, some friends and I used a butter knife to occasionally break into the weight room late at night. I always looked for an edge.

During the 1999 season, I got into one game. We were playing Itawamba. I remember just one play: The running back burst out of the backfield on a sweep. I had held my ground on the corner and now swooped in to make the tackle. As I lunged to hit him, one of our linebackers simultaneously closed on the ball carrier and got to him first. I brushed the running back as he fell. I didn't even check the stats to find out if I was credited with half a tackle. I was just thrilled to have had that single moment. I didn't know it then, but my college football career was over.

When we opened spring practices in 2000, I was bigger and felt more comfortable on the field. One moment during a scrimmage still stands out. The quarterback faked a pitch to the running back, held the ball, and made a bootleg sprint toward the sideline. He was coming right at me. It was time for me to be accountable to my teammates, but on this play, no other tackler beat me to the punch. I closed fast on our elusive quarterback and smacked him hard, knocking loose the button on his chin strap. I felt like I was on my way to becoming a starter. There was just one problem: the coach who recruited me to East Mississippi,

Shelton Gandy, had just left for another job at Southern Miss. My new coach didn't see the same potential in me. When the revised roster was tacked to the bulletin board after spring practices, my name was not on it.

I was devastated and unsure what to do next. Football was everything to me. More than anything, I loved being on a team, part of something bigger than myself. I enjoyed the practices, the bus rides, and the locker room banter. All that was gone. I continued with spring classes at EMCC, but by the late summer of 2000 I decided to enroll at another school, East Central Mississippi Community College in Decatur. I had a new game plan: play one season at East Central and then hopefully transfer to Southern Miss and play for Coach Gandy. Everything seemed to click for me at my new school. In the weight room, I outlifted the incumbent crop of defensive backs. On the field, I outran them. Before the fall roster was finalized, the coach called me aside.

"I want you on my squad," he said. "But these other defensive backs are already on scholarship. I'd like to put you on scholarship in January."

I am the first to admit I'm not a patient person. This is a character flaw that I continue to work on. I want to reach my goals and reach them now, so the coach's words didn't soothe me. My college football dream already had been stalled for a year. Even more, I had outhustled and outperformed his players. There was still another complication: I had just suffered an agonizing breakup with a girlfriend, the first true love of my life. The split hurt me deeply. Suddenly, at age twenty, I didn't have the game or the girl, and I needed to get away. I felt I had only one option. In October 2000, I enlisted in the U.S. Army. They would be my next team. They would expect from me the same kind of accountability that had always motivated me.

That decision may seem abrupt but it was filled with good logic. In the military, I could earn money for an eventual return to college. I saw myself hitting the gym, getting even stronger, and someday playing college football again. I also could get a taste of the career I wanted to pursue, medicine. In time, I hoped to become a physical therapist or a radiologist. The army would train me to become a medic. In addition to those reasons, there was one intangible factor—I could mature beyond the cozy confines of Davis Road and rural Mississippi. I could become a man who stood on his own. I wouldn't be depending on my parents anymore. I could take care of myself.

Since my childhood, I had watched one uncle and one cousin truly blossom in the military. Whenever they made return visits to Mississippi in their crisp uniforms, I recognized how sharp they were, how together they seemed. They had moved beyond a small town where many people worked hard just to get by, and where others simply lived to drink and party. These two guys were traveling the world and working for their country. I had always been impressed by that.

I spent most of my first year in the military stationed at an army base in Schweinfurt, Germany, located in the Bavarian region of that country. On September 11, 2001, word of the terrorist hijackings and airline crashes in the United States reached us rapidly in Germany. The World Trade Center attacks in New York occurred at 2:45 P.M. and 3:03 P.M., Central European Time. I remember watching footage of the jet colliding with the tower on a TV at our barracks. By dinnertime it felt like we were at war.

Although I'd been trained as a medic, I was immediately assigned to guard the arms room at the base while carrying a little 9-millimeter gun. I remember thinking: *If the enemy invades and gets all the way to me, man, we're done.* I wasn't scared. I just knew that if something bad happened and I had to single-handedly keep an advancing force from raiding the arms room, things were not good. Beyond my day-to-day duties, I seemed to mesh well with the army's disciplinary culture. I understood that when a higher-ranked person told me to move, I moved, and I asked no questions. That discipline was second nature to me. My mom and dad's strict parenting style had prepared me for it years ago.

My next international stop was in Kosovo, the Baltic province bordering Serbia that had been under United Nations control since 1999. Starting in 1996, the Serbian (formerly Yugoslav) government waged war with Kosovo's main population, ethnic Albanians, to gain control of the province. While the wars in Iraq and Afghanistan rolled on, I arrived in Kosovo as part of a UN peacekeeping force. I worked as an evacuation medic, but the soldiers whom I treated and transported to the aid station were all hurt in noncombat incidents like car wrecks and barracks wrestling matches. More often, I helped set up medical distribution centers at public buildings in the community. There I would hand the locals over-the-counter drugs like cough medicine or ibuprofen.

As American soldiers fought the rising insurgency in Iraq, the neighborhoods in Kosovo remained quiet. I took advantage of a relatively normal work schedule and immersed myself in college correspondence classes—algebra, oral communications, anatomy, and physiology. Another medic—my superior officer and friend, Sgt. Mario Rodas—pushed me to continue my education. I had known him since my days in Germany. Six years older than me, Rodas was a family-oriented guy with a wife and two girls. I got to meet them during a cookout that Rodas held for his soldiers. His youngest daughter, about three at the time, called me "Tiki." Rodas still refers to me that way. When my parents flew to Germany to visit me in 2002, Rodas and his family were heading back to their home in Los Angeles for a short break. The sergeant was gracious enough to let my parents stay at his home on the base so they wouldn't have to spring for a hotel room. He told me later he wouldn't have trusted any other soldier in his platoon with that same privilege.

In both Germany and Kosovo, Rodas had been my boss. Like a big brother, he taught me how to be a good army medic, including how to care for and maintain an army ambulance. He also made sure I was taking the right classes to advance my career. As a result, I earned a promotion to sergeant E5 in barely more than two years, a fast pace for a medic. Rodas always looked out for me. In time, I would count on his calm support to guide me through the worst two moments of my life.

In March 2004, I was sent to Iraq with the 1st Battalion of the 8th Cavalry Regiment, attached to a platoon in the Bravo Company. Camp Falcon, a high-walled compound in a hostile section of southwestern Baghdad, was my new home. I understood that my life was now very much in danger. Watching that innocent Iraqi man die in the hail of gunfire at the police station only heightened those feelings. During my first month in the country, 52 American soldiers were killed—the highest U.S. body count in four months. In April, it got much worse—135 American soldiers died. At the time, that marked the single bloodiest month of the war for U.S. troops. Since then, only one month has surpassed that figure: November 2004, when 137 American soldiers lost their lives.

Almost every day, I called my parents back in Mississippi. They were worried but they did their best to reassure me.

"What's going to happen is going to happen," they often told me. "There's no stopping it."

I hit the gym, did my job as a medic, wrote about my faith in the little pocket diary I carried, and did my best to stay alive.

By watching CNN in the chow hall, we all knew that the war was growing more and more unpopular back in the States. I never let that get in my head, though. I couldn't afford to. If I allowed myself even one brief distraction while on patrol or while conducting a raid, it could cost the life of one of my buddies. No matter how often we heard that the reasons for this war were wrong, that we had no business in Iraq, that we were only jeopardizing our lives to protect an oil supply, I kept a sharp focus on my true purpose for being there. We were called servicemen and servicewomen, and I took that name to heart. I had come to help. I wasn't fighting for oil, I was fighting for the guy next to me. Or for the wounded soldier I had never met.

At my core I'm a family guy. Each day in Iraq, I ached to get back home to my parents and my daughter. Almost all of the soldiers around me shared that same urge. The biggest reason I grabbed my aid bag and often ventured into the angry Baghdad streets, risking everything, was to help the other soldiers get back to their families. People were depending on me, including the woman I wanted to marry.

I had first met Candy Gibson when we were in the fifth grade. I gave her a shiny necklace and wanted to be her boyfriend. By the time we reached high school, we remained close friends, although we didn't date. She was pretty and smart, and I always felt like Candy had my back, that I could trust her and depend on her. I had her best interests at heart, too. After I enlisted and later on, when I went off to war, we stayed in touch through letters and phone calls. I still had strong feelings for her. Three weeks before that hidden bomb rearranged my body and my world, I began thinking about life with Candy. I would soon be home. I would be able to finally spend quality time with her, to really commit to her. As my days grew short in Baghdad, I decided to propose to her. Late one night, I called her father from Camp Falcon and asked for his permission to marry Candy.

"If that's what you kids want to do, I support you one hundred percent," he said.

A couple of nights later, I called Candy.

"Did you talk to your pop?" I asked.

"No, I haven't," she said. "Why?"

"Well you need to talk to him."

"Why?"

"Because . . . I asked for his permission to marry you."

"You're playin'!" she said with a smile in her voice.

"Just talk to your dad."

Candy did. And then she said yes to my proposal. We were both so excited. We would set everything up as soon as I flew home from Iraq. I couldn't wait to slip a diamond ring on her finger. But as I hung up the phone at the base, there was one part of the engagement plan I didn't yet know: I would be making that trip to the jewelry store in a wheelchair.

3

Missing Pieces

With the damaged chopper gone and the injured and dead lying still on the road, a fresh quiet filled the air. A sharp slap to my cheekbone broke the silence.

"Wake up! Wake the hell up!" Staff Sgt. Bryce Rigby, my platoon leader, screamed while kneeling over me. He had just sprinted to me from across the highway. He saw what remained of my right leg, and he saw that I was slipping away.

Another hard blow to my face.

"Kortney, stay awake! Where are you from?"

The two rips in my leg arteries had gushed away some of the twelve pints of blood that once filled my body. My circulatory system was slowly shutting down and grayness filled my head. I was dying.

Rigby saw my eyes roll back.

"Kortney! What's Mississippi like?" he asked loudly while groping inside my right leg, pushing on the torn artery. "Tell me about your girlfriend."

I wasn't in any pain because my body was going into shock. I knew I had been hit by the bomb but I didn't know how badly. I could hear Rigby's anxious voice but I couldn't see his face.

"What can I give you? What can I give you?" he asked, knowing that as a medic I could help treat myself.

Instinctively, I thought about the remaining morphine pin I had stuck in my vest pocket while aiding Vang. I didn't need it but since Rigby had asked, I started patting my chest, searching for that pin. I never found it. Rigby told me later that he was almost overcome by the smell of my burned flesh.

Both of my legs were bleeding, but the right thigh seemed to be losing more fluid, so Rigby focused on that. He kept his hand on the artery while grabbing field bandages from his pack. He wrapped one pressure dressing around my right thigh, but with so much blood soaking into the material, the soggy bandage snapped. He quickly slapped a second dressing around the thigh, pulling it taut to stop the flow before time ran out on me. That bandage also tore.

"The tourniquets keep breaking!" he yelled.

Lying on the highway fifteen feet away from us, full of shrapnel and feeling the piercing ache of a compound leg fracture, Sgt. 1st Class John Shatto heard Rigby's shouts.

"Use a belt!" Shatto hollered.

Rigby yanked the belt off another soldier who was now standing over me. He looped it around my leg while a third guy from my platoon, Staff Sgt. Matthew Bittenbender, tugged it tight and then buckled it in place.

The crowd of Iraqi people, many of whom scattered after the explosion, now grew even bigger and began to press closer. On the bridge above us, some of them stopped and took pictures.

In one lane on the highway, a single Iraqi vehicle began to roll toward us. One of the Minnesota soldiers guarding the perimeter fired his M-16 two or three times over the vehicle to force it to stop. As a group of Iraqi bystanders simultaneously started to step in our direction, another Minnesota MP squeezed off a round of machine-gun fire just above their heads to scare them back.

When the immediate area was secured, the second Medivac chopper landed on the highway. As its rotors spun, bits of sand pelted my face. Rigby looked again at the lower part of my right leg, attached by just a few strands of skin. He noticed that three toes also were missing on my right foot. As the air medics rushed toward Shatto and me, Rigby carefully wrapped my mangled foot and right lower leg in a white field dressing. He knew there was no way to save the leg. But he believed I still had a chance.

This guy has got to live, Rigby thought.

The medics and other soldiers loaded Shatto, Vang, and me onto stretchers and carried us across the highway to the chopper. This time we got to the Blackhawk's side door without a bomb going off. The medics clipped the straps on our stretchers into hooks on the helicopter wall to secure us for the short ride to the CSH, or "cash" as everyone called it. Shatto's stretcher was below mine.

"Hang in there, bro," he said.

As I moaned, Shatto reached up and put his hand on my shoulder.

When word of the attack first reached the Tactical Operations Center in the Green Zone, my cousin Debbie Poe was standing by the radio.

"We've been hit and there are soldiers down!" the pilot of the first Blackhawk hollered into his microphone. "We're coming in!"

"My cousin was just here," Debbie told the other soldiers inside the TOC. "I sure hope that wasn't him."

Soon our chopper was airborne. It landed on the helipad at about 8:45 A.M. I had been hemorrhaging from two arteries for almost fifteen minutes and remember nothing about the short flight.

Medical teams loaded our stretchers onto four-wheel ATVs and whisked us to the emergency room. Doctors immediately surrounded me, looked at my leg, and knew they had very little time.

"We need matching blood over here! We're going to need X-rays, a CT scan!" one doctor yelled. "We're taking him to surgery!"

"Please don't let me die," I said. "Please don't let me die."

Other medical teams simultaneously worked on Vang and Shatto, both of whom were conscious.

"Go help my medic!" Shatto shouted at the doctors who hovered above his battered legs. "I'm going to be okay! Go help my medic!"

"No, they're working on him, and we're working on you," one of the ER staff told him.

Shatto watched as the nurses jabbed IVs into my arms to begin replenishing my fluids. How close was I to death? Right at the edge. The medical staff pumped as many as five bags (or pints) of blood into me. The average healthy man has about twelve pints of blood in his body. That means I lost roughly 42 percent of my overall blood volume: a "class IV hemorrhage" in medical terms. When you donate blood, a nurse will take a pint, or about 10 percent of what's surging in your veins. Anything more and you would feel woozy. I had lost four times that amount. In a class IV hemorrhage—anything greater than 40 percent—patients are often unconscious and their skin becomes pale and cold. With that much blood loss, according to the American College of Surgeons, "the limit of the body's compensation is reached and aggressive resuscitation is required to prevent death."

After that first transfusion, the medical staff pushed my gurney through emergency room doors toward the operating room. A few minutes later, Debbie hustled into the ER to collect the names of the wounded soldiers. She still didn't know that I'd been hurt.

Someone handed her a sheet of paper with our names. She held the report without glancing at it, talking to the medical staff about our conditions, gathering the necessary information that she would need to send to the Pentagon. Finally, a voice in her head urged her to look at the paper in her palm.

"Oh, my God! Kortney!" Debbie said. "When did he come in!?"

"He came in on this call," an attendant told her.

"Where is he?"

"He's up in surgery. He just left."

"I've got to get up there," Debbie said.

"Wait, there's something you need to know before you go up there," the attendant said.

"What?"

"They're going to have to take his right leg off."

Debbie began to cry. Then she walked to her barracks to pack some clothes. Wherever I was headed next, my cousin was going with me.

The explosion had mutilated my leg, leaving the surgeons no shot at saving it. The lack of blood flow below the ruptured artery in my right thigh had killed much of the tissue beneath that point. Surgeons sawed through the femur above my right knee and then sealed off that artery. Later, I learned that the surgeons had used a portion of the artery from my right leg to create a bypass around the slashed artery in my left leg.

After they closed me up, Debbie called Mississippi. The sun was just rising in Little Rock.

"Hello," my father answered, still a little shaken from his nightmare about the explosion.

Debbie was crying.

"Mitch, it's Debbie. Kortney was just in an accident."

"Mmm hmm," he said, sensing that much worse information was about to follow.

"Well, Kortney got hurt. They had to take his leg off."

"Oh, my God. Really?"

"Yes," Debbie said. "Please tell Lois for me. They're taking Kortney to a hospital in Germany. I'm going with him."

My first memory after the surgery is brief and hazy. I'm not sure of the day or the time. I was in a hospital treatment room, gazing into a warm light directly over my face. I heard quiet voices all around me. People were cleaning the wounds in my legs. I closed my eyes and faded back to sleep.

After my amputation, a chopper had flown me—still unconscious—to Balad Air Base, also known as Camp Anaconda, about fifty miles north of Baghdad in the violent Sunni Triangle. The place was nicknamed "Mortaritaville" because of the frequent mortar shells that land and explode at the base. Also on board that helicopter, as promised, was Debbie. She had received special permission from her superiors to accompany me, although I can't think of an army commander who wouldn't have granted that favor. Our last stop would be the Landstuhl Regional Medical Center, a sprawling army hospital in southwestern Germany. But after arriving at Balad on Monday afternoon, our pilots had to wait for the cover of midnight darkness to fly the evac plane up and out of Mortaritaville.

The transport craft also carried two badly burned Marines. Nurses had taken the seats closest to the patients, leaving Debbie to keep an eye on me and my gurney from across the plane during our six and a half hour flight.

It was Tuesday morning when we finally reached Germany and began the bus ride to Landstuhl, a gigantic facility sometimes referred to as "the Iraq War's German front." Since 2003, more than eight thousand soldiers and military personnel from the Iraqi and Afghan theaters have been treated at the complex. With all that practice, Landstuhl blossomed from a small, sleepy military hospital into one of the best trauma centers in the world. A central hallway connects fourteen buildings. In an emergency, the hospital can hold up to a thousand beds, although 140 beds is the standard setup. Those 140 or so patients are cared for by more than two thousand hospital employees working two shifts. In a typical day, Landstuhl serves 1,178 meals, doles out 1,598 doses of drugs, and handles 23 new patients. In a time of war, the hospital is a nonstop swarm of emergency medicine.

That Tuesday morning, my old friend, Sgt. Mario Rodas, was just finishing his overnight shift at Landstuhl. About the same time that I had been deployed to Iraq in March 2004, Rodas was assigned to Landstuhl where he worked as a patient liaison. In that role, he talked with wounded soldiers fresh off the Iraqi battlefields, seeking to answer all their questions, gathering personal hygiene items for them or scrounging up any small creature comforts that they had requested. Rodas also spoke with each of their doctors, asking about their specific medical plans so he could keep their superior officers apprised of their healing. Rodas was a gifted medic and a genuinely nice guy, a straight shooter who also could make you laugh. But a recent event in his life had even further softened his bedside manner. In October 2003, at the age of twenty-nine, he had suffered a heart attack.

The chest pain had started when he was on leave in California, attending his sister's wedding. He thought nothing of it and flew back to Germany with his family. While driving his car away from the airport, the pain returned. This time it was far worse. Instead of continuing on to his house, Rodas raced straight to an American hospital in Wuerzburg and soon was transferred to the intensive care unit at Landstuhl—the same ward I was placed in after leaving Iraq. The doctors found no underlying health issues in Rodas to explain the heart attack and chalked it up to a medical anomaly. But the event left a deep imprint on him, he told me later. He emerged with a greater appreciation for life. Lying in that hospital bed, thinking of his two daughters and knowing that he could die that night, Rodas vowed to be a better father and husband. The illness forced my friend to be placed on a six-month medical evaluation that prevented him from shipping out to Iraq when I did. In late 2007, Rodas would ultimately be deployed to Iraq, stationed in the International Zone.

As the blue-painted bus carrying me and the burned Marines rumbled toward Landstuhl, Rodas was driving out of the hospital parking lot, tired from his all-night shift. Five minutes after he left work, his cell phone rang. His captain was calling from Landstuhl.

"Hey, isn't Kortney Clemons one of your soldiers from before?" the captain asked.

"Yeah, yeah, that's one of my guys," Rodas said.

"Hey, I've got some bad news. He's coming in."

Rattled, Rodas pulled his rented Audi A4 station wagon to the side of the street and parked.

"What's his condition?" Rodas asked quietly.

"He has lost his leg."

In his one year of work at Landstuhl, Rodas had spent many tough nights with the families of wounded or dead soldiers. He empathized with them as they cried, but he had built up an emotional wall in order to do his job properly. When he heard about me, Rodas cried for the first time since taking that liaison job, he told me later. His wall was broken.

"I'm coming back to work," Rodas said to his captain. "I want to handle him personally. He was my soldier."

After I was carried from the bus to a bed in the intensive care unit, I remained unconscious for the rest of the day. I didn't know it, but I was finally out of Iraq.

The doctors slowly began weaning me off the sedation drugs. As I slept, Debbie popped into my room and sat with me for hours at a time, anxiously asking the nurses when I would awake.

That same day, Shatto rolled his wheelchair up to my ICU room to see me. He had been airlifted to Landstuhl for treatment on his shattered leg and the dozens of other shrapnel wounds he took to his face, hands, and torso. He would eventually return to Fort Hood, Texas, and spend two months in a wheelchair, enduring nine surgeries, including a procedure to insert a ten-inch metal plate in his right leg. In time, Shatto would walk again. When he peeked in my room, I was still out cold. He saw the breathing machine, the tube in my throat, the monitor wires taped to my body. And he saw the stump. From the doorway, he asked God to make sure I made it. Then he wheeled his chair away in silence.

If I soon wondered what I had done to deserve this, and wondered what I might have done differently, I was not alone.

Rigby wrestled with his own feelings of guilt from that day because I had nudged him off the back corner of the stretcher. It was my job. Still, that decision haunted Rigby. The real truth is that he saved my life.

Years later, while talking with guys from the Minnesota platoon, I would learn that Vang also carried a similar emotional burden because his crash and injury eventually put me and the other four stretcher bearers on top of that IED. In that case, too, Vang was simply doing his job, driving an army truck. A patch of loose gravel led to his Humvee accident. But to professional soldiers, these rational explanations and reality checks don't much matter. They look at the final, fatal tally and reach the conclusion that bad things should never have happened on their watch. But in war, bad things happen.

For Shatto, that internal battle would thankfully start to soften as time passed. In his mind, he had made the decision for us to haul the stretcher to that precise spot on the guardrail. Long after the detonation ripped apart his legs, he continued to beat himself up mentally. He thought he should have somehow sniffed out that hidden bomb, should have ordered us to execute the rescue in a safer spot.

"It's only natural to feel like you're responsible," Shatto would say later, essentially seeing the stubborn guilt for what it is—real and painful, but not based in reality. No one there could have detected that bomb before it was triggered. No one was to blame, except the insurgents. As my parents always tried to tell me, what's going to happen is going to happen.

Debbie, too, was dogged by guilt although it came from a slightly different angle. She mistakenly believed that my reason for visiting the Green Zone was simply to see her. She thought that I had altered my driving plans and my schedule that morning just to hug her and catch up a little, and that those few precious minutes had put me on a return route right toward that bomb. How she lived with that anguish, I can't imagine. She didn't share those feelings with me for a long time, and eventually Debbie would seek counseling to come to terms with what happened. But that day in my hospital room, halfway around the world from the Mississippi dirt road that we knew so well, Debbie sat near my bed, looked at my missing leg, and felt like it was all her fault.

When I woke up, it was Wednesday night. I was alone. My head rested on a pillow. My room was dim and quiet except for the beeps of machines that monitored my heartbeat and breathing. I was not in pain. The door was closed. From the lighted crack beneath it, I could see people moving back and forth in the hallway. I lifted my head and looked down at my body.

On the left side, I saw the usual long bulge of the leg and foot beneath the bedcovers. On the right side, below my thigh, all I saw was a perfectly flat white sheet.

Back in Baghdad, my sleep had been filled with nightmares. In one recurring dream, I sat atop a building and watched bright mortars fall silently around me. I figured what I was experiencing in the hospital was just another bad dream. I lay back on the pillow and shut my eyes.

I'm going to wake up, I thought, *and my leg will still be there.*

A short time later, I awoke for the second time.

What happened to me? I thought. *Man, I must have really got hit.*

I tried to wind my mind back to that deadly patch of highway and to our rescue attempt.

I looked down at my body again and saw that the sheet on the right side of the bed was still flat. It was no dream. A torrent of emotions began to well up—fear, sadness, anger. Was my life over? Would I ever be happy again? Would I ever have a family of my own? How could I live without being able to run? Who was I now?

The door opened. A nurse walked in.

"What happened to me?"

"You were in an accident," the nurse said. "You lost your leg above the knee."

I dropped my head back on the pillow. Now it was real.

"You have someone outside to see you."

Rodas had been visiting some of his other patients in the ICU, and now he was checking to see if I had finally awakened. Earlier, he had called my parents in Mississippi and told my mom than I wasn't going to be alone at Landstuhl. The nurse asked him to step inside the room. He took a deep breath and entered.

I was in tears, sitting partially upright in the bed. When I saw Rodas, I asked him the one big question that had been ricocheting through my head.

"Why did this happen to me?" I asked, sobbing. "Why did this happen to me?"

Rodas was speechless. How could he or anyone begin to find a reason? He didn't say a word as I continued to ask the same question over and over. Instead of providing an answer, he gave me some perspective.

"I really can't tell you why. I really don't know why," Rodas said. "But God does things for a reason, man. And even though this happened, just remember that God is good, man. No matter what, God is good."

It helped to hear those words. But I still couldn't get my head around why this had happened or, more to the point, what I had done in my life to deserve it.

Instead of trying to figure out the unanswerable "why," Rodas and I started talking about the "what." I replayed what I could remember of the attack. I told him about stopping for the over-turned Humvee and about loading up the injured soldier on the stretcher. I told him about the blast and the faint memories I held of lying on the highway with the smoke and dust swirling around me.

"All I remember is crawling to the Blackhawk, trying to get myself to the Blackhawk. I knew I had to get there," I told Rodas, starting to cry again. "I was crawling. I was trying to get there. I didn't want them to leave without me."

Back in Kosovo, Rodas and I used to deliver medical supplies to areas ravaged by the old war. We had given cold medicine to people who were down with the flu and over-the-counter pain reliever to folks with minor scrapes that had grown infected due to the filthy conditions. Now I was the patient and my old pal was the one offering me care.

"Man, you're a good guy. You're a smart guy and you're strong," Rodas said. "You can overcome anything with the attitude that you have. Everything is about attitude."

Soon after our chat, Rodas left to finally get some rest. Then Debbie came back to my room.

"How you doing?" she asked.

"Okay."

"You finally woke up, huh?"

"Yeah."

Later, she confided that she really wasn't sure what to say or how to approach me.

"Man, I had just seen you," she said. "And then I heard about the IED on the radio."

I was silent.

"You know you were in an accident?"

"Yeah."

"You know you don't have your right leg?"

"Yeah."

"It's going to be all right. There's a reason for everything," Debbie said. "How do you feel about it?"

"Well, I'm okay. I'm glad to be living," I said, meaning it. "I'm just glad to be alive."

Well, Debbie thought, *you don't know the half of it. You don't know half the stuff you just went through.*

Over the next couple of days, I was moved to a private room as I healed and regained my strength. Fortunately, I was not in much pain, probably due to all the medications I was taking. I did feel the phenomenon called phantom limb pain—a dull ache that seemed to be coming from my missing lower right leg. More than half of all amputees go through phantom pain at some point, some of them for long stretches. Doctors used to believe that this pain was caused by an irritation in the severed nerve endings, and that these torn nerves sent abnormal signals that the brain read as pain in the old appendage. But according to a new theory, what I experienced may have been the brain rewiring itself, making up for the lost limb by creating new pathways to receive sensory input from other parts of my body. Whether that's true or not, I'm just glad that phantom pain eventually faded. I already had enough to deal with.

When I was with other people, my laughter began to return. A visit from seven or eight of my old platoon buddies from Germany cheered me up. They were medics and mechanics. They noticed how much bigger my body had become from all the weightlifting. I just smiled and made a muscle with my arm and said, "I still got it." To boost my spirits and add a little life to my drab, one-window room, Rodas poked through the bin of donated items at Landstuhl and brought me a CD player and a disc of mixed gospel hits. I played it when my friends stopped in to see me.

The tears flowed again, though, when my parents called my hospital room. I loved hearing their voices but when I tried to speak to them, I only sobbed. I just handed the phone back to a nurse and she said good-bye for me.

During the times I was alone in the room, all those hard questions about my future continued to race around my head. When I heard that three of the Minnesota soldiers had died in the blast, the news stung me like a punch to the gut and gave me still more questions to ponder: Why had I survived? Was there another purpose for me in this world? Lying flat on my back in a German hospital bed, I began the most important journey of my life—a mission of discovery to learn who I was and what I stood for.

I didn't know it yet, but I had to lose my leg to find myself.

4

Into the Void

My body had begun to heal, but my head had a lot of work to do.

One day before checking out of Landstuhl and departing Germany for American soil, I still had not summoned the courage to throw back the blankets and take a good, hard look at what the bomb had done to my right leg. I had seen the empty space below the sheets, but that's as far as I had taken the exploration. I was now four days into my new life as an amputee. I was dealing with it by not dealing with it.

In preparation for my trip back to the States, the hospital staff had moved me to a transitional holding area inside the medical complex. This ward was full of portable beds on wheels. Some held wounded soldiers who soon would face their loved ones looking nothing like they did when they went off to war.

My temporary sleeping area contained all of the medications and devices that would travel with me on the plane, including a morphine machine that trickled a stream of the numbing drug into my body to soften the many aches radiating from my waist down. As our time in Germany grew short, the soldiers in the ward greeted a parade of visitors who wished them safe travels and better days. One of the people who stopped by my bedside was Shatto, who rolled up with a smile and some great news.

"The guy on the stretcher made it," he told me.

I was thrilled to hear that. My final mission had been a success after all. I now wanted to see Vang and talk with him, but I was told that he had not been shipped to Landstuhl. I have not seen him since the moment the bomb went off.

Shatto and I said good-bye. He, Rigby, and I would soon be reunited during a welcome-home ceremony for our platoon at Fort Hood. But the events on the ground during those terrible few minutes on February 21 would forge a lifelong friendship between us.

All of my travel details seemed set. The doctors had asked me where I preferred to do my rehab work—Walter Reed Army Medical Center in Washington, D.C., or Brooke Army Medical Center in San Antonio, Texas. I chose Brooke because it was closer to my family. My few belongings—including that spiritual pocket diary—had been collected and crated back at the Green Zone hospital, ready for shipment to my parents' house in Mississippi. Months later, that box would arrive and my father would pull out a piece of my battlefield clothing—the green armored vest. He would inspect it and find a spot in the upper left corner of the chest where the material had been shredded by a sharp chunk of flying metal—part of the bomb that took my leg. He would poke his finger through that hole in the vest and think how lucky his son was to be alive. My dad also would pluck out the digital Timex watch that I had been wearing on my wrist that last morning in Baghdad. Despite the massive explosion, the Timex was still ticking. Just like his son.

I had one other odd souvenir to bring home with me—a plastic cup that rattled with a few hunks of shrapnel the surgeons had picked out of my body. The biggest bit was a one-by-one-inch, copper-colored lump of metal etched with a row of vertical lines—like the markings on the bottom of a mortar shell. Also in that cup were a fragment of black asphalt and a smaller metal scrap that still carried a tiny dried slice of my tissue. Each of those three pieces represented the split second when my life took a new turn: one stood for the massive violence of the moment, one for the battlefield where it all went down, and one for the permanent injury that I sustained.

As I reclined in my holding-area bed, Rodas also dropped by for a last visit. He had been talking on the phone with my mom, updating and reassuring her. Rodas had heard the fear and sadness in her voice back in Mississippi. He now understood that I had a job to do when I landed in Texas. I needed to help my parents through this ordeal.

"Have you looked at yourself yet?" he asked.

"No. I can't. Can't do it."

"You're about to go to the States. Your parents are going to be there. You need to try to be strong for them," Rodas said. He knew that switching my focus toward helping someone else would actually help me.

"You might want to check yourself out so that when you do get home, you meet your family on better terms," Rodas told me.

He was right. I had to be emotionally prepared for this homecoming. The time had come to pull back the sheet.

When I was alone again, I took a deep breath, placed my hands on the fringe of the blanket, and lifted the covers above my waist. For the first time I saw the massive damage in my left leg that was wrapped in heavy gauze. I saw the staples the doctors had inserted in my groin, which had taken a shower of metal. Then I looked to the right side. I saw the thick white bandages covering the rounded stump. The leg ended at what used to be the middle of my thigh. No knee. No ankle. No foot. What I saw most was the void. I stared for a few seconds at the empty spot on the mattress.

I dropped the sheet, lay back, and swallowed hard. I didn't know much about the new me or this new life, but I knew I would put on a brave face for my parents. And they would do exactly the same for me.

Rodas wanted to fly with me to San Antonio, to talk with me during the thirteen-hour flight and steer me away from gloomy thoughts. But there were too many other casualties heading home from the war. With fifteen soldiers and several nurses booked for passage, there was just no room for a healthy soldier. As it turned out, I could have used the company.

As I waited to be loaded onto the blue bus that would haul us ten minutes away to Ramstein Air Base, I noticed for the first time how cold it was outside. Patches of snow covered parts of the ground. This was winter in Germany, after all. Iraq and its palm trees suddenly seemed even farther away.

Once we reached Ramstein, the bus drove us onto the tarmac and each soldier was rolled outside, then wheeled up through a rear hatch on the massive cargo plane. The stretchers were stacked two high. I was on the bottom. A catheter hose had been attached to me so I could urinate without leaving the mattress. The soldier above me had suffered bad burns, probably during a roadside bomb explosion, but he could get out of his bunk and move around.

After we were airborne, the burn victims on board stood, chatted, walked to the restroom, or just gazed out the frosty windows.

I had not been upright in almost a week. Lying on my stretcher, I felt more confined and restless than I ever had at Landstuhl. I ached to stand and move around, maybe even remove the catheter and use the plane's bathroom for myself. I asked one of the nurses for a pair of crutches.

"Sorry, you're not ready to get up yet," she said.

I felt totally helpless.

So I lay back, sipped some orange juice, and listened to the low hum of the plane's engines. There was nothing to do but think. My thoughts bounced from dark to sunny to dark again. Sure, I was happy to be alive. Hearing that the three guys on the other side of the stretcher all had been killed only reinforced just how fortunate I had been to survive. I could have been coming home in a flag-draped box instead of on a stretcher. But thinking about being alive soon led me to thinking about the future. That wasn't a good topic at the moment. I worried about what would happen to me after I reached home. I had never known anyone with an amputation. Would I be in a wheelchair for the rest of my days? And what about all those plans I had? I'd begun the week with such excitement, anxious to see my family, return to school, and restore my college football career. I'd ended the week missing a limb. What next? What would I do with my life now? Would Candy still want to marry me? Would any woman want to marry me?

When these questions became too overwhelming, my mind automatically drifted off to easier topics, like the fact that I was coming back to American soil. I even managed to sleep a little. But when I woke up and looked around the plane, again seeing all the soldiers who had been wounded like me, I found myself returning to those same questions. Where was I really headed in this world? When would I feel like myself again? Back and forth I went, all the way home from Germany: a few hard minutes spent trying to imagine my future, then a few easy minutes daydreaming about hugging my family, then back to focusing on the cold reality of the moment. I only knew one thing for sure.

I'm done for, I thought.

Brooke Army Medical Center was built for war, and for the gruesome things that happen to human bodies when nations decide to fight. In the army, we refer to the place by its acronym— BAMC or "Bamzy." The emphasis is on "Bam." Located just outside of downtown San Antonio, the current version is a seven-story, 450-bed facility that is considered the army's most technologically modern hospital. At BAMC, the doctors, nurses, physical therapists, and prosthetists had tapped into a new wave of gadgetry and computerized therapies to help people walk just weeks after amputation. Yet the place also is deeply flavored with military history.

If you step into the sprawling parking lot and look far to the west, you can still make out the original Brooke Army Hospital. In 1870, the city of San Antonio donated forty acres of land for an army post to be called Fort Sam Houston. By 1886, the compound contained a log-cabin medical dispensary, and by 1907 it boasted an 84-bed hospital. Army surgeon Dr. Roger Brooke took command of the Fort Sam hospital in 1929. Dr. Brooke specialized in infectious diseases like tuberculosis and he brought an impressive resume to the job. He was credited with being the first army doctor to use routine chest X-rays in exams. Brooke held the top job at the hospital for four years. In 1938, the army built a new, 418-bed medical facility at Fort Sam that soon began treating soldiers who had been hurt fighting the Germans in Europe and the Japanese in the South Pacific. In 1942, they renamed the place Brooke General Hospital. During the Cold War, Brooke General filled a chilling niche in America's defense system. In 1949, with Russia and the United States each manufacturing huge arsenals of atomic bombs, American leaders began thinking about the horrific aftermath of a possible nuclear attack. They imagined a scenario in which thousands of people survived, yet suffered from severe radiation or blast burns. At Brooke, the military put together one of the first clinics designed to treat traumatic burns.

In 1996, the army replaced the original hospital with an updated and enlarged Brooke Army Medical Center in its present spot. Not long after the wars in Afghanistan and Iraq began, BAMC began taking the overflow of amputee cases from Walter Reed.

For centuries, wars have had an eerie by-product—improvements in weaponry led to increases in killing power, which gave way to advances in medicine. That's also been true for this present conflict. More of us survive our battlefield injuries but are coming home with devastating and lifelong scars. In World War II, 70 percent of the soldiers who got hurt survived their injuries. In Vietnam, the survival rate climbed to 76 percent and it stayed there for the Persian Gulf War. But in Iraq and Afghanistan, 91 percent of the injured soldiers have survived. Superbly trained medics, like the guys in my unit, have helped bring that number up. We can get soldiers stabilized on the battlefield, then in the air, and into a bed at Walter Reed or BAMC in just thirty-six hours. Army doctors also are more mobile and better equipped, able to do field surgery out of backpacks if necessary. But the biggest factor in the higher survival numbers is the army's use of better helmets and heavy, Kevlar-lined vests. This gear has helped protect soldiers' vital organs during attacks, spreading the damage to arms, hands, legs, feet, and faces. About two-thirds of the wounds sustained in Iraq and Afghanistan are to those unshielded body parts.

At BAMC, the huge flow of amputation cases inspired better and faster ways to get these men and women back on their feet. I was part of that new wave. Exactly five weeks before I lost my leg, BAMC opened the army's second Amputee Care

Center. (The first was at Walter Reed.) The care center occupied more than 29,000 square feet of space where it combined recent prosthetic inventions with a World War II–era team approach: wound-mending surgeons, orthopedic specialists, psychologists, physical therapists, and prosthetists all working together on individual cases. There's a small, computer-aided prosthetics factory at BAMC that cranks out artificial limbs made perfectly to order. There's a physical therapy lab where the grunt work is done— frail bodies are restrengthened on floor mats and one-legged or no-legged people learn how to walk again. There are separate recreation rooms for upper-body and lower-body amputees, a 90-degree therapeutic pool, and a simulated apartment with a bedroom, kitchen, and shower where maimed soldiers can relearn everyday tasks like washing up, cooking breakfast, or unscrewing a jar of peanut butter. While I was hospitalized there, BAMC also had begun building a "gait lab" that would use computer-sensitive floor panels to measure patients' weight and pressure as they walked, and cameras to record the intricacies of their strides—all to help the prosthetists build even better artificial legs.

After the thirteen-hour flight and a long bus ride through a chilly San Antonio, I was wheeled into BAMC, placed on a padded exam-room table, and left alone as doctors began looking at the other guys who came in with me. Each of my mangled legs was uncovered, ready for scrutiny. I couldn't get up. As the minutes ticked by, I grew more uncomfortable in the quiet of the little room.

Where is everybody? I thought.

Soon the door opened and a hospital chaplain walked into my exam room. I have to admit, the sight of the man startled me. When a chaplain arrives at the hospital, it usually means someone has died, but he quickly made it clear that he was just there for reassurance, not to deliver bad news. We chatted for a minute before the doctor knocked and entered. Without saying much, she carefully scanned the open gashes and surgical incisions in my left leg. The surgeons in Iraq had purposely not stitched up my left leg, choosing to keep those wounds simply packed with gauze and wrapped with Kerlix, a white gauzelike bandage. By keeping the leg wounds somewhat open, it allowed the BAMC medical staff to frequently wash them out to prevent infection. The doctor also checked the remnants of my right leg and then looked at the surgical staples in my groin. The shrapnel had hit that area hard. Beyond wondering whether I would ever walk again, the groin wounds brought another question to my mind.

"Will I be able to have kids?" I asked the doctor.

"Were you able to have them before?" she responded.

"Yes. I have a daughter."

"Then you can have them again."

Her answer gave me a little relief. But starting a family was strictly a long-term plan, so I didn't dwell on that good news.

After my exam, I was wheeled to the hospital room where I would spend much of the next month. As I entered, I saw a bathroom to my left and then, straight ahead, I saw my adjustable bed, affixed with side guards to keep me from rolling out. Just beyond that, four windows overlooked a green pasture full of horses that belonged to the Cavalry. Above the bed hung a thick metal triangle on which I could pull myself up. Next to the bed, a small TV was attached to a moveable arm. Between the bed and the windows sat an upright medical machine and an IV bag to pump morphine into me when necessary. Three other beds were in the room, each separated by curtain-dividers.

A medical attendant helped me from the wheelchair to the bed. I thought about the three Minnesota soldiers who never made it home. I tried to focus on the fact that I was lucky to just be a patient at this hospital.

"It could have been worse," the attendant said in a warm voice, trying to cheer me up.

Yeah, I thought, *but it could have been better.*

What I hated most of all was not being able to do anything for myself. I had become an independent guy during my years in the army. Relying on other people for the smallest tasks, like going to the bathroom, only highlighted my new limits. This reliance bothered me deeply. I asked the attendant for some crutches so I could at least hobble to the restroom after I was alone.

"Sorry, not yet."

Man, I thought, *I can tell I'm not going to like this.*

The next day, my family arrived at BAMC. They had flown up to San Antonio and would be able to stay in their own room in a hospital wing reserved for visiting families.

As I lay in bed, they walked in together wearing big smiles—my dad and mom, my fiancée, Candy, and my daughter, Daytriona. They had brought some get-well cards that had been delivered to their house. We set the cards up on my windowsill. They also gave me two balloons, one with an American flag and the other with a single gold star. Because I had just returned from a war zone, the hospital had put me on "contact precaution." For a short time, any visitor to the area around my bed had to wear a light blue hospital shirt and hospital pants plus white latex gloves to protect them and me from any battlefield germs that I could have still been carrying on my body. I was wearing a short-sleeved, powder blue hospital gown.

We were all thrilled to see each other, even in those circumstances. But my daughter, Day, seemed scared to touch me, maybe because she thought she would hurt me. I paid close attention to her as they chatted about my injury and what had been going on in their lives. I inched Day to my bedside and then scooped her up and held her on my chest like a baby as she giggled. The old family instincts kicked in. Soon we were all laughing. For the first time in more than a week, I began to feel a flash of hope replace some of the worry and fear that had filled my head. I knew I would not have to go through this alone, and that was a giant boost.

My mother was only looking at my face, I noticed. She wouldn't look down at the flat space below the sheets on my right side. She was trying to get her head around this injury, too.

At least he didn't come home in a black bag, she thought as she looked at me. *And there are all those other mothers who will never see their kids again. Still, will he walk again? How is he going to cope with it?* Then she spoke.

"You're going to be fine. You're going to be fine," my mom said. "Everything happens for a reason. God doesn't put anything on you that you can't bear. So I know you can handle it. You just have to be patient and let yourself heal."

"I know," I said.

But inside, I was thinking, *I hope you're right.* I wasn't sure they could fully relate to what I was feeling or going through. All I really wanted to know was how and whether I was ever going to walk again. At that moment, I saw a bleak and limited future— returning to my parents' house on Davis Road where I would spend the rest of my life fetching the mail or attending church in a wheelchair or on crutches.

During the next few weeks, my mom, my dad, and Candy would make sure that one them was always in that room with me to help keep my mind from wandering down troubling paths. Early the following morning after that first visit, my dad sat in a chair near my bed wearing blue hospital garments and his baseball cap. I wanted him to believe that his son was ready to find his way back to happiness.

"This is just a bump in the road," I said, thinking back to what Rodas had told me about being strong and positive for my family. I figured if I showed weakness, they might lose faith in my recovery. My father, who had taught me how to play sports as a kid and who cheered all my football accomplishments, had decided to put on a brave front for me as well.

"It may be a difficult journey," he said. "But if you run into a wall, I'll help you get up. I'll help you get up so you can run into that wall again."

Not long after that, a soldier walked into my room to greet me. He was in his early forties, wore close-cropped hair, a gray "Army" shirt, and black shorts. He stood close enough to my bed that I couldn't see below the bottom of his shorts.

"Hello Kortney, I'm 1st Sgt. Dan Seefeldt. I'm an amputee."

At first I was surprised. I had never seen anyone walk with an artificial leg, and I had not noticed anything different about Dan's stride as he entered. Then he took a couple of steps back and let me see his prosthesis. I inspected all the fancy components in his leg.

Dan, who was from Manitowoc, Wisconsin, had been driving out of Sadr City in Baghdad, escorting a damaged Bradley fighting vehicle back to camp, when his Humvee was ripped apart by an exploding bomb next to the road. The blast had immediately blown off his left leg above the knee. Like me, Dan had been flown to BAMC. After he arrived, doctors had measured the remnants of his left leg and crafted a hard plastic socket to wrap around his stump. The smooth piece would support his body weight and allow him to turn, cut, and stride freely. Two days later, they measured Dan while he stood in an artificial leg, tweaking the fit, and a couple of days after that, he was learning how to walk again. He had been wounded only about six months before me.

"This is a C-leg," he said. "It has a microprocessor in the knee that makes little adjustments for me as I walk. You will get one of these, too. You'll be up and walking in no time."

The C-legs, which cost about forty-five thousand dollars apiece, could be customized by the prosthetists to perfectly match my normal gait, Dan said. A small computer runs the leg's hydraulic system, which, in turn, bends the knee, controls the kick forward, and allows the leg to straighten and push off again: the mechanics of one basic step. Besides mimicking my gait, the C-leg would let me pivot and cut through a crowded room, climb and descend stairs, and even ride a bike. Once I learned how to trust the leg, I wouldn't have to think about every little step. The computer-programmed knee would do the thinking for me.

I was fascinated by the technology. Even more, I was ecstatic to hear about Dan's recovery and to feel his confidence about my future. This gave me another big dash of hope. It also helped that Dan was almost twenty years older than me. I figured that if he could return to the world of the walking, I could get there just as quickly, being an athlete in my prime.

"They can't give you your leg back," Dan told me. "But we've got really good technology now that will let you do things without your natural limb. You can still do whatever you want to do."

That's what I needed to hear, but I was still scared because I was dealing with a badly damaged left leg in addition to the missing right leg. I wondered how long that would that hold me back. The left leg was full of holes—the one in my thigh was almost five inches long and two inches wide. The left leg, foot, and toes still held some shrapnel, and surgeons had just rebuilt and rerouted the artery that supplied all the blood to that leg. It was a mess. One of my doctors wrapped the entire left thigh in beige gauze and taped it tight. Then he wrote on it in black marker: "PLEASE DO NOT DISTURB THIS DRESSING or you will feel my squirrelly wrath!" It made me laugh. And no one disturbed it.

After about a week, the doctors began using a wound vacuum to treat my left leg. The portable machine consisted of a sponge with a long tube that attached to a shoebox-size suction motor. Each day, they placed the sponge into the exposed tissue in my thigh, turned on the machine, and pulled out the unwanted fluid. It kept the wound clean and dry and helped it heal more quickly.

But the left leg was not finished acting up. I also dealt with "compartment syndrome." This can happen after surgery or following an injury. Inflammation creeps in at the wound site or in the tissue nearby, swelling a confined space in the body and blocking the flow of blood to the rest of the limb. My calf had ballooned so badly due to all the destructive injuries in the leg that I was facing nerve damage or muscle death in my left foot if doctors couldn't fix it. Instead of losing one leg, I could have lost the ability to use both. Surgeons sliced grooves into both sides of the leg, running from just above my ankle to the underside of my knee. Medically, it's known as a fasciotomy, and this reduced the swelling. They eventually closed the leg again with forty-three staples. I know because I counted them many times while lying in bed.

In all, I would undergo surgery five times at BAMC to help reconstruct my body. As a result, I was on heavy doses of pain killers—Percocet, Vicodin, morphine, and, later, methadone—to wean me off the morphine. Eventually, I would decide that I was simply done with all the pain meds. I would stop taking the methadone pills cold turkey, causing me to get chills, sweats, and hot flashes just like a heroin addict going through withdrawal. But that would all come later. For now, I had to focus on getting better. As I said, I am not a patient guy.

I couldn't wait to get upright again. According to the doctors, that big moment was probably weeks away—when my wounds had healed enough to allow my left leg to bear weight. Maybe it was my army-medic training, or maybe it was just my natural eagerness, but I had other ideas about standing. One day, during my early weeks at BAMC, one of the other three amputees sharing the room had a family member visit. Not long after she arrived, though, the woman fainted. From our pillows, all four soldiers saw the woman collapse. We each instantly forgot about our missing legs and our other wounds. In my case, I also was pumped so full of pain drugs, my head was almost swimming. But we each hurled back our sheets, bounced out of our hospital beds, and began hopping toward the fallen visitor. Had she opened her eyes to see this bizarre sight—four guys with white-bandaged stumps leaping feverishly to her rescue—I wonder if she might have fainted all over again. I was the first one to reach her side to check on her and comfort her, my old battlefield skills taking over. My wounds were not ready for any kind of activity, but I never hesitated. That was the first time I had stood since the explosion in Baghdad.

Not long after that, I decided I was going to stand up again and use the bathroom like a man, and I was going to do it without crutches. I would hop to the toilet. My family was in the room, and so was a nurse. I pulled myself up and out of bed using the metal triangle, put all my weight on my left foot, and briefly stood on the hospital floor, jumping a bit to keep my balance. But just as quickly, I lost my balance and fell backward. The nurse and my parents caught me before I hit the floor. I just didn't want anyone to help me.

After that day, I would routinely wake up at four or five in the morning, climb from my bed into my wheelchair, and roll to the sink to wash up. Then I would slip back into bed before any of the doctors or nurses came in. My independence—not to mention my stubborn streak—was becoming well known at the hospital. I was in a dog fight to get better, and I planned to win. Maybe football was now, permanently, just a part of my past. But in my future, I was going to live again.

5

Baby Steps

My comeback began on a spongy black mat in a bright room filled with broken people.

Inside the hospital's amputee care center, physical therapist Matt Parker eased me from my wheelchair down to the floor, placed some light dumbbells in my palms, and launched me on my long, slow road from bedridden soldier to running man. More than two weeks into my stay at Brooke Army Medical Center, the time had finally come to rebuild my body. This was a major moment in my life, a grand turning point. There was just one problem: I could barely keep my eyes open.

As a result of all the pain medications I was taking, my head was light and my mind was sleepy. I would sometimes doze off when my mother pushed my chair through the hospital hallways. In the ensuing days, I would snooze on the exercise mat or doze while cranking out reps in a handcycle—a stationary bike operated by the hands instead of the feet.

"Don't fall asleep on that thing," Parker would shout from across the room with a smirk, "you'll slam your head on the pedals."

Early on, this was my rehab reputation. The other wounded soldiers in the room would sometimes razz me when I lay on my back for abdominal exercises: "Yo, you sleepin' over there, Clemons?" But it wouldn't be long until I was needling them about their workouts.

This was my "crawl phase." The early therapy sessions with Parker were designed to fortify my upper body as well as the core muscles in my stomach, hips, and lower back—all the parts of my body I would need to get me upright and walking again. I was at my most frail, but the doctors had examined all my wounds, sutures, and staples, and confirmed that the various holes and slices were healing at a decent pace. They had cleared me for exercise, although I still needed to tote my portable wound vac into the therapy clinic. I was not supposed to be unplugged from the little machine for more than thirty minutes at a time. After all the bed rest, it was now Parker's time to get me in motion.

Dark haired, in his mid-thirties, and a native of Washington State, Parker was the kind of physical therapist who cared not just about muscles, flexibility, and endurance but also about a patient's mental side.

"How are you today?" Parker would ask an amputee arriving for his daily therapy in the first-floor rehab clinic.

"Fine," he would say.

"You can't tell me you're 'fine.' And I'll tell you why," Parker would say. "There's an old Aerosmith song called 'F.I.N.E.' The title is an acronym. Now, I won't say what the 'F' stands for. But the 'I' stands for 'insecure,' the 'N' is for 'neurotic,' and the 'E' is for 'emotional.' So, are you 'fine?'"

"Uh, no," the solder would say. "I'm okay."

"That's better. But now you have to tell me what's really going on."

Parker just wanted the amputees to know he was fully aware that all of the soldiers in his clinic had been trained to never complain or show weakness. When it came to physical therapy, though, that kind of brave silence didn't help anybody.

Our first days of rehab were spent mainly on the mat. Since I was not ready to stand on my gimpy left leg and foot, Parker had me perform sit-ups and crunches, working my abdominal muscles. He stretched my hips and measured the range of motion in my legs. He gave me a pair of hand weights and told me to do bench-press lifts while I kept my shoulder blades elevated off the floor. I also used the weights for some of the same exercises I had done as a football player—pumping up my chest, back, biceps, and triceps. Parker didn't need to teach me anything when it came to hoisting dumbbells, but he did critique my style, making sure I didn't hurt myself. As a guy temporarily confined to a wheelchair, the last thing I needed was a shoulder injury.

The goals of those first workouts were simple. The first was to build my core strength, to make sure I was physically stable when the day came to finally stand in my new prosthetic limb. The second was to make sure I stayed occupied.

"You need to find something to keep you busy—and keep you out of your room," Parker said.

Sweating again felt good, almost normal. The gym had always been a refuge for me, a place where I excelled. But unlike my workouts in Baghdad—or those in college when my teammates and I used to break into the fitness center with a butter knife—I wasn't quite ready to be social with the other twelve or so patients with whom I usually shared the therapy clinic. During those initial sessions I wore my headphones to rehab, listening to a little serenity music while I pushed my body. One of my favorite artists at the time was Smokie Norful Jr., a gospel singer and pianist whose biggest hit, "I Need You Now," was written after his wife was told she had cancer, his father had open-heart surgery, and his grandmother was facing serious medical issues. In that song, Norful reached out to God for healing and comfort. I could relate.

While the words and melody soothed me, I could see that the other soldiers across the gym appeared to be laughing, joking, and clowning around. What was that all about? I decided that during my next appointment, I'd leave my headphones back in the room. I wanted to check out what was so funny. I wanted to be part of that. What I eventually heard was good-natured trash-talking, the essence of sports conversation and part of any great locker room.

As a high school and college football player, one of the things I loved most was simply being part of the team, those bonding moments when everyone pulled in the same direction for a common good. Central to that was the banter between the guys. With their chuckles and one-liners, these other patients were forming a team, too, all egging one another on, pushing one another to get better. But on another level, their constant ribbing was a healthy way for these soldiers to taunt their tough situations, to stare down the injuries, to scream, "This won't beat me! This will never beat me!" I was ready to join in.

Our rehab room was occupied only by lower-body amputees. Patients who were missing arms or hands exercised in another area at the hospital where the equipment suited their specific needs. In our gym, there were two clear subsets: the ones whose legs had been severed above the knee, and the ones who had lost their limbs below the knee. In the amputee world, still possessing your knee offered a huge recovery edge, especially when it came to walking or running. With its elastic web of tendons and ligaments, and its rubbery, shock-absorbing cartilage, the knee is a natural mobility machine that can cut left or right, thrust you into the air, propel you forward, or simply take the pounding of everyday life or everyday sport. Without a knee joint, the impact of walking—not to mention running—is aimed directly at that residual stump, and in my case, there is no natural cushion left. When the surgeons removed my lower leg, they pulled my hamstring muscles from the back of my thigh, stretched them down and over the stump, then attached those strands to the bottom of my sawed-off femur. They also took what was left of my quadriceps muscles in the front of my thigh and sewed them to the bone as well. Between the skin on the outside of my stump and the end of the femur inside, there is about an inch and a half of tissue.

When above-the-knee amputees walk, we generate seven to nine times the force of our body weight right into the point where the prosthesis meets our residual leg. For me, that's almost 1,500 pounds slamming into the socket. But that's not where that energy and those frictions stop. When someone with an above-the-knee amputation walks or runs in a prosthetic leg, the weight-bearing forces from those steps are purposely passed up the remaining femur to the ischium—the bone that forms the lower back and part of the hip. You can walk and run again, but it feels like you're carrying a person on your back. By the numbers, above-the-knee amputees expend 280 percent more energy when we walk as compared to a person with both legs. In time, the back and hips can start to ache. But this physical disadvantage became the perfect fuel for my rehab jabs down in the therapy clinic room.

The two amputee groups had tagged themselves with nicknames: we were the AKs (above the knee), and they were the BKs (below the knee). At the hospital, these groups became sort of like our teams, a way to create a little healthy competition and fire up the spirit, and this was my way into their trash-talking world.

"Hey, all you BKs, we gotcha, man!" I said one day. "Us AKs, we're out to get you!"

They laughed and barked back.

"Yeah? What are you gonna do?" they said. "You ain't got no knee over there!"

"Man, you're not even amputees," I said. "What are you missing, like a couple of toes? Come on."

"Yeah, that's why we're gonna take you AKs out. We'll be outside running while you're over there sleeping on your mat, Clemons."

"Well, ya'll might as well just stand up then, ya'll might as well come on because the AKs are on top. We got it goin' on!"

The back-and-forth jawing was funny and it did inspire us to work harder. We all understood and appreciated the value of competition. We all thrived on the notion that we were the kind of people who met life head-on and devoured all the challenges in our paths. This was how we ticked. This was how we had been trained by the army.

The AKs wanted to prove to the BKs, to the therapists, and to the world that nobody was going to outhustle or outwork us. The BKs had that same edge, that same desire to outperform the AKs, or any able-bodied person for that matter. The patients in that room were professional soldiers, meaning most of them were highly motivated, mentally tough, physically strong, bold, and brassy. Internally, many of us were battling private demons: worries about our future, questions about our identity, and all of the invisible brain-related conditions that we had dragged home from the battlefield, like posttraumatic stress and depression. But outwardly, most of us projected that same soldierly attitude: gritty, confident, amped.

The physical therapy clinic also provided a kind of sanctuary where we could again feel somewhat normal instead of feeling like sudden outsiders in a two-legged world. Each of us was missing something. In the clinic we weren't different. It would take me years to feel comfortable with my new appearance in public places, at first hiding my amputation with long pants and, later, cloaking it with skin-colored artificial limbs. Getting used to the stares would take time.

With that kind of instant bonding, the rehab sessions created some tight friendships. One of my earliest hospital pals was an army master sergeant named Jonathan Hart. Twenty-four years older than me, Hart had been sent back from Mosul, Iraq, right around the time I was being airlifted home from Germany. He was dealing with a serious kidney condition, sleep apnea, and a torn meniscus, or knee cartilage. At Camp Diamondback in northern Iraq, he had run the dietary department at the base hospital, headed troop morale efforts by staging basketball tournaments and dances, and, as an ordained minister, held Sunday gospel services that blared church music into the surrounding desert. A big man with a big laugh, Hart stuck his head in the exercise room one morning while I was working out.

"All right, Kortney, what's goin' on?" Hart boomed.

"Well, the BKs over there think they got it goin' on, man," I hollered. "But they're trying too hard. We got it goin' on, and we don't have to try too hard. We're the AKs. BKs can't hang with us."

Hart roared and clapped his hands. Across the room, two of the BKs threw their heads back and howled. Army specialist Albert Ross, a twenty-one-year-old Louisianan who played the trumpet in his high school marching band, had lost the lower part of his right leg on August 23, 2004, when a rocket-propelled grenade landed near him and detonated while he was on patrol in Baghdad. Robert Roeder, a Tampa Bay Buccaneers fan and navy seaman, had been standing on the deck of the USS Kitty Hawk aircraft carrier on January 29, 2005, when an F/A-18F Super Hornet landed and snagged one of the arresting wires designed to stop incoming fighter jets. But the thick steel cable had snapped, whipped around, and sliced completely through Roeder's lower left leg. Ross and Roeder—along with Hart, myself, and a few others—soon would form a little hospital posse, seven wounded people who stood behind one another while we each tried to find our way in bodies decimated by war.

Most of my new friends were a little further along than me in their recoveries. Ross, already was walking in a high-tech prosthetic leg that fit into a laced-and-tied white running shoe. I couldn't wait to get up and moving like Ross, and when it came to standing again, I had a single date, March 24, circled on my calendar. On that Thursday, an army general would pin a Purple Heart medal on my chest and salute my sacrifice. On that day, exactly thirty-one days after my injury, I wanted to stand on two legs to receive the honor.

But in mid-March, my main mode of transportation was still the wheelchair. Not that I was complaining. For some reason, the hospital had given me the biggest, widest chair it had in stock. Parker called it "the eighteen-wheeler." The medical staff eventually realized their mistake and wanted to swap it for a more suitable size, but I wouldn't give that thing back. Even though I'd have to cruise down the hallways with my arms stretched wide to reach those wheels, it was a comfortable ride. There was even enough room to let me stash some extra clothes on both sides of the seat, in case I needed to make a quick change during the day. Hey, I still wanted to look good.

After all the weightlifting and rehab sessions with Parker, my core muscles were now robust enough to help me rise from that wheelchair and keep me stable as I stood in a prosthetic right leg. I knew that standing again would feel amazing. But even more, I was antsy to take my first steps, to see the culmination of all those workouts. My parents and Candy, who had celebrated each of my small recovery victories during their three-week stay at BAMC, were also excited and ready to see a huge milestone.

On March 19, a Saturday, tens of thousands of Americans protested the second anniversary of the U.S. invasion of Iraq. People demonstrated in 765 cities and towns. They carried signs decrying the evils of war. They carried signs supporting the troops. In San Francisco, twenty thousand people protested and rallied.

In New York City, ten thousand gathered to demand an end to the Iraq War and a return of our soldiers. In the Oval Office, where I would someday stand and talk with the commander in chief, President Bush marked the occasion on his weekly radio address.

"Good morning. On this day two years ago, we launched Operation Iraqi Freedom to disarm a brutal regime, free its people, and defend the world from a grave danger," the president said. ". . . To all the brave members of our Armed Forces who have taken part in this historic mission, and to your families, I express the heartfelt thanks of the American people. . . . Because of our actions, freedom is taking root in Iraq, and the American people are more secure."

On March 19, I walked for the first time since losing my leg on a Baghdad highway.

John Fergason, the chief of prosthetics at BAMC, had evaluated my rehab progress and decided the day had come to fit me with my first prosthetic socket—a clear plastic sheath that snuggly enclosed the rounded end of my right leg, also covering what remained of my upper right thigh. This was the first piece of the full prosthetic leg I eventually would receive. The socket's main job would be to gently absorb the force of my body weight, transferring that energy to the rest of the artificial limb and then to the ground.

Fergason's formal plan that Saturday afternoon was to attach the socket to my leg, stand me up between a set of parallel bars in his prosthetics lab, and then closely examine the socket's fit and feel.

In Fergason's mind, I was still days away from walking. My body wasn't quite ready, he believed, and my new artificial leg wasn't ready, either. But me and my family, well, we had other ideas.

The prosthetic socket encasing the end of my right leg was a true piece of art, and the artist was standing with me inside the parallel bars. Fergason was one of the best in the world at crafting these protective shields. He was a stickler and a perfectionist when it came to his creations because he knew that if they didn't fit, we didn't walk.

A wiry man in his midforties with close-cropped hair and a dry sense of humor, Fergason had recently left his job as the head of prosthetics-orthotics at the University of Washington, Seattle—long considered a nerve center for advances in artificial limbs. As the wars in Iraq and Afghanistan continued to rob hundreds of soldiers of their arms and legs, a friend at Walter Reed had alerted Fergason that BAMC was about to open a new ward to care for the overflow of battle-related amputations. Fergason didn't wait around to be recruited by BAMC brass. He called them. Becoming the army hospital's prosthetics chief would be an ideal career move on two counts, he believed. One, the area was home to his wife's family. Two, he could build the artificial limb program without any worry about financial constraints; whatever expensive parts and components the returning soldiers required, Fergason knew that money was no object and insurance companies would not stand in the way as they often do in private medicine. In that setting, he could work wonders. This was his calling, his chance to serve.

Fergason often cracked jokes to keep his patients loose, but he was sentimental, too. He was a father of three young children, and he had never forgotten their first steps as toddlers. When the grown men under his care made their first strides in the legs he had assembled, Fergason used to say, "It never gets old to me."

His prosthetics lab at the hospital looked like a cross between a NASCAR garage and an arts-and-crafts studio. This was the leg factory. Like any good mechanic, he had a stack of four red toolchests containing drawers that brimmed with clamps, propane torches, saw blades, and drill bits. Bags of plaster sat open on a workbench. Fergason and his five-member team also used a wide array of industrial machinery: saws, drill presses, sewing machines, and a computerized carver.

Job one in Fergason's lab was to create the sockets—made to order and perfectly matched to each bump and groove in what remained of an amputee's leg, yet also designed to fit in the future. When casting a socket, Fergason had to calculate how his patients' activity levels would change as they became more mobile, what they weighed in the present, and what they might weigh in two or three months. Fergason would then use all these variables to determine the socket's stiffness and strength.

At this point, two main manufacturing methods were available—by the numbers and by basic human feel. In the high-tech version, Fergason would take a precise set of measurements from a patient's residual limb and plug those numbers into his computerized milling machine, which in seven or eight minutes would then churn out a foam model for a socket the soldier soon would wear. Next, a vacuum machine pulled liquid plastic over the model and, after the liquid dried, technicians knocked away the foam, leaving a fresh plastic socket.

But some mangled legs required a more hands-on approach. For Fergason, this low-tech method of socket-making was like a return to art class. First, he would cover the soldier's residual leg in plastic and cloth strips. Then, using a blue marker, he would plot out where severed bones pushed upward and where the remaining limb had indentations from shrapnel wounds or from the amputation surgery. Bandages covered with plaster were then moistened and pasted around the limb. As they dried, the blue ink seeped into the underside of the plaster cast, showing Fergason just where he needed to scoop out extra space to accommodate small bulges in the stump, or where he needed to add plastic to fill in low areas. The idea was to create a socket that perfectly replicated the intricacies of a limb, almost like a relief map. Later, the rest of the prosthetic leg would be fastened to the socket.

"Without question, I do embrace much of the older-school style of practice because, when the day is done, I know that thing is going to fit," Fergason would say when explaining his work. "And I also use technology when I know it's going to augment my current skills. Prosthetics isn't as scientific as we'd all like to think. There is a lot of artistry to it that affects your results."

His sockets were the single most important piece of any artificial leg, whether you were talking about a computerized walking leg or a super-light sprinting leg. They cradled and protected the tips of our severed limbs at the very point of impact. If the sockets didn't fit just right, patients would be in pain during their rehab sessions and would lose critical time in their quests to walk or run again. If we suffered aches where the socket wrapped our legs, we were never told to "just get used to it." At the same time, though, a new leg could never completely replace the one God gave us, Fergason would say. While he worked overtime to make the sockets as comfortable as possible, the feel could never be described as "great." They were more or less tolerable.

Once the sockets were done, Fergason would order and buy the rest of the leg components—including knees and feet—from prosthetic makers like Ossur. Just as he did with his socket designs, Fergason would select knees based on how active he thought his patients would be three months into the future. Physical therapists like Parker and the patients themselves would help him with those projections.

Once the leg parts had arrived at BAMC, Fergason would align the entire limb, positioning the socket in perfect relation to the knee and foot. To do an alignment, Fergason and a physical therapist would simply watch an amputee walk, studying each tiny segment of his stride—the artificial foot on the ground, the leg moving forward, the leg moving backward—what prosthetics people call "the phases of gait." If Fergason saw that a toe needed to be turned more toward the outside of the body, or that a foot needed to be pulled farther up or pointed farther down, those changes usually could be made with a 4-millimeter Allen wrench, simply by tightening screws on the inside or outside of the knee. When Fergason needed to align a computerized knee, he could just plug his laptop directly into the knee and get an instant visual rendering of eight possible adjustment parameters. As the patient did a test walk, Fergason's computer screen would show him the precise knee position and the amount of force—or "load"—on his heel and toe during every phase of those steps. Physical therapists like Parker also would scrutinize the patient's gait and direct Fergason to speed up or slow down the knee. To do that, Fergason would simply left-click his mouse on a bar on his screen and pull it to the left or the right, either increasing or decreasing the knee settings. (These days, the computer adjustments are done wirelessly.)

"The alignment is critical," Fergason would say. "If the alignment of your car is off, you're not going down the road straight. You're going to wear out your tires and it's dangerous. Same thing for us. If the alignment isn't right, I'm hamstringing how far the physical therapist can take you."

Because Fergason's workshop was located right in the hospital, I could stop by the lab anytime and ask him to adjust the fit of my leg. This was common practice in the amputee world. Often, the bones in our residual legs continued to grow, which caused painful spurs and also changed the entire shape of the sockets we needed. He made as many as six sockets a year for some soldiers. His room was always a flurry of leg-making and leg-tweaking, with patients coming and going. But even with such serious reasons for our being there, Fergason always kept things light.

"Whether you agree with the political aspect of the war is inconsequential in here," Fergason told the *Austin American-Statesman* in a 2006 interview. "Rehab is the only thing that's consequential. We want the guys who walk in these doors—or roll in—to walk out of this hospital and get back to their lives as fast as possible."

Sometimes Fergason brought his three young kids with him to the lab. They would meet and talk with the soldiers.

"They do understand that war is a difficult thing; soldiers protect our country and some of them get hurt doing it and dad helps them get well again," Fergason told the *San Antonio Express-News* in 2006. "They see a soldier with an artificial leg and they'll ask, 'Dad, did you make that one?'"

Fergason had cast my new socket. Now he planned to meet me in a fitting room where he would attach it and check the socket's snugness and comfort. But when he turned the corner and entered the room, he was stunned to see my mom, my dad, and Candy waiting with me, plus a TV news crew from Seattle that happened to be videotaping a story on the hospital.

What Fergason had envisioned was a routine fitting. What he saw were faces filled with expectation.

They think Kortney is going to walk today, Fergason said to himself. *But his prosthetic leg isn't even ready. We are* way *ahead of schedule here.*

My dad, Mitch, greeted Fergason with a broad smile.

"You know, I wasn't there for Kortney's first steps," Dad said. "I wasn't going to miss these!"

"You bet he's going to take some steps today!" Fergason said, his mind reeling. "I'm glad you could be here."

Then he thought, *I'm not going to be the one to kill this party.*

Now Fergason had to find a leg fast. He stepped outside the fitting room and racked his brain. He had just finished working with another soldier named Evan Morgan, a double amputee, who might have been his best chance to beg a leg.

Evan was still hanging out nearby in the prosthetics lab, shooting the breeze with some other soldiers. Fergason approached him with a question that you probably only hear in an amputee ward.

"Hey, Evan, your knee would work out really good for Kortney. We don't have another one lying around that would work for his height and weight. Do you mind if we use your leg to get him up, so he can take his first steps?"

"Not at all," Evan said without hesitation. "Go for it."

How often in life does another man loan you his right leg?

Evan was a twenty-one-year-old marine from Boulder, Colorado, who had wanted to join the U.S. Marine Corps since he was eight years old. His older brother was a marine, too. Evan had wrestled a bit in high school and also loved to go on distance runs, a passion among people in Boulder. Just eleven weeks earlier, Evan had been attached to a U.S. Army Special Forces unit, riding in a Humvee in Al Qaim—a town in Iraq's northwestern Anbar province near the Syrian border. This region, the army believed, was part of a smuggling route and a sanctuary for foreign fighters. On January 1, 2005, a flatbed army truck—riding in a supply convoy—had hit an IED and become stuck in the desert. Evan's platoon had been told to escort a tow truck that would fetch the damaged flatbed. After delivering the tow truck, Evan had asked his driver to do a U-turn and head back to camp. But his Humvee's right front tire—just below Evan's seat—had run atop a second explosive devise during the turn, triggering an orange fireball. The blast had cost him his right leg above the knee and his left leg below the knee. It also stole the vision in his right eye and left him with a broken right arm, broken nose, and fractured fingers. While recovering and rehabbing at BAMC, Evan had received two new feet and a prosthetic right knee. On the day he took his first steps, he and Fergason had cried together.

Because Evan was an above-the-knee amputee on his right side and about my size, his leg would be a decent fit for me. He sat down in a wheelchair as Ferguson used an Allen wrench to loosen the four screws—one in back, one in front, and two on each side—that held the mechanical leg to his socket. Evan's leg had a black knee. A yellow metallic rod stood in for what would be the shin or lower leg. On the foot of his limb there was a yellow Reebok running shoe, its laces permanently tied into a bow. For a single-leg amputee to wear two shoes, the artificial foot must match the size of the natural foot, so when I need a prosthetic foot, I order it in a size nine. Limb components—especially those in carbon-fiber running legs—come in a limited variety of manufacturer colors, often black or gray. You can customize a walking leg by ordering a cosmetic, skin-colored covering. But if you want to really add some personality to your prosthetic limb—if you want to pimp your leg—the best spot to do that is in the socket. Those glossy pieces can be laminated with wild designs or bright colors. I've seen guys with army camouflage or pictures of their kids adorned on their sockets. Later, I would have a Penn State Nittany Lion logo painted on my socket.

After returning to the fitting room, Fergason attached my socket as I sat in a light fiberglass chair between the parallel bars. He then fastened Evan's leg to my socket, tightening the same four screws. The limb now dangled from just under my dark blue gym shorts.

"Okay, Kortney, let's try it. Go ahead and stand up," he said.

"Keep much of your weight on the parallel bars so your limb doesn't have to take all the weight," he coached.

I pushed myself out of the chair, using the waist-high parallel bars. The track was about fifteen feet long with a rubbery black tread that gave the beginners some needed traction. One end was bordered by three full-length mirrors in which we could watch our form as we tried those initial shaky steps. The other end opened to the rest of the room. That's where my small crowd of supporters—Dad, Mom, and Candy—anxiously waited for me to learn how to walk for the second time in my life.

Fergason, kneeling in front of me and wearing blue latex gloves, held both sides of my waist as I slowly found my balance with my original foot and the loaner on my right.

"How does that leg feel?"

"Not as bad as I thought it would," I said.

Standing in an artificial limb was a strange experience. It certainly didn't feel like a part of me. It's not like I suddenly had the sense of possessing a full leg again. What I had was this cold contraption I somehow needed to control and maneuver. I couldn't feel the knee bend, although that's what it was built to do. Mainly, I was worried about falling once I got moving.

Fergason had me stand and grab the outside parallel bar, looking out toward the room. Evan had rolled his chair to the door to peek inside. He was smiling. Then Fergason stood behind me and turned me again toward the open end of the track, in the direction of my parents and Candy. Time to walk.

You can do it, my mother said to herself.

With Fergason's left hand on my waist and his right hand gripping the artificial limb just below my socket—and with me firmly clutching each bar, palms sweating—I took step number one as an amputee.

"Get your right heel out in front of you," Fergason said.

Using the muscles in my right hip and right hamstring, I kicked the borrowed leg forward, planting the yellow running shoe on the black tread below me. I then brought my left leg ahead, even with the right.

A few feet ahead of me, my dad broke into a smile as tears rolled down his cheeks. People in the room clapped.

"If it gets too uncomfortable, take more of your weight in your hands as you hold the parallel bars," Fergason said.

Uncomfortable? No. I was walking. A massive grin spread across my face.

I repeated the motion—push and plant, right leg forward, left leg forward—as he continued to guide me. Then we turned and faced the mirrors. For the first time, I could watch myself step into this new life.

On the back of my black T-shirt—in the middle of a yellow square patch—my family could see the logo of a flying Blackhawk helicopter, like the one that had rescued me from the battlefield twenty-six days earlier. Next, Fergason let me go solo, standing in front of me and reminding me how to move the leg and how to distribute my weight. Foot by foot, I made it to the mirrors. Then I turned again and made another lap, still using those bars for support. That day, I completed about fifteen or sixteen steps. In the past few years, I had traveled around the world and survived excursions through a war zone. Yet that tiny trip in a hospital rehab room was one of the biggest journeys I will ever take.

Between the parallel bars, I never stopped worrying about taking a tumble. But I didn't go down. I pulled it off because I never doubted myself. I felt all along like I could accomplish this feat. I knew it would be hard, and it was. I just fully concentrated on each step. One at a time.

Man, that was dangerous, I thought after it was all over. *I can't believe I can stand up on my own. I can't believe I can walk again.*

"Hey, man, how'd you like that yellow shoe?" Evan asked, knowing it didn't quite mesh with my style.

"I've got to get me a pair of these!" I said sarcastically.

"Thanks, man," I added, "for letting me get up on your leg."

Two years later, Evan would be competing in triathlons with his two artificial limbs. Sports would become the juice for his stunning revival. In his races, Evan would routinely beat two-legged athletes to the finish line, something that he said made him feel "*real* good!" To increase his traction for those road races, Evan would eventually peel the yellow soles off those Reebok shoes and paste them onto the bottom of his high-tech running feet. I'm glad that I was able to take a little test-drive in one of those same yellow soles.

Five days later, with my own artificial limb securely in place, I rolled my wheelchair into an auditorium at BAMC. The portion of the leg just above the knee was decorated with red and white stripes and the blue star field of the American flag. I had come to receive my Purple Heart medal. I would stand for the ceremony just like I planned.

My official Purple Heart certificate—signed by Francis J. Harvey, secretary of the army, and C. William Fox Jr., commanding general of Brooke Army Medical Center—said I was receiving the award "for wounds received in action." One line also offered a nugget of Purple Heart history: the honor was "established by General George Washington at Newburgh, New York, Aug. 7, 1782." That's a story worth telling. As commander of the Continental Army, Washington understood two critical pieces of battlefield psychology: the morale and motivation of the common soldier. Those qualities, he knew, were the cornerstones of fighting a grueling war. Whenever one of his front-line troops demonstrated true valor in action, Washington gave that man an officer's commission or a promotion, plus a bump in salary. But by the summer of 1782, money was running short to pay the soldiers, much less all the new officers, so the Continental Congress told Washington to stop the practice immediately. The general came up with a creative and cheap alternative. In an order written at his Newburgh headquarters, Washington directed that "whenever any singular meritorious action is performed, the author of it shall be permitted to wear on his facings, over his left breast, the figure of a heart in purple cloth."

In the late 1920s, the U.S. War Department decided to revive the Purple Heart decoration for troops who were hurt in battle. In 1931, General Douglas MacArthur took over that project. Under MacArthur's direction, the new award bore a gold likeness of Washington's profile against a purple background, all framed by a gold heart-shaped border. The accompanying ribbon was also purple, trimmed in gold. It looks exactly the same today. The Purple Heart is the oldest military decoration still in use and the first to be made available to the common soldier. The medal's motto: "Some gave all . . . all gave some."

The year before the September 11, attacks, the federal government ordered a new batch of Purple Hearts. The old supply, which was running low, had been made in preparation for the planned invasion of Japan in 1945, at the close of World War II, according to the History News Network. Military leaders had expected the U.S. infantry assault on Japan to last until nearly 1947, with thousands of probable American casualties. The invasion was scrubbed when Japan surrendered following the atomic bombings of Hiroshima and Nagasaki. After the wars in Korea and Vietnam and the first Gulf War, that stock of Purple Heart decorations had been depleted. In August 2007, the *Houston Chronicle* reported on a shortage of the medals as a result of the wars in Iraq and Afghanistan. According to the *Chronicle*, a navy veteran in line for the honor was told by Navy Personnel Command that he would have wait for his Purple Heart or buy his own for forty-two dollars because the military was "out of stock."

The Pentagon's rules on the awarding of Purple Hearts are detailed but do contain some gray areas. In a nutshell, military personnel become eligible when they're hurt in action against an enemy of the United States. Any injury to any part of the body qualifies, although the wound must require treatment by a medical officer. What doesn't qualify? Frostbite, heat stroke, non-enemy-caused accidents, and more. My new rehab buddy, Robert Roeder, fell into that no-man's land of Purple Heart glory. Because Roeder lost his leg outside the designated combat zone, he did not earn a Purple Heart.

"We're in a current conflict. I would imagine that, you know, everyone would be considered combat related just because everyone is training up to the point where they're going to be in Iraq," Roeder told CNN in November 2006.

We both were serving our country at the time of our injuries. We surrendered our legs to the cause. How can you draw a line between those two traumatic events and say that one was worthy of a medal and one was not?

The presentation ceremony was packed. The other Purple Heart recipient that day was Sgt. Johnny R. Wilson, who had sustained severe injuries to his lower left leg and ankle when his truck was damaged by a roadside bomb in Iraq. Dad, Mom, and Candy sat together in the audience. I sat in my wheelchair at the front of the room, just below a poster of the 2003 *Time* magazine cover that named "the American soldier" as its person of the year.

I wore a gray "Army" T-shirt and black shorts. I listened as the commander of my army division, the 1st Cavalry, told the crowd that our sacrifices had helped change history in Iraq, where 52 percent of the people had recently voted in national elections. Purple was the color of the day in Iraq, too. Voters had held up purple-stained index fingers—a mark to show they had cast their ballots; even more, the purple smudges were a sign of defiance against the terrorists.

"In Baghdad people understand the value of democracy and they would not have it without these great American soldiers," said Major General Peter W. Chiarelli.

As the general approached me with medal in hand, I slowly stood from my wheelchair.

Just don't fall down, I said to myself as Chiarelli pinned the medal to my shirt, on the left side of my chest. My mechanical knee had the ability to bend and also the ability to buckle. Because it was not one of the knees with a microprocessor, it wouldn't lock in place for me. There was nothing to keep me from tipping, except my own balance. Again, though, I was able to stay upright. All of my falls would come later, when I tried to run.

I was proud that my parents and Candy saw me receive the medal, and witnessed a formal military ceremony. But in truth, if I could have my leg back, I would gladly have returned that Purple Heart to the army. I would make that trade any day.

That's not to say the medal didn't carry meaning for me. I appreciated it as a token of my duty and my accomplishments. It also reminded me that I was still around to accept it. The three guys on the other side of the stretcher were not. On the day the army honored David Day, Jason Timmerman, and Jesse Lhotka with their Purple Hearts, somber generals handed those medals to their three grieving wives—Amy, Teresa, and Stacey.

Still, if I compared my situation to a Purple Heart recipient who had suffered, say, a bullet wound, there was a profound and inescapable difference. The hole in that soldier would eventually heal and close over. My leg would never grow back. In other words, I would never need a ribbon to remind me or anybody else what I had given up for my country. When I walked down the streets long after that ceremony, everyone would see my sacrifice.

Today, the Purple Heart rests in its case, tucked in a box at my parents' house.

Back in the same room where I had launched my recovery— Matt Parker's physical therapy clinic—I began the exhausting task of truly relearning how to walk.

Although I had already cranked out several steps to the sound of applause and the sight of tears, this part of the process required me to simply stand, on both legs, between the parallel bars. There wasn't much fanfare for that. But Parker's first task was to get me used to bearing weight on the new knee as well as on my left side, which had been so damaged by shrapnel and swelling. I worked on shifting my weight from right to left and back again. Just by staying upright between the bars, I was boosting the overall endurance in my lower body.

Next, I took steps between the bars.

"You don't have to overpower the prosthetic leg," Parker told me. "We're going to work on smoothing out your gait so that it looks more natural."

From the bars, I soon went to crutches. Parker taught me how to practice a "four-point gait"—first planting the right crutch, then the left foot, then the left crutch, then the right foot, almost spiderlike. This practice would prepare me for being able to stand independently on each leg. It also taught me how to put the right amount of pressure on the prosthesis so I could get the knee to bend whenever it was the proper time for that within my gait. Here, the overall idea was to get my walking to appear symmetrical again.

I moved through those drills quickly. I remember Parker looking surprised when, not long after that, I was holding the crutches in my hands but not touching them to the floor. I had learned to stabilize my new knee. I was on my way forward again.

While I took those positive steps, I still had wounds that few could see—and only I could feel. One I would deal with for years: post-traumatic stress disorder. The other I struggled with in those first months home: a serious concussion. Together, they packed a mean punch and caused me to make a major detour in my life's plans.

Both were easy to explain, given the blinding violence of my last minutes in Iraq and the endless threat of bad things in an angry land.

The concussion seemed to sap my short-term memory. I was misplacing objects and forgetting names, and when I looked in the mirror, I could see subtle evidence of the concussion. In the photo for my new army identification badge, taken on March 31, 2005, I had dark circles around my eyes—what some people call "raccoon eyes," a temporary trait associated with some head injuries. I also had suffered a ruptured eardrum in the blast, which was just another indication that I was practically standing on top of the bomb when it blew. According to the Mayo Clinic, a concussion occurs when the brain—which has all the consistency of gelatin—slides forcefully against the inner wall of the skull. This sloshing and banging can cause bleeding in and around the brain as well as the tearing of nerve fibers. Falls and car accidents can send the brain into sudden motion. So can bombs.

Post-traumatic stress disorder, or PTSD, is a life-altering anxiety that can be triggered when a horrific event happens to you or when you see unspeakable injuries happen to other people. In Iraq, "horrific" and "unspeakable" were the norm. I came home with PTSD. So did tens of thousands of other American soldiers. According to an October 2007 *USA Today* article, out of the more than 100,000 combat vets who had sought help for mental illness since the start of the war in Afghanistan in 2001, almost half were PTSD cases. Because so many troops are seeing extended duty and multiple tours, medical experts believe the diagnosis rate among Iraq veterans will ultimately top the 30 percent PTSD rate faced by Vietnam veterans. About 1.5 million U.S. troops have served in Iraq and Afghanistan. If the expected diagnosis rate holds true, the war will create about 450,000 PTSD cases—even more if the conflict drags on for several years.

The symptoms are frustrating and sneaky. On the Mayo Clinic's list of PTSD warning signs are flashbacks, or reliving the traumatic event for minutes or even days at a time; shame or guilt; upsetting dreams about the traumatic event; trying to avoid thinking or talking about the traumatic event; feeling emotionally numb; irritability or anger; changes in relationships; self-destructive behavior, such as drinking too much; hopelessness about the future; trouble sleeping; memory problems; trouble concentrating; and being easily startled or frightened. Depending on who I talked to, I had at least six of those symptoms.

My nightmares were bad. For years after I returned to the States, I had a recurring dream: I am riding a bike through the crowded streets of Baghdad, lost and separated from my unit, frantically searching for my friends while mortars fall all around me, causing no sound as they erupt into fireballs. What does it mean? Well, I can only look at the pieces of the nightmare. The bike might be a symbol of my childhood when I rode up and down Davis Road. Being lost from my unit could represent feeling exposed and vulnerable—something that was part of everyday life in Baghdad. The silent bombs? I never heard the explosion that took my leg. I suppose the dream might mean that I'm trying to escape to my younger days when I felt safe and had both of my legs.

I don't necessarily try to avoid thinking about the trauma I experienced in Iraq, but I make it a point never to watch CNN or any other war coverage. Seeing those images bothers me and seems to spark those nightmares. And as a result of spending nearly a year staying ready and prepared for attacks, I still visibly jump whenever someone slams a door or whenever I hear other unexpected loud noises. True relaxation is hard for me to find.

The memory lapses were another issue, but in the spring of 2005, it was hard to tell where the concussion stopped and the PTSD began when it came to my forgetfulness. I should note that if a soldier suffers a concussion while in action, he or she is eligible for the Purple Heart. Under the Pentagon's rules, however, a diagnosis of PTSD does not merit a medal.

Probably the toughest PTSD-related problem I faced, and still occasionally face, was the feeling of hopelessness about the future. There were times after I returned from Iraq when I thought, *Maybe it would have been better if I had died on that highway.*

I wasn't in any pain. Maybe I should have died. There would be days during the summer of 2005—after my family left and returned to Mississippi—when that depression really took hold. I just wouldn't want to be around other people and wouldn't get out of bed. I have read the accounts of other soldiers with PTSD who said they had the urge to close themselves off from the world. Some of those soldiers drank excessively or did drugs to soothe those empty, forlorn feelings. My coping mechanism would eventually become sleep, hours and hours of sleep. This would mark one of the most dangerous periods of my life, a stretch when I might have allowed my future to slip away in a haze of lonely depression. Thankfully, my posse of hospital friends, especially Jonathan Hart, would help pull me out of that funk.

The doctors at BAMC prescribed me with an antidepressant drug to try to curb the PTSD symptoms, but I didn't feel like myself on the drug and stopped taking it. After I made that choice, I actually felt some of my old energy return. The best medicine for me is being around people.

Despite the posttraumatic stress and the tiny baby steps I was taking in the physical therapy room, I was determined to continue life as close to my original plans as possible. During those first weeks in the hospital I had a friend drive me to a San Antonio mall to buy an engagement ring for Candy. I made the purchase from my wheelchair. Candy was spending every day with me during my recovery, and I wanted to marry her. We were childhood sweethearts. But my parents urged me to wait. They felt I needed time to heal, that I should concentrate only on getting better. Eventually, I saw that they were right.

Candy and I put the marriage plans on hold. We would remain the best of friends. She would still be looking out for me, and I for her. But we both had our lives to lead, and our separate goals to conquer. The decision to wait was painful.

At the very core of my recovery was the sheer will to forge ahead in life, the refusal to let one terrible moment on a battlefield drain my hopes or kill my spirit. In my journey of self-discovery, this was one of the first things I learned about myself: I don't quit. As long as I was going forward in this world, everything was good. But sustaining that inner fire would take all my strength. I seemed to be moving away from the amputation each day, with every step I took in my new limb. But the mental wounds? They were already holding me back.

Family members dressed up for the funeral of my dog, Blackie. I'm on the left, being held. Taken in the early eighties on Davis Road in Little Rock, Mississippi.

As a young boy with my dad, Mitch, and mom, Lois, in Little Rock, Mississippi.

During a break, I grab a laugh with some friends in Germany, in May 2003. I'm the one in the front.

My good friend and fellow army medic Charles E. Odums II, twenty-two, of Sandusky, Ohio, who was killed on May 30, 2004, when his convoy struck an improvised explosive device.

Taken during the memorial service for Charles Odums at my base, Camp Falcon, in Baghdad. I spoke at this service, reading a Bible verse for my friend.

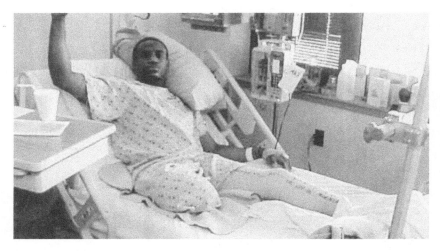

In my hospital bed contemplating my new life not long after returning from Iraq. Here, you can see the full extent of my leg injuries.

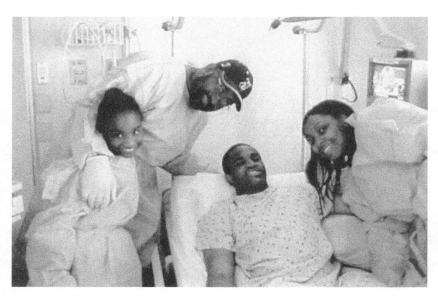

In my hospital bed at Brooke Army Medical Center (BAMC) surrounded by (left to right) my daughter, Daytriona, my father, Mitch, and then-fiancée, Candy, on their first visit after I was flown to San Antonio in late February 2005. My family members are wearing hospital scrubs and gloves because I was temporarily on "contact precaution," meaning that I might have carried germs home from the battlefield.

With my cousin Tony Stinner and my mother. Tony paid me a visit at BAMC in March 2005. Here, I'm grinning big from my wheelchair, leaning back casually and trying to make it seem like I was at ease with the injury. Actually, I was just trying to appear strong for my family. Behind my smile, I was very worried about my future.

With Candy and Tony Stinner.

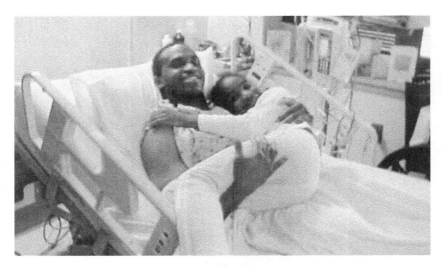

I snuggle with Daytriona in my hospital bed at BAMC during my family's reunion after I returned from Iraq. Daytriona initially wasn't comfortable with my injury.

Thurman Lewis, a former teammate at East Mississippi Community College, visited me at BAMC in 2005. Back in college, Lewis, a wide receiver, and I, a defensive back, competed against each other on the practice field. We were also close friends.

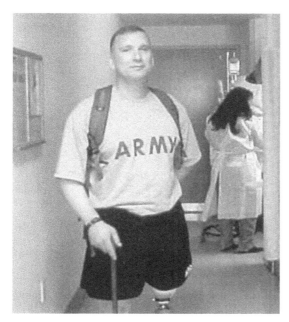

1st Sgt. Dan Seefeldt, who lost his left leg when a bomb exploded next to his Humvee while in Iraq, paid me a bedside visit shortly after I arrived at BAMC. Dan wore an artificial limb with a computerized knee—the first time I'd seen anyone walk in a prosthetic leg. The visit gave me hope.

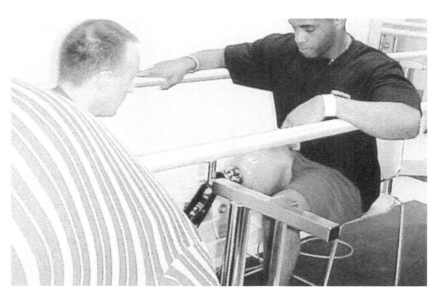

Preparing for my first walk as an amputee. Kneeling in front is BAMC prosthetist John Fergason. My mother and father and Candy are also in the room, watching and crying.

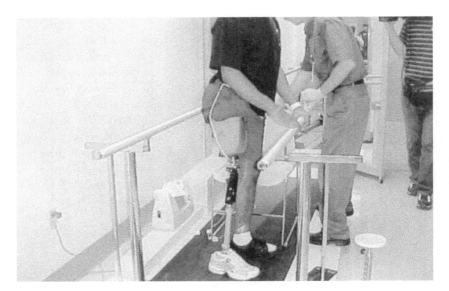

I take my first steps in a prosthetic leg borrowed from a wounded Marine. I am working with prosthetist John Fergason at BAMC in early 2005.

With my track coach, Teri Jordan, at Penn State.

Some of my fellow army medics and I enjoy a reunion party at Fort Hood in Texas, circa March 2005. I'm in a walker. On the table are photos of medics Charles Odums and Taylor Burk as well as the Purple Heart medals each man received posthumously.

Getting my Purple Heart from 1st Cavalry Division Commander Maj. General Pete Chiarelli on March 24, 2005, at BAMC. To receive the medal, I rose from my wheelchair and stood for one of the first times on my artificial leg.

I am running on the indoor track at Penn State. Dialing in my sprinting form has been my toughest battle as a runner. The better the form, the faster I hit the finish line. Because of the prosthetic leg on my right side, my right arm has a tendency to flare out too wide during a full sprint. That wastes energy and time. I still must focus on keeping my right elbow tucked in tight to mimic the motion of my left arm. The bracelet on my left wrist contains one word: "Courage."

While jogging in place, my goal is to keep my prosthetic leg directly beneath me on each stride. If the knee lands too far in front, I have less control over the prosthesis. Also, I am working on boosting the amount of knee drive in my sound leg.

I run on a Cheetah foot, custom made by Ossur for sprinting on a track. The prosthetic socket on my thigh is held on by suction and by a power belt that straps around my waist. When I run, I use a polycentric knee that matches the back-and-forth motion of a natural knee, built for bursts of speed by Otto Bock. When walking, I use a bionic Rheo made by Ossur, which contains a microprocessor that constantly reads and reacts to the surrounding terrain and my stride.

PART II

WEARING THE COLORS

6

Vision of Hope

s I learned how to walk, I saw a one-legged man run. For me, that changed everything.

One morning in early April 2005, I was in the prosthetics lab—sitting on a table and getting an adjustment to my new, computer-powered leg—when John Fergason mentioned that a visitor was wandering through the Amputee Care Center.

"He's above-the-knee, like you," he said. "And he's going to run today."

"He's going to *what?*" I asked, stunned. "An AK?"

I couldn't imagine someone with my level of injury running, feeling the wind in their ears again. I'd heard about guys like this, but I needed to see it with my own eyes.

I jumped off the table and began searching the clinic for this mystery visitor. Even with my new C-Leg—a futuristic wonder that used sensors to read the precise angle and swing speed of my knee fifty times per second—I was hardly smooth as I rambled through the hospital hallways. Since I couldn't feel my knee bending with each step, I didn't yet trust the leg to stay stable and keep me upright. To compensate, I cocked my right hip and brought the limb around in an almost circular motion, sort of like I had a solid wooden leg.

Where is this dude at? I thought while searching the ward. *I know he's walking with a limp. I know I'm going to be able to tell that he's an AK just by the way he walks.*

Unable to locate him, I returned to the prosthetics lab and sat on the table again. That's when the visitor found me. He walked in: a tall African American man wearing a relaxed smile, a polo shirt, slacks, and dress shoes. Two things struck me immediately. First, the walk. Effortless and fluid. Second, the shoes.

Man, get this, I thought. *Where did an amputee get dress shoes?*

I'd been thinking that I'd never wear dress shoes again. How could my artificial limb accommodate a nice piece of footwear? The next day, I would take my favorite old pair of dress shoes to the prosthetics lab, hand them to Fergason, and ask him to adjust them so I could again wear the right shoe, just for now, over a metal foot. The visitor had already showed me something—losing your leg didn't mean losing your style. He'd already earned some points.

"I'm John Register," he said, extending his hand. "I'm an AK and I'm going to run today. Are you coming out to the track?"

"Yeah," I said, impressed with the confidence this guy carried. "I'm coming out."

The outside track at BAMC was little more than a small, rubberized walking path about a hundred yards from the physical therapy ward—far enough that I had to make the short trip in my wheelchair. The quarter-mile loop cut through a clump of leafy trees. The other soldiers and I, about fifteen in all, settled into a shady stretch of grass next to the track's straightaway. The morning was sunny. The air was warm and full of expectation. In front of us, Register sat and attached his running leg to his socket. It was sleek, built for speed. Below his hydraulic-powered Mauch knee, he wore a silver-colored FlexFoot, which looked something like a metal spatula but J-shaped. After he introduced himself, he began to tell us his story.

"Gentlemen," Register said, "life goes on. There are no limitations. You can still do what you want to do. For proof, take a good look at me. I am just like you. I once was a soldier who fought in the Middle East. I once was a runner. And then I lost a part of myself. They took my leg off right here at BAMC.

"But now, I am a runner again."

Register said he had always loved the hurdles most. In each fifty-second burst, he tasted real life: a series of barriers to clear, your own precious lane to follow, an accompanying pack of grunting rivals sharing the same singular goal. A happy and easy run, interrupted by a series of thigh-stretching leaps.

"It's such a fast race but it's not necessarily the fastest guy who gets there first," Register liked to say. "It's the one who stays on the ground the most."

Staying grounded. That's something Register deeply believed in. Find your path and passion—whether that's sports, music, art, or auto mechanics—and dash headlong toward the finish line as if your life depended on it. Don't look left toward the bad times. Don't look right toward the self-doubts. Just fixate on the hurdles ahead. His own path, he once hoped, would take him to the 1996 Summer Olympics in Atlanta. He had surrendered his entire world to try and get there—enlisting in the army just to work with a top track coach, going to war to fulfill his military obligation, living away from his wife for months just to shave slivers of seconds off his best running time.

But as he pushed age thirty, Register could hear the big clock ticking. With two years remaining before the Atlanta Games, he figured he could probably make one hard, final run for his dream. He clogged his head with sprinter's math: he had to slice a half second off his 400-meter hurdle time each year. He had already run a 50-second race in Texas. He needed to be at 49.5 seconds by the end of 1994; 49.0 by the end of 1995; and 48.5 by the time the Olympic track trials were held in the late spring of 1996.

"Then, I thought, I'm not only in the ballpark of making the trials, but making the finals. And anything can happen in the finals."

Register was always sunny like that. Born into a 6-foot, 3-inch body with lean, explosive muscles and a mind ready to accept the pain of training, he was used to winning. He expected things to work out. He was a man with an all-day grin.

He grew up in Oakbrook, Illinois, an upscale Chicago suburb with a polo club, swam at the local YMCA, and played baseball on the local diamonds. But speed and song were his real talents. In high school, he won the Illinois State Championship in the 300-meter hurdles and shaped his singing voice. He earned music and track scholarships to the University of Arkansas, where he sang in the choir and became a three-time All-American in the long jump and the 4×400-meter relay. He qualified for the 1988 U.S. Olympic track trials in the 110-meter hurdles but decided to stay at Arkansas to finish college. He also realized he needed to grind more time off his stride if he wanted to realistically run for gold. He figured that his time would come at the Barcelona Games in 1992, so after graduating from Arkansas, he enlisted in the army and grabbed a spot in the World Class Athlete Program, an army feeder system for future Olympiads.

Register earned a slot on the All-Army Track Team, coached by Major Charles Greene, a former world-record sprinter and lead runner on the 4 × 100-meter U.S. relay team that took gold at the Mexico City Games. Greene preached that his runners and jumpers were "soldiers first." In their day jobs they wore army uniforms, snapped salutes, and worked to defend the country. But even on the track they were expected to train, run, and win in the name of the flag. Register never expected a war. But when Desert Storm flared in 1991 he did his duty, routing army radio communications from a bunker in the Saudi Arabian desert. He had to come home to get seriously hurt.

When the Gulf War ended, Register had only five months to qualify for the American track team headed to the Barcelona Olympics, too narrow a window for proper training. So he reset his aim for the 1996 Atlanta Games where he planned to compete in the 400-meter hurdles. Still a soldier and back on the All-Army Track Team, Register returned to his prewar obsession: cutting bits of seconds off his best 400-meter time.

On May 20, 1994, he planned to leap through another set of hurdles at his army base in Bitburg, Germany. The track was rubbery. His legs felt alive. As he blasted out of the blocks, he was thinking only about his time. The fifth hurdle got him.

One foot tangled with the metal bar, knocking him off balance. All of his two hundred pounds slammed down on his left knee, which twisted 30 degrees, turned inward, and popped out the back of his leg. He crumbled. He didn't know it at the time, but the violent leg twist had ripped an artery in the knee joint.

On the track, floating in a sick, gray fog of pain and misery, Register began singing church hymns out loud. With each note, some of the stomach-turning ache eased. He looked down and noticed his leg bent into an L shape, but he didn't begin to truly worry until he was flown back to San Antonio, Texas. There, at Brooke Army Medical Center, surgeons were unable to restore proper blood flow to his lower leg. A doctor put a hand on Register's shoulder and offered two grim choices.

"You can keep the leg, but we have to permanently immobilize it. That means you live in a wheelchair. Or," the doctor said, "we can amputate just above the knee."

Register didn't flinch. He chose to sacrifice the limb with hopes of walking again.

Five days after Register clipped that final hurdle, BAMC surgeons took away the left leg that was supposed to carry him to the Olympics. Friends phoned his hospital room to check in and offer cheerful words. Register made them laugh. Inside, though, he was terrified. His old identity—father, husband, soldier, sprinter—had been carved away with his leg.

Register's comeback began in a neighborhood swimming pool. As part of his physical therapy, he reeled off hundreds of arm-burning laps in the warm, chlorinated water. He certainly wasn't thinking about sports glory, just about shedding a few pounds and putting his body back in motion.

He had learned how to walk in a prosthetic leg and then received his discharge from the army. He had found his niche as a civilian sports specialist in the World Class Athlete Program. As he began to mend physically, he and his wife moved to Alexandria, Virginia, where Register recruited promising soldier-athletes and gauged their progress toward future Olympiads. For exercise, he occasionally jumped into a local public pool. One day a lifeguard noticed his amputation and saw his choppy stroke. She helped him refine the swimming motions and taught him how to tighten his flip turns. He began to cut neatly through the water, kicking with one leg. His lap times melted. Soon, Register took his exercise hobby to new heights, hiring a swimming coach, Marc Stanley. He began to think again about Atlanta—this time, at the Summer Paralympics, the largest sports festival in the world for people with disabilities. The Summer Paralympics immediately follow each Summer Olympics in the same host city, drawing about four thousand athletes who vie for medals in twenty-one sports.

At the 1996 U.S. swimming trials—the races that would determine the Paralympic team—Register reeled off his fastest time in the 50-meter freestyle, 30.03 seconds, and a personal best in the 100-meter freestyle, 106.06 seconds. He made the U.S. squad and swam the anchor leg in the 4 × 400-meter medley relay at the Paralympics. He didn't medal, but when he had a chance later to sit trackside and watch the amputees run the hurdle events in Atlanta, Register caught track fever again.

In 1998, Register was fitted with his first running prosthesis, one that absorbs pounding and allows athletes to run on their toes for more speed. He worked for a year and a half in the leg, first learning how to sprint, then learning how to leap. In 2000, he qualified once more for the U.S. Paralympic team and headed to Sydney, Australia. This time, he competed in track and field and earned a silver medal in the long jump.

On an off day in Sydney, he wandered to the Paralympic pool to cheer on his old teammates. As he watched the 100-meter breaststroke, he noticed something about the Chinese swimmer who had opened an early lead. Baoren Gong had no arms. At the turn, Gong used his head to push off the wall, then blitzed the rest of the field to finish first in the heat. Under the sport's rules, swimmers must stay in their lanes in the water while the rest of the athletes finish, so Gong kicked and floated and waited. As he did so, his legs began to cramp, and with no arms to help, his head repeatedly drooped under the surface. He was now in danger, but he kept bobbing. A race judge jumped in and held Gong afloat while the heat finished and the crowd began to chant his name. He gave everything to win.

From the bleachers, Register soaked in the moment. He learned a lesson that he often preaches today, especially when he talks to freshly wounded U.S. soldiers.

"We always look for someone else to get us moving," Register will say, "when we really have that within ourselves."

As the wars in Iraq and Afghanistan began sending home hundreds of soldiers without limbs, Register found a new calling. The United States Olympic Committee hired him in 2003 to lead its Paralympic Military Program. Part of his new job was to meet with injured soldiers and tell them about all the available military-led sports programs—from American Legion rec leagues to the Paralympic Games. He held sports clinics at the military hospitals, a safe place for the soldiers to dip into the wide array of Paralympic events like wheelchair basketball, seated volleyball, powerlifting, sled hockey, cycling, and running.

He never came to recruit athletes for the U.S. Paralympic team. For broken men and women fresh from the battlefield, he knew that grand concept was just too large a mental leap; they still had to learn how to walk, care for themselves, and live independently. But if Register's travels and clinics helped find a handful of elite soldier-athletes who might someday vie for Paralympic gold, well, that was just a beautiful by-product.

Mostly, Register preached the wonder of sports as a tool to replenish and restore the soldiers' bodies and minds. When the game was on, he often said, disabilities almost vanished amid the sweating, score-keeping, trash-talking, and laughing. Competition and camaraderie were like double-doses of good medicine, an instant return to the days when the soldiers were whole. Now they just had to play those old games a little differently.

In his talks, Register could break the magic of sports into four categories:

"Number one, it's chemical. You get the endorphins going in your brain, a chemical reaction. You get that euphoric feeling.

"Number two, it's social—you're having fun, developing friendships and partnerships.

"Number three, you have the mental aspect. You're not only thinking about how to play the game but you're thinking, 'I have a physical disability so, in this new state, how do I play this game

I used to know? How can I overcome that challenge?' It's a mental state. It transcends the limits.

"And of course, fourth, you have the physical," Register would conclude. "How can I get myself better, stronger, and faster; how can I get myself in better condition? And not just better at sports, but just being healthy—lowering your heart rate, eating better, taking care of yourself. That translates into your therapy.

"You can go to PT every day, but until you put those muscle groups into action by doing something relevant, sometimes it's hard to see the end result. The therapist can see it, but sometimes the patients can't see where they're going with this. They can't see what the end state looks like until they test out their bodies in the vehicle of sport."

Out on the track, on the road, in the gym, or in the pool, the soldiers suddenly will get it, Register would tell us. They will suddenly see a world outside the hospital walls. They will see life.

If Register's personal story didn't grab our hearts and shake our souls, his next steps surely would. From a standing position, he bolted forward and sprinted sixty yards down the track. As he ran, his body leaned slightly forward. He ate up ground quickly, with no extra head or shoulder movement, just pure, sweet strides. His artificial limb and natural leg worked in perfect, symmetrical tandem: the prosthetic knee bent and thrust upward, causing the artificial foot to kick forward, grip firmly on the surface, and rocket him ahead. This guy was running—a full dash followed by a neat, firm stop. Then he did it again, and again. I was in awe.

After each trip down the track, Register would walk back toward our shady spot, talking to us as he approached.

"That's how you run, leg over leg. You manipulate the knee," Register said. "Use your prosthetic limb as a part of your body. You control the leg. It doesn't control you."

He and I made eye contact during that first demonstration. He saw that I was studying his technique like a defensive back studies the quarterback's eyes. I was absorbing it, stamping it into my brain for future use.

On an athletic level, these wind-sprints fascinated me. On a human level, the moment truly changed me. Weeks earlier, my very identity as an athlete had seemed to disintegrate in the horrible, hot power of the insurgent bomb. Now, I was watching a man with the same injury—and, once upon a time, the same dreams—showing me that I could run again. And run fast.

But there was something deeper at play. Register was so much more than a quick guy in a prosthetic leg. He was a successful guy with a productive life and an important career. In his professional life with the Olympic Committee, he traveled, taught, and helped compile new talent for the U.S. Paralympic team. He was still involved, still contributing, still serving people. Register's impact on me was enormous.

There still is life, I thought. *This guy has it good. I know of guys with two legs back home in Mississippi who don't have all that he does.*

Register finished his visit that day by teaching a few of the amputees how to run some strides in their new limbs. For the more recently injured patients like me, he showed us how to maneuver around the track in aerodynamic racing chairs. I did make one loop around, but that lightweight chair wasn't my speed. And Register could see that. I now had my mind set on running again, maybe even running for my country while wearing the red, white, and blue U.S. Paralympic uniform.

Maybe I can get in, I thought. *Maybe I can be part of a team again.*

"What you can be," Register told us, "is part of a legacy. The birth of disabled sports—what eventually became the

Paralympics—that all started during World War II, with one doctor who believed in the healing power of sport."

Sixty years ago, in an English hospital filled with war wounded, the atmosphere was quiet, somber, and forgotten—far different from the one at BAMC. Each man in the ward had piloted a Spitfire fighter plane for the British Royal Air Force and had been shot down by Nazi aircraft while defending the skies of his homeland, suffering permanent paralysis when their planes crash-landed. In the 1940s, any chance at further life for these patients was dim; spinal cord injuries killed eight out of ten people within a year, usually when infections from pressure sores or urinary toxins ran wild in the body. Often, though, the patients simply gave up.

In the London suburbs, Stoke Mandeville Hospital was teeming with young, once-athletic pilots who were suddenly confined to mattresses. The facility also was home to a neurosurgeon with some radical ideas on treating these men. His name was Dr. Ludwig Guttmann, a German Jew, and he knew a few things about taking chances.

His most daring moment came on Kristallnacht. During the November 1938 surprise attack on Jewish people, shrines, and businesses, Nazis destroyed thousands of synagogues and arrested some thirty thousand Jewish men. That night, Guttmann was making the medical rounds at his Jewish hospital in Breslau, a Prussian city under Nazi control. When word spread of the swift assault on Jews, Guttmann admitted any man who showed up at the hospital, no questions asked. The next day, German secret service officers walked in, saw the crowded wards, and grew instantly suspicious. Without blinking, Guttmann escorted the Nazis past each bed, assigning made-up illnesses or injuries to his new "patients." Guttmann's stunt saved more than sixty men from being herded to German concentration camps. The next year, Guttmann fled to England.

At Stoke Mandeville Hospital, Guttmann dug into the cases of British pilots paralyzed during the war, convinced he could not only extend their lives but preserve their spirits.

"If the body is thrown into chaos, the soul must follow," Guttmann said in a 1976 interview, his German accent still thick after nearly thirty years in England. "The people develop adverse psychological reactions. They lose activity of mind; they lose self-respect. They encapsulate themselves into enforced isolationism. Now, it really grieved me that nothing can get these people out of this."

Guttmann pioneered a fresh medical tactic—rehabilitating not just broken backs but whole people. Sports were the centerpiece of his bold philosophy. He believed the men had to exercise again, to somehow reignite their competitive furnace. He organized water polo games, which allowed the men to use their buoyancy to regain some movement, followed by wheelchair basketball.

In 1948, after a twelve-year hiatus due to the war, the Summer Olympics returned. To help spur the rebuilding of London, the International Olympic Committee awarded the Games to the British capital. And that gave Guttmann an idea. On July 28, as the Olympics opened downtown, sixteen paralyzed pilots were helped up to the hospital's helicopter pad where they each fired arrows at straw-bale targets and played snooker, darts, and table tennis. That competition became the first Stoke Mandeville Games. Four years later, when the Olympics opened in Helsinki, wounded Dutch servicemen joined the Brits on the same tarmac.

The Stoke Mandeville Games took root. For a logo, Guttmann borrowed on the concept of the six Olympic rings, adopting three intersecting wheelchair tires as his emblem. But it hinted at his bigger dreams: an Olympic-like sports festival for people with disabilities.

Eight years later, Guttmann's sports competition was relocated to Italy—host of the first Paralympics. They were held in Rome just a few weeks after the Summer Games there closed. Twenty-three nations sent four hundred athletes. It wasn't about therapy anymore. It was about competing against the world's best and, of course, winning medals.

In 1964, the Paralympics moved on to Tokyo where wheelchair racing was introduced. By 1972, the West Germany–hosted Paralympics attracted more than a thousand athletes from forty-four countries, and people with quadriplegic spinal injuries and blindness competed for the first time. As the international gathering bloomed, it attracted still more athletes who were injured not in military conflicts but at work or at play—car accidents, cliff diving, horseback riding—as well as people born with birth defects. Longer stretches of peace had changed the face of the Paralympics. In September 2004, the Athens Paralympics drew nearly four thousand athletes from 136 countries. They participated in nineteen sports, including cycling, powerlifting, sailing, and wheelchair rugby—the gritty game captured in the Oscar-nominated documentary *Murderball.* A handful of athletes also earned medals in archery—the sport Guttmann had used to help treat British pilots on a hospital tarmac during World War II.

The wars in Afghanistan and Iraq are expected to partially return the 2008 and 2012 Paralympics to the event's original military focus. More than six hundred American soldiers, men and women, many of them former high school athletes, have lost arms, hands, legs, or feet in the desert conflicts. Among the three-hundred-member U.S. Paralympic team bound for the Beijing Paralympics, Register forecast a roster that includes nine or ten Iraq War veterans. By the time the Paralympics enjoy something of a London homecoming in 2012, the American team may contain forty-five soldiers who were wounded in Iraq and Afghanistan.

We are coming.

Some of us are aiming to rock the athletic world, challenging records and showing fans that the true beauty of sports doesn't lie in winning or losing but in refusing to die.

When all of my leg wounds had fully mended, I was able to transfer from my hospital room into a family dorm on the BAMC grounds where my parents and Candy had been staying. Their suite had a small kitchen with a microwave, a living room, separate bedrooms, and wheelchair-accessible bathrooms. More than anything, though, it contained people who loved me. From late March until early May, I was never alone there. We laughed together. They kept my mind occupied and held the PTSD–related depression at bay.

All of the soldier-patients at BAMC were entitled to take a convalescent leave of up to thirty days. I had not seen Mississippi for almost two years. A big helping of Southern cooking and Southern hospitality on Davis Road would do me a world of good. Seeing my relatives and friends, sleeping in my old bed—all those things would provide a happy break from the grueling days of rehab. After six weeks of hard work and medical treatment at BAMC, my doctors and therapists were now urging me to take that vacation at home. But I had drawn a line in the sand: I wanted to return to Little Rock just like I had left there, standing and moving under my own power.

"I didn't leave home in a wheelchair," I told the hospital staff. "I'm not going home in one."

By early May, I had finally reached that lofty goal. I was still miles from running, but my ability to walk had been pretty much restored. It was time to take a little drive. My dad had already flown back to Mississippi to return to his job. My mom, who had not earned a salary during the two-month absence from her company, would join me on my ride home. Candy, who had been by my side during some of my darkest days, would ride with us.

Earlier, my folks had driven my 2005 Nissan Pathfinder from Little Rock to San Antonio so that I could eventually be able to drive it home, operating the brake pedal with my new C-Leg.

On May 6 at about eleven at night, we crammed all our bags into the back compartment of the SUV and hit the road, heading northeast. I drove into the Texas darkness and motored straight through until dawn, waiting to see that Mississippi border sign. Every mile toward home put a little distance between myself and that world. By ten Saturday morning, we had reached Jackson, Mississippi, a little more than two hours from my parents' house. I had no idea what was waiting at the end of our journey.

By twelve thirty, we were cruising through the thick pine groves of Little Rock. My mom and Candy were oddly quiet as we turned from Mississippi Highway 491 onto Chunky Duffey Road, the last bit of hard pavement until we hit home soil. As we turned left onto gravel-packed Davis Road, I finally understood their silence. And I smiled. Dozens of cars were parked bumper-to-bumper on both sides of the road. I saw bundles of red, white, and blue balloons floating on strings. I saw excited people thrusting hand-painted signs into the air: "WELCOME HOME KORTNEY." And then I saw the assembled crowd, hundreds of people. I was shocked. There were family and neighbors and friends. Old and young. Big and small. I was walking into a giant hug.

I made it, I thought. *I am home.*

With spatula in hand, my dad waved and smiled from the grill outside our house. He was sizzling up fat rows of sausages and hotdogs, cooking some fried green tomatoes, and smoking thirty pounds of freshwater fish and forty-seven slabs of ribs. A feast for a celebration.

I stepped from the driver's side door of my truck, kicking up some of the red Mississippi dirt with my two feet—the one I had been born with and the new one that would carry me through the rest of my life.

There were kisses and handshakes and salutes and tears. But the best thing I heard that afternoon, over and over, was "Thank you for your service."

We partied and ate and embraced until about eight o'clock that Saturday night. Then I nestled back into home life for a few restful weeks—a vacation from the land of broken soldiers.

In early June, I drove back to BAMC to resume my treatments and physical therapy. As the odometer in my Pathfinder clicked off the miles, my mind danced with all those exciting future possibilities. The new hopes inspired and enticed me: running for my country, running for a gold medal, running to show other wounded soldiers that life can continue at full throttle. But dead-ahead in my path, I knew some mighty big hurdles still loomed. And I was just hoping that one of those hurdles didn't trip me in mid stride and cause me to crash.

As the summer sun cooked San Antonio into a steamy haze, the old questions in my head roared to life. They filled the empty hours I suddenly faced with my family now back in Mississippi: Why had this happened to me? Why had God let my world to blow up when I had been so committed to my faith? Had I done something bad in my life to deserve this? If so, what? Was I just fooling myself into thinking I could run again, even compete again?

If early March had been my "crawl phase" in rehab, the months of June, July, and August 2005 marked my dark phase. Depression caused by the PTSD kept me in bed for hours on end. Unanswerable questions kept me searching for answers. A private conversation with God was tinged with anger and confusion.

After my return to BAMC, the army moved me from the family suite to a private room in a hospital barracks. The dorm was designed for new amputees. A bathroom just to the left of my front door contained a roll-in shower stall. Since I was still using my wheelchair quite a bit, that was a nice amenity. The small kitchen had a minifridge and a microwave plus a pantry where I could store boxes of my favorite cereal, Honey Bunches of Oats with Real Strawberries. There was a roll-in closet for my casual clothes and dress clothes. I set up my computer in the living room, put my little TV on a dresser in the bedroom, and made it as homey as possible. But the room soon became more like a cave, a retreat from the world.

Many days fell into the same numb, high-calorie pattern. I often left my prosthetic leg in the room and, using crutches, hobbled down to my SUV in the parking lot. Using my left foot to operate the pedals, I drove to a nearby McDonald's, where I bought bags of biggie-size treats in the drive-through lane. I then returned to my room, devoured the burgers and fries while lying on my bed, and eventually fell asleep with the TV on. Later, I'd wake up with McDonald's wrappers covering my chest. Between all those fast-food binges and midday naps, I always showed up for my physical therapy appointments to avoid getting in trouble with the hospital staff.

In the PT room, I continued to smile, laugh, and crack jokes, but privately I felt like an actor. Around others, I was pretending to be okay, but back in my bedroom later, alone with my thoughts, I was somber, frustrated, and so sad. Sometimes I would cry. The depression seemed to be a combination of the PTSD symptoms plus all the spare time I now had to stare at my limitations. I was discouraged by what had become a poorly fitting prosthetic limb; my residual right leg was still going through changes and, as a result, it sometimes hurt to walk. I was still trying to come to terms with the loss of football, and I still wasn't sure where this new life was going to take me—maybe just back to the tall pines of Mississippi.

I had to find some meaning in this situation, a reason for my injury, some purpose in my world. My thoughts again turned to

God. In Iraq, my spiritual commitment had led me to keep that journal of faith. On the day I got hit, I had never felt closer to God, so, to be honest, I was upset that this had happened while He watched over me. When you have a relationship with somebody and things go wrong within that relationship, you get upset. I got upset with God. I saw other soldiers in Iraq who were doing things they shouldn't have been doing, but I had really been striving to do the right thing, to keep Him first. I knew I wasn't perfect, but I had been trying to walk the straight line. I naturally had a lot of questions. And I wanted some answers.

I began to ask myself why I had been so devoted to my faith while in Iraq. What was my motivation? Was it because I was in the middle of a war? Was I just scared and looking for some comfort? Or was I simply trying to do the right thing for myself and become a better person?

I began to examine my entire life, hunting for mistakes I had made, something I had done in God's eyes to deserve my injury. I questioned my ways. Had this happened because in the past I had been too blunt, too direct with people? The Bible says God will forgive all our sins, so how could these wounds be the result of my sins? How could they be a punishment of any kind? I thought back to the moment after the explosion and came to believe—and still believe—that God had helped me crawl across that highway, and that He had led me to safety even though I didn't know where I was headed. I thought about the surviving soldiers who had sprinted to my side, looked at me on the pavement, watched the color rush out of my face, and said to themselves, *This guy is dying, just like our three friends over there.* God had saved me. But why? In those lonely moments early that summer, I couldn't come up with answers.

It turned out that many of my new hospital friends—burn victims, amputees, and depression sufferers—were wrestling with the same questions and the same unknowns. Ravaged bodies meant ravaged feelings of self-esteem. Devastating wounds meant pain, and trouble getting around, and dealing with stares whenever we left the hospital grounds. We slowly began to lean on and rally one another. We became the voice of optimism and strength, giving each other what we couldn't give ourselves.

I remember the first time I met Connie Spinks. She was twenty-two, had a North Carolina accent, and had recently run seven-minute miles. When our paths crossed at BAMC, she was in a wheelchair with blast burns on her face that had temporarily seared her brown skin white. She and I rehashed the tales of our injuries to each other, as many soldiers do. On October 13, 2004, Connie had been riding in the gunner's turret of an armored Humvee, returning to Camp Freedom in Northern Iraq, when a man in a small explosive-packed pickup truck drove straight into her vehicle and sparked a huge explosion. Two U.S. soldiers inside the Humvee died. Connie ended up momentarily hanging from the Humvee's open door, snagged by a piece of her uniform. She had a broken femur, a fractured fibula, a shattered ankle, broken fingers, and second- and third-degree burns on her hands, wrists, and head. When she was rescued, other soldiers dragged her across the dirt road, filling her open wounds with bacteria. During her first four months at BAMC, she was quarantined—she had to wear a yellow gown plus gloves and a mask if she left her room—as doctors tried to keep the germs in her body from spreading to other patients. She would undergo twenty-two surgeries.

Some of Connie's prized possessions were her photos of Denzel Washington. During a visit to the hospital, the actor had not only presented Connie with her Purple Heart, he had leaned down and given her a kiss on the cheek at a time when she was very worried about her looks.

"My self-esteem isn't the greatest because of my scars," she confided to me one day. "I thought I used to be really cute and sexy."

"With your personality, your beautiful smile, and your good heart, any guy can look past your scars," I told her. "They can see how special you are on the inside. Just give it more time because you are going to heal. Then you'll be back to your old self."

In truth, I needed to hear those exact same words. We all did.

I had Candy in my life, but at the same time I wondered whether she or any woman would really still want me. I shared those concerns with Connie.

"You don't have to settle for anything or anybody but the best," Connie said. "God will send that person—if He hasn't already—and He will give that person a clear heart and a clear mind so she can deal with being with an amputee, and deal with being married to an amputee.

"No one here looks at you or the other patients like cripples. I feel sad because you got hurt but I don't feel sorry for you. None of the therapists feel sorry for you. You can do anything that any other person can do."

Connie stood by her words in a big way. She already had become emotionally attached to one of my rehab buddies, Albert Ross—the twenty-two-year-old trumpet player from Louisiana who had lost his lower right leg in an explosion while on patrol in Baghdad. She looked past the injury and saw the man. One day she had spotted Albert walking in a hospital hallway and noticed a little hitch in his step. She introduced herself and asked a bold question.

"Why are you pimp-walking at the hospital? This isn't the place to meet girls," she asked.

"I'm not pimp-walking," Albert said. "I'm an amputee."

He had to pull up his pant leg to show her the evidence. Eventually, Connie and Albert would get married. In the spring of 2008, they would have their first child.

Our little posse included Connie and Albert as well as Jonathan Hart, the staff sergeant who had been sent back from Mosul due to his kidney problems, sleep apnea, and bad knees. "Big Sarge," at 6-foot-2, 290 pounds, was the noncommissioned officer in charge of the hospital's Soldier Family Assistance Center, or SFAC. With seven computers, two big-screen TVs, Xbox and PlayStation consoles, DVDs, a fish tank, and a spread of donated munchies and soda, the SFAC was one of our main hangouts in the evenings. Big Sarge would organize game nights, bingo parties, and barbecues in the SFAC. Our clique also included Leon Watson, an army reservist from Cleveland who had been burned in a suicide bombing on the same day that Connie had been wounded. One of Leon's legs had become infected and he was still waiting to see if the doctors would have to amputate. Maybe the funniest member of our group was Robert Roeder, the navy seaman who had lost his leg on the deck of the *Kitty Hawk*. After his thirty-day convalescent leave, Roeder had returned to the hospital unshaven and sporting a long mullet that spilled from the back of his ever-present baseball cap.

"What happened to Roeder?" everyone asked. "Is he still in the navy or did he get out?"

The mullet was just a wig.

We all got a big laugh. But as the summer wore on, people noticed that I wasn't hanging around the SFAC as much. Hart noticed, too. He noticed when anybody in our posse dropped off the radar. Hart would instruct one of us to knock on that person's door and make sure they were okay. So Big Sarge knew just where to find me. One day he burst into my barracks room in the middle of the day and saw that I was still in bed.

"Get up, get outta there!" he yelled. "You ain't going through this, man. I'm not going to allow that."

Hart would definitely keep me moving over the following summer weeks, driving me in his gray Mercury Grand Marquis to dinners or civilian-organized cookouts off the base, to San Antonio Spurs basketball games, or downtown to parades. Sometimes we would just drive and talk. Other times we would sit in my room and talk. Big Sarge, who also was an ordained minister, worked hard to get me to open up, listening to me talk and giving me some inspirational words as I ate my cereal and milk.

"There's no way I know what you're going through because I'm not missing a leg," he said. "I wasn't there when the IED hit. But I do know that the Good Lord is going to keep you. Life does go on. You're young enough that this won't get the best of you."

We talked about Candy and my decision to put our marriage plans on hold. We talked about football and how much I already missed the game. We talked about my running again someday. All summer long, I had kept the picture in my head of John Register sprinting down that hospital track in his prosthetic leg.

"You need to take that adrenaline you used to get from football, that desire, that type of satisfaction, and get all that from competing as a sprinter," Hart said.

We also talked a lot about my faith, including all those deeper questions that had been rolling around my head.

"You have to remember that God is the creator," Hart told me. "He's the one that brought you here."

"I know," I said. "And I know it was God who drew me across that street after the explosion."

Not long after this conversation, Hart packed our posse into his Grand Marquis and drive us about eleven miles to attend Sunday services at Emmanuel Pentecostal Church of God and Christ. A receptionist at the hospital regularly attended Emmanuel and she had invited Connie to come check it out. Connie, in turn, had taken the posse along. These trips became a Sunday ritual. At first I used to walk into that church on my crutches. Eventually, I limped in on my prosthetic leg and the entire congregation stood and cheered. They would do that same thing for Leon after the surgeons decided to remove his leg, causing him to walk in a prosthetic limb.

My talks with Hart slowly helped me turn a corner in my private battle. So did my decision one day to pop in a hospital videotape that contained footage of Paralympic powerlifters competing in a past event. The sport is the Paralympics' version Olympic weight-lifting: athletes lie on a flat bench beneath a loaded bar that rests on a rack placed at eye level. After a judge gives the athlete a com-mand to lift, the athlete removes the bar from the rack, lowers it to his chest, pauses, pushes the bar to a full-arm extension over his head, and then returns the bar to the holding rack. Competitors are given three attempts to lift their chosen weight, the amount of which is based on each athlete's body weight.

Man, I thought while watching the lifters, *I can do that.*

Weightlifting had become one of my passions as a football player and as a soldier. I immediately began using my free time at BAMC to hit the hospital gym, to try my hand at powerlifting, and to push my bench press numbers higher. I saw this as another way I could compete again and feed my sports appetite.

I envisioned the three dead Minnesota soldiers looking down on me with approval and appreciation; they had not made it home but I had. They wouldn't want me to waste my second chance. If I did, I would be disrespecting their memories and their sacrifices. The Paralympics, I realized, was an event where I could honor everything those men had given up. At the same time, I began to find new meaning in my injury and in my life. I came to understand and grasp one fact—what's going to be is going to be. The only thing I could do, I thought to myself, was live every minute to the best of my ability, and to have faith that I was on the right path.

I came to the conclusion that before losing my leg, I had tried to control too many things in my life. I had been too set in my ways, maybe too stubborn to accept the fact that life was laced with little detours.

There are going to be side roads you're going to have to go down, unexpected turns you're going to have to take, I told myself. *There are things you have to go through that you need to experience. When obstacles come up, you need to understand that these hurdles are supposed to be there.*

The battlefield injuries taught me that I really don't have control of anything. I can have wishes. I can have expectations. But at the end of the day, what's going to unfold is what God wants to unfold. I stopped asking "Why me?" I started looking at my situation as if I had been chosen. I stopped thinking I had done something wrong to deserve what had happened. I started understanding that God had a mission for me, something bigger, something beyond me.

7

Off and Running

I jammed down the throttle and turned up the Ray Charles music as the Texas prairie became a flat, green blur in the car windows. Big Sarge looked pretty calm in the passenger seat, even though I was at the wheel, and my right leg was lying somewhere in the back.

We were headed north to Oklahoma for the Endeavor Games, an annual June sports festival for disabled athletes of all ages and talents. The hospital therapists had mentioned it to the soldiers, encouraging us to take the trip and test ourselves at sitting volleyball, softball, and wheelchair basketball—a little confidence-booster or maybe just a chance to work up a sweat in our new legs. A few other BAMC patients also were en route to the event, including our friend Albert Ross. They were taking a passenger plane, but because I recently had undergone surgery on my punctured eardrum, the doctors had grounded me and ordered me to drive.

Jonathan Hart—Big Sarge—had offered to give me lift in his Grand Marquis. Letting me drive was his idea. I had a grin on my face most of the way there.

When Hart and I reached the host site—the University of Central Oklahoma in Edmond—we saw some of the three hundred participants walking or rolling through the tree-lined campus. About twenty of those men and women, each down a leg or an arm, were veterans of the wars in Iraq and Afghanistan. Those recovering soldiers would scoop up loads of medals in the coming days—a glimpse of the Paralympic future. Dustin Tuller, an army sergeant who had lost both his legs after getting shot four times while leading a raid in Baghdad, took first place in five swimming events. Army Staff Sgt. Michael McNaughton, who had stepped on a land mine in Afghanistan, grabbed a gold medal in the 100-meter dash and a silver medal in the 200-meters. And Brian Wilhelm—who remained on active army duty after a leg amputation—finished second in the shot put and did some sprinting, too.

"A lot of people feel sorry for me when they see I'm missing a leg, but then they start cussing me when I outrun them," Wilhelm told the *Oklahoman* that week. "And I don't let them catch up, no matter what I do. That's just the way I want to be—driving on, never stopping, no matter what."

I admired that fiery resolve. I'd love to have lined up on the track with Wilhelm, but I wasn't ready to run yet. My event at the Endeavor Games would be powerlifting, the bench-press sport that had grabbed my attention when I'd watched that Paralympics videotape back at BAMC. Still, track-sprinting was in my soul and, I hoped, my future. Until that day arrived, though, I figured I could return to my gym-rat roots and use my upper-body muscles to get back into competition. Now wearing my blue-and-silver computerized walking leg under my shorts, I strolled with Hart into the powerlifting venue, the twenty-five-hundred-seat

Hamilton Field house. As I got ready for my lifts, we noticed a big guy strolling into the gym without a hitch in his stride. We watched as the guy shed his sweatpants, unclipped each of his prosthetic legs, and dropped to the floor.

"Look at him," Hart said. "Can you believe this dude?"

The man then hopped onto the padded flat bench, wrapped his hands around the bar, and shoved the weights toward the ceiling. He won the powerlifting medal for his body-size division.

When it came time for my lifts, the two spotters or "loaders" slid 275 pounds of circular metal plates onto the racked bar as I eased onto the bench. I was certainly no stranger to this activity. I had lifted 300 pounds before on the bench. But this was my first time in an official powerlifting competition, and the rules were all a little odd to me. I had to learn both the commands and the proper technique. In powerlifting, once the referee calls the athlete's name, he (or she) has two minutes to complete the lift. Once that clock is moving, the athlete lies on the bench and extends his arms upward while the loaders remove the weighted bar from the rack and place it in his hands. His legs—or in my case, leg—must be lying straight and still on the bench as well. The lifter then must wait with elbows locked for the chief referee to make a downward movement of his hand and give the command: "Start!" The lifter must lower the bar to his chest, hold it motionless on his chest for about a half-second pause, and then press it upward with an even extension of the arms. At that point, the bar must be held steady until the referee gives the final command: "Rack!"

I really had to pay attention to the signals and not get ahead of myself in any phases of my lift. But once the command was barked, I slowly lowered those 275 pounds and made sure to pause for a beat with the bar on my chest. Then, with a big breath, I squeezed my elbows together and drove the bar up again, clanging it back on the rack. Big Sarge clapped and yelled. In my division, the weight amount was enough to earn me a gold medal, which the referee draped over my head.

The lift stoked my Paralympic dreams. I again felt the rush of adrenaline and the fun of conquering the moment. But it wasn't completely satisfying, I had to admit.

I still have both of my arms. This is what a two-armed person is supposed to do, I thought. *But someone with one leg and a half, or one leg and a quarter, isn't* supposed *to run.*

My whole life, I had tried to surprise people by doing not what was expected, but something more. Something surprising, maybe even something awe-inspiring. That had always been how I'd motivated myself. Awe-inspiring would just have to wait.

In addition to powerlifting, I took part in sitting volleyball—batting back shots while my artificial leg leaned against a gym wall. I also tried fencing while sitting in a chair. For some laughs, I reattached my leg and played a little one-on-one against Hart and his two bad knees. Facing away from the basket and dribbling the ball at the free throw line, I had a little fun with Big Sarge.

"I'm gonna get you! I'm gonna back you down!" I said. "See, I'm settin' you up, man!"

I planted my prosthetic leg, which was attached to a low-cut running shoe, then used the limb to spin around toward the hoop, scooping the ball up and through the net.

"Didn't see that comin', did you?" I asked.

After shooting hoops for a bit longer with Hart, we wandered outside to the campus track and watched athletes lacking natural legs fly down the lanes. To me, it actually looked easy.

I could do this, I thought.

In time, I would find out that the runners were just making it look easy. Chugging a straight, 100-meter line in an artificial knee and a metallic foot would be one of the hardest things I'd ever attempt.

That day, our BAMC buddy Ross lined up in the blocks and, at the gun, reeled off a 100-meter sprint. He didn't win, but the only thing that mattered to Ross was that he finished.

"That was amazing," he said afterward.

Even more stunning, we saw a man with two prosthetic legs and no arms motor around the track.

"If this guy can do it, why can't I?" I asked Hart as we sat in the bleachers and soaked in that staggering feat. "Why would I ever feel sorry for myself? Look at these folks. I've *got* to be able to do it."

"Hey, when you race again, I'm going to be right there at the finish line, waiting for you," Big Sarge said. "You're my sidekick, man. So you'll see me at the line. I'll be that little extra nudge you need."

Since my earliest days at BAMC, Matt Parker had bolstered my body's core to brace me for my first steps. Now the therapist turned his attention to my only leg, preparing me to fly.

Everybody in the amputee clinic knew I was hungry to sprint again. I had been talking about little else since returning from Oklahoma in mid-June. Parker and John Fergason were thrilled that one of their first above-the-knee patients was gunning for that giant milestone. They would share in that victory when the moment finally came.

In July, Parker guided me through a new hopping exercise to prepare my lower body for running. Standing on my left foot, I would leap as high into the air as possible. Then I would land, hold, and repeat. And repeat and repeat. Parker was building and reawakening my natural leg, prepping that half of my body for what I would soon face.

"Your sound side has to be really ready for the forces that come with running," Parker said.

The hops were part of a training regimen called plyometrics—
a system that's supposed to bridge the gap between strength and
speed, designed to boost muscle power and help you produce
instant force. Some people also call it "jump training." The hops
simulate quick, explosive movements—like bursting out of the
starting blocks. This was true running science. The exhausting
drills were aimed at rewiring the tiny sensors in my muscles,
tendons, and joints called proprioceptors. These little nerve endings detect body motion, limb position, and joint angle as well as
where parts of the body are in relation to objects around us, like
the ground. With plyometrics training, you try to shorten all those
inner communications. That, in turn, revs up your quickness.

With my running muscles getting honed and hardened, the
next step was to tweak my equipment—my artificial right knee
and right root. For that, Fergason brought in one of the world's top
leg men. Peter Harsch was a prosthetic expert and Ironman competitor whose blond hair, TV looks, and athletic skills would, just
one year later, earn him a spot on the CBS show *The Amazing Race.*
His partner in the network program was Sarah Reinertsen, a motivational speaker with whom he had trained. They also dated. Sarah
was an amputee and the first woman with an artificial leg to finish
the Hawaii Ironman Competition. Harsch, then a sales rep for the
Iceland-based prosthetics maker Ossur, was a straight-talking dude
from Laguna Beach, California, with a deep passion for running.
He also excelled at cycling and swimming. But running, he later
told me, was a "huge release for me, and a time to reflect."

"If somebody said, 'Peter, you can't run anymore,' I don't
know how I'd handle it," he confided.

For that reason, he and I connected. I thought I had lost
running forever. But that summer, Harsch began jetting in from
California every other week at Fergason's request, to make extra
sure that I and some other soldier-amputees soon would rejoin
the world of runners. On his trips to Texas, he would bring an

incredible bag of gadgets. There were knees with artificial intelligence that learned how a user walked, understanding and reacting to quick changes in speed and terrain. There were bionic knees that powered people out of chairs or up flights of stairs. There were bionic feet capable of independent thought, responding and changing when their sensors picked up subtle shifts in the topography. Priced as high as eighty thousand dollars per component— and paid for by the U.S. Army—those space-age leg parts were for everyday use, for just striding through life.

But when it came to the running, Harsch also brought the goods. The Ossur Total Knee was a mechanical wonder that imitated natural knee motion. It contained built-in shock absorbers that simulated the flexing action of normal knees, the slight bend you see when a person bounds down a 100-meter track or a basketball court. The Mauch Knee was another type. It ran on a mini hydraulic system and was built for multitasking, whether a user wanted to ride a bike, run, or just stroll through a mall. The Flex-Foot, layered with a light-weight carbon fiber similar to material used in modern aircrafts, had a heel that absorbed the pounding of running.

During a July visit, Harsch was sitting with me one night in an empty hospital hallway outside the prosthetics lab. Everyone except Fergason had gone for the evening. Before packing up their wrenches and screwdrivers, Harsch and Fergason wanted to make a slight adjustment to my Rheo walking knee—a computerized unit that was smart enough to adapt to my stride. Harsch was working on the knee's speed, asking me to take quicker steps up and down the hallway to see how it felt and how the knee performed.

"Walk really fast," Harsch instructed.

I did. Down and back. The knee seemed okay. But then he surprised me while I was still in motion.

"Just try to run."

"What?" I said. "Run?"

"Yeah, just take off," he said with a gleam in his eye. "Just see what happens."

I had not yet been taught anything about running in an artificial leg. I had only watched John Register and the athletes at the Endeavor Games do it. But I picked up the pace and clomped down the hallway, more of an ugly, slow jog than anything else. I stopped, turned, and came rambling back to Harsch and Fergason.

"Whoa," I said when I reached them. I was scared and excited at the same time.

The impromptu moment planted the seed in all of our minds to do something more, something faster—and soon.

In August, Harsch was back at BAMC, and this time he brought the parts to build my first running leg. As we sat in the prosthetic lab, he attached a Total Knee to my socket. The mechanical joint was shiny and silver-colored, almost robotic looking. Next, he fitted me with a Flex-Foot, which was dark gray with a blue accent but shaped like a natural foot, with a flat heel and a grooved toe area, rising less than three inches to the mechanical ankle. The entire foot, despite its shock-absorbing innards and carbon plates, weighed barely more than a pound.

In Paralympic sports, your prosthetist can be just as important as your coach. Athletes can seek the latest technological advantages to snip seconds off their times. In that vein, the Paralympics isn't like NASCAR, where every car has to run within strict mechanical guidelines. That said, Paralympic track rules do outlaw motorized knee joints. They also limit the length of artificial limbs for double amputees because the longer your legs, the longer your strides, and the faster you run. (For a single amp, like me, the length of the artificial limb matches the natural limb). But beyond that, if you can design and build the fastest fake feet on the planet, more power to you—and that is already happening.

Consider the case of Oscar Pistorius of South Africa. Born without the fibula in his lower legs, Pistorius runs with curved, carbon-fiber blades on his feet that make him competitive with the top two-legged sprinters in the world. His nickname is "the Blade Runner." But in January 2008, the International Association of Athletics Federations—the world governing body for track and field—determined that Pistorius's springy blades were technically superior than human feet, that they allowed him to use 25 percent less energy expenditure once he reached his top speed. The IAAF banned Pistorius from running at the Summer Olympics in Beijing. That led Pistorius to hire a New York–based legal team to appeal the ruling to the Court of Arbitration for Sport in Lausanne, Switzerland. If he wins his case, he plans to run at the 2012 Olympics in London. In the meantime, Pistorius could compete in the Paralympics if he chooses. The case offers clear proof that the gap between disabled sports and able-bodied sports is closing. My prosthesis, too, would need to be perfectly tuned up and dialed in.

To tighten the alignment of my running leg, Harsch asked me to walk. It felt like putting on a pair of new shoes. After observing my hallway steps, he slightly rotated the knee to match my individual gait. It felt good, a step closer to my dream. Harsch thought my slow stride seemed smooth. Being a running leg, though, there was only one way to make sure all those moving parts were lined up correctly: he needed to see me run. I was thinking that might happen in the coming weeks, maybe after some training out on the BAMC track, but just as they had a month earlier in the same hallway, Harsch and Fergason looked at each other and hatched a spontaneous plan.

"Hey, let's go outside and we can really light it up," Fergason said.

We walked through the clinic doors and out to a barricaded parking lot—no cars, just an empty stretch of hot asphalt. The track, located at the front of the hospital, was too far away for this quick test run, they decided.

I stood on a random spot of the parking lot as Fergason and Harsch offered me some simple, last-second tips, telling me to plant the prosthetic leg so that the Total Knee was straight and locked before pushing forward and shifting my weight to the left foot. They wanted me to stay in control, to just do a slow jog— not the all-out sprint I was aching to do. Still, I was nervous. I had been wearing the running leg for such a short time. This test was a little like plopping someone down behind the wheel of a race car and telling them to just hit the gas and zoom around the first turn. Below me there was some fancy, expensive machinery that I didn't have a clue yet how to control. Even more troublesome, a small group of patients was watching this little scene from a smoking tent just outside the hospital.

I bet you he eats it, I imagined one of them saying before taking a puff of his cigarette.

"Okay, Kortney, go for it," Fergason said.

I lurched forward and began an awkward, careful trot in the Texas sunshine.

"Man, just take off!" Harsch urged.

I bumped up the speed a notch, still keeping it at a jogging pace. The sole of the running shoe on my left foot slapped the asphalt as the Total Knee pulled the Flex-Foot forward from its tucked position behind me, near the back of my right thigh. The artificial foot continued to swing until it was beneath me. Then the knee locked and the Flex-Foot smacked the parking lot with a slight scrape. I leaned slightly ahead, using the spring in the artificial foot to drive myself forward another step, with my weight shifting back to the left foot. Then I repeated the cycle again. Slap, scrape. Slap, scrape. Slap, scrape. Even at that slow pace, I could hear the warm wind rushing past my ears. It felt incredible. And then, as I kicked the Flex-Foot forward again for another stride, the carbon-fiber toe snagged my left calf, tripping me. I belly-flopped on the asphalt and my palms smacked the blacktop, leaving some skin behind as I skidded to a stop.

The guys in the smoke-break tent were right. I ate it. Bad.

Mortified and stunned, Fergason and Harsch rushed over to me. But unlike the last time I lay face-down on a slab of pavement, I was smiling when the guys reached my side. Before they could say anything, I jumped back to my feet.

"No problem. No problem. Just tell me what I did wrong," I said. "And let me do it again. I know I can do better."

"I know exactly what's wrong," Fergason said. "That won't happen again."

They spent the next thirty minutes turning the Total Knee a bit more toward the outside of my body. The faster people run, the more their feet tend to point inward—a pigeon-toed effect. I was no different, so this new alignment would help keep my right foot away from my left calf. Once the leg was set, I tried it again—this time without pain or drama or chuckles from the smoke-break tent.

The little parking-lot jog was a breakthrough, but it only fueled my fire to truly run, to really let it fly. Before losing my leg, I had been a speedy football player with NFL ambitions. Deep inside, my muscles still remembered that light-as-air sensation, that electric burst of sudden power, what it was like to tear away from the pack, to roar forward down the field. *That's* what I needed to feel. Peter Harsch understood. With arms folded as he watched me jog carefully in a hospital parking lot, he knew exactly what I wanted, where I wanted to be, and very soon he would deliver me to that place.

Our BAMC posse crammed into a borrowed hospital van and headed into the streets of San Antonio on a mission of mercy.

It was all Big Sarge's idea, but each soldier in that vehicle was more than ready to donate a little kindness after months of being on the receiving end of so much love and attention.

We each had watched in dismay a week earlier as Hurricane Katrina raked the Gulf Coast and unleashed a killer flood that ravaged a region and rattled the entire country. I worried about my parents, who had to weather the storm as it barreled north through Mississippi, still packing big winds and dropping buckets of rain. Beginning with a convoy of fifty buses, 250,000 Katrina refugees had slowly rolled into Texas. Officials in San Antonio had agreed to take in 25,000 of those people, and thousands were given a safe place to bed down inside a huge warehouse at KellyUSA, an old Air Force Base in the city. At BAMC, we wanted to help the displaced folks but weren't sure how.

"Look, here's what we're going to do," Hart said. "We're going to sign out the van and drive to the shelter. We're going to go inside and each one of us is going to pick out a family. Then we're going to take those families to Wal-Mart and we'll spend a hundred dollars apiece on them."

"Yeah, let's do it. Let's do it. I'm in," each of us said.

With Hart at the wheel, and with Connie, Albert, Leon, another BAMC patient, and myself riding along, we drove to the former air base and planned to make some new friends. We must have been quite a sight as we pulled up to the old airplane hangar and piled out of the van—three amputees and one woman in a wheelchair. After escorting a dozen or so of the refugees to Wal-Mart and bankrolling their purchases of fresh clothes and bathroom supplies, we took them to a buffet meal at the Golden Corral. We pushed three tables together and, over our plates of salad and steak, we traded horror stories. One at a time, they told their tales of withstanding a natural disaster, then fleeing both the rising waters and the death scene in New Orleans. One at a time, we described how we had lived through enemy bombs in a faraway land. Every person at that dinner was a survivor. But we all would carry our scars for the rest of our lives.

After an intense conversation like that, it helped that I could quickly return my mind to sports, especially my sports. The Paralympics, the Olympics for disabled athletes around the world, symbolized the best part of the human spirit—the will to thrive after we think everything has been lost. At an Olympic track, the loudest cheers come when a sprinter breaks a record, but at a Paralympic track, every race is an amazing race. A big step in my Paralympic journey had arrived by late September. John Register, the former soldier and Paralympic medalist who had inspired us with his sprints back in April, was now staging his first Military Sports Camp in Colorado Springs, Colorado. Hosted by U.S. Paralympics, the event brought together thirty-four injured military personnel—some fresh from the battlefield—plus the top U.S. Paralympic coaches for four days of sports show-and-tell. The coaches taught the amputees and paraplegics the finer points of sitting volleyball, handcycling, and seated fencing while simultaneously scouting the next wave of talent for the Beijing Games. Register organized the gathering to lure former high school and college athletes back to sports, to teach them that competitive sweat can restore a healthy life. But he also asked some of the soldiers to imagine how it would feel to chase gold medals on foreign soil.

At an indoor ice arena, I sampled sled hockey, firing pucks while pushing myself across the slick surface with a pair of wooden sticks. On an outdoor road course, I pedaled a bicycle for the first time since losing my leg.

There are people with two legs who can't do this, I thought, *But I can still do this.*

In these two sports, I was well out of my comfort zone. Hockey? I'd never played it. Cycling? I had barely learned how to walk again, and now I was zooming down a hard-surfaced trail at

6,035 feet above sea level. But the injury would never change one thing about me: it was only when I was out of my comfort zone that I felt I was accomplishing something.

When the sports camp shifted events to the Fort Carson Army Base in Colorado Springs, Register tried some old-fashioned recruiting, walking around a gym in shorts to show off his own artificial leg and flashing a disarming smile to help coax nervous war heroes to keep trying these children's games. Without the legs they once had, some soldiers were scared about looking foolish in front of a crowd. Register was concerned that if they didn't shed these self-conscious worries, they might never feel confident enough to take other risks in their lives.

By then, some of the competitors had nicknamed one another "rollies" or "hoppies," depending on their battlefield injury and their mode of movement. Soldiers in wheelchairs were the rollies. I was a hoppie. After a sitting volleyball game—during which all the lower-body amputees left their artificial limbs leaning against the gym wall—I hopped to the rifle-shooting targets and then to the Ping-Pong tables, too excited to stop and reattach my right leg. The electricity was thick inside the base gym at Fort Carson—a small town of its own with gas stations, a Burger King, guard posts, and a breathtaking view of Pikes Peak and its golden aspen trees. The bleachers around us were filled with small groups of cheering soldiers, most of them wearing green or sand-colored camouflage. That day, every competitor was playing for the home team.

At lunch, I had a chance to grab a sandwich with Register. He was seeing a different guy across the table compared to the one he had encountered that April day at BAMC. I was off all the pain medications, so the fog was gone from my eyes, replaced by the look of a man with a new urgency. Register later said that he saw in me a younger version of himself, someone with mammoth opportunities ahead in the world of sports, so he wanted to clue me in on all the things he had been forced to learn on his own about running knees, prosthetists, and sprinting techniques.

"What you have to remember is that running and training as an above-the-knee amputee is not much different from running as an able-bodied guy," Register said. "It's the same stuff. When you run, you want to be the most efficient you can be, expending the least amount of energy for the fastest time possible.

"Hey, the only real difference is the equipment," he said. "Back when I was running track for the army, I would bring out my flat shoes for bounding drills and my spikes for hurdles. Today, I still bring out my flats and my spikes when I go to the track. Now, I also bring my running leg."

Sitting next to me, my dad listened to Register's words and nodded with a smile beneath his ball cap. Because U.S. Paralympics had paid for the participants' airfare, food, and hotel expenses, I had brought my father on the trip. His presence was maybe the best thing about that sports camp. My dad had never been on a plane until he had flown to San Antonio after my injury. This was an opportunity for both of us, a chance to travel together and see a different part of the country. But I also basked in his support because it went straight to the heart of my passion for football, why I had mourned the loss of the game, and why I got choked up whenever NFL or college games came on TV. Let me explain.

When I was growing up, my priorities were to please God and my family. These were the main themes of life on Davis Road. One of my early inspirations was my cousin Dexter McCleon, who lived next door to me for a time. As a high school student, Dexter had thrilled his family with his football feats, earning a scholarship to Clemson University where he became a star cornerback, also my position. I remember his parents driving out of Davis Road in their van to go watch their son play in those college games. Later, Dexter graduated and went on to the NFL where he logged ten seasons, including the 2000 Super Bowl with the St. Louis Rams. He often brought his parents to the games. This was the life I'd wanted my parents to have, too. Not just so I could share any financial rewards from football, but because anything good that I accomplished on the football field would have reflected on my mom and dad, shouting to the world how well they had raised me. When I lost my leg, football died, and so did that vision.

Now the Paralympics had emerged as a possible way to achieve that vision. Running or lifting in Beijing—maybe medaling in a foreign land—could restore that dream and give me another chance to pay my parents back for everything they had done for me.

All the other soldiers were gone, relaxing in their dorm rooms, watching TV in their hospital beds, or surfing the Web upstairs in the activities center. Fergason and Parker had each driven home to see their families. As the sun set on another day in the amputee clinic, only two people remained—Harsch and me.

On this trip to BAMC, he had brought something only a prosthetist would pack: a box of custom feet. During his short stay, Harsch had fitted some of the other patients with these feet and worked his magic on bionic knees and ankles. He also had spent time fine-tuning my running leg, trying to find the perfect settings to match my hydraulic knee on the right and my natural knee on the left. November had come and my time at BAMC was winding down.

"Man, it's been a long road," I said. "All I want to do is run again."

"Well, let's make you run," he said without a hint of hesitation. "Let's take a couple of hours and go out to the track right now."

I'm sure my eyes lit up at the suggestion.

"Yeah? You'll take the time to do that?"

"Kortney, I'm only in town for a couple of days," he said. "We got this far. Why don't we go to the track?"

Harsch gathered up his hand tools—screwdrivers, T-handles and Allen wrenches—and we walked together toward the front of the hospital. The track, with its reddish clay surface, sat next to a parking lot, a reminder of my previous jog and the spill I had taken. We sat on the grass and stretched as the sky began fading toward dusk. This was right where Register had sprinted seven months earlier, dazzling us and also tempting us with what the future might hold for a bunch of broken soldiers. Ever since that day, I had imagined the joy of cruising down the track in the first lane. A return to running was the little carrot that dangled in front of me during all those weeks of rehab. Suddenly, the moment had arrived. As Harsch verbally walked me through the complex rules of running in an artificial limb, I only grew more jumpy, like the butterflies I had felt in my belly before a big football game with a big crowd waiting outside the locker room.

"Here's what I want you do to: get that knee out there, get that Flex-Foot on the ground as fast as possible, and then drive through the knee and drive through the foot. I don't want the prosthesis to run you. You need to run the prosthesis. I want you to relax your upper body and swing your arms."

We stood up and I stepped onto the track. As he set up a video camera, I took some deep breaths, stared down the long lane ahead of me, and flashed back on how far I had already come—from a blood-soaked Baghdad highway to that terrifying moment of looking at the new me in a German hospital bed to a Texas physical therapy clinic where I had tried to be brave for my family and my family had tried to be brave for me. On the long plane ride home from Germany, I had wondered who I had become. Now I was starting to see who I was: an athlete again, a guy who deeply appreciated his family, a guy at a peace with life, a guy about to take off.

Then Harsch said the three words I had been waiting to hear for so long.

"Just go now."

I began with a fast walk for the first few yards, just building my timing. I pumped my arms at my sides for power and fought the urge not to extend my arms for balance, like a man on a tight-rope. That would only slow me down, and I wasn't having any of that tonight. The Total Knee was whipping my foot from front to back a little too quickly, but it didn't feel unstable. In fact, it seemed pretty strong. As I jammed the Flex-Foot into the track with another step, the artificial toe grabbed nicely and I felt my body spring forward. I pulled my left knee higher, increasing the speed on that side and slapping my left running shoe on the track. My weight shifted back to the right side as I suddenly floated into that old normal rhythm, left, right, left, right, picking up steam, eating up ground, and feeling the smile spread across my face.

Sixty meters later, I stopped and thrust my right fist into the air.

"I ran!" I screamed.

I began walking back toward Harsch, whose grin easily matched mine. I saw the ground I had just covered and also saw my future.

"I'm going to run again," I told him.

"How did that feel?" he asked.

"Man, it was awesome."

As a guy who himself lived to run, Harsch beamed.

"It felt *great* to run again," I said. "I didn't think I was ever going to run and now I can sprint again."

That remark made Harsch stop and think. He later told me that it reminded him of all the wounded soldiers who desperately needed to follow in the same steps I had just completed.

"A lot of these guys, they were lying on a battlefield not long ago and they didn't even know, number one, if they would be alive, or number two, if they were going to walk again," he said. "And running? They don't think they're ever going to run again. So we have to fulfill that dream. We've got to give them opportunities to compete in life."

Back to earth and his job after my brief dash, Harsch rewound the video he had just shot. Then we broke down my form, frame by frame. While the glow of my personal triumph was still white hot, I entered a new, more calculating phase of my life: the obsession to find and fix the flaws in my gait, the eternal search for ways to shed tiny bits of seconds from my sprints. That obsession would last for years. Over time, the adjustments by Harsch and others would include a blur of equipment tweaks and knee recalibrations, component swap-outs and foot upgrades—like an all-day, all-night pit stop for me and my artificial leg.

At that early stage, though, finding the flaws was easy. I had the basic motion of a power runner in that first sprint, but one thing Harsch already wanted to do was reduce the rise of my right heel during the back swing of my leg. Basically, I was overpowering the hydraulics in the knee, which was causing the right heel to fly so high that I was almost kicking myself in the butt. While that may sound like good, aggressive running—or the punch line to a really bad joke about an amputee sprinter—it was throwing off my timing. Here's why: When someone runs with two natural legs, his knees are flexed at about 5 to 10 degrees when his heels hit the ground beneath them. That bend in the knee absorbs shock and helps spring the runner forward. But when an above-the-knee amputee runs, if the prosthetic knee is slightly bent when the heel lands, the knee may buckle and the runner may fall. In my world, I had to make sure my right leg was fully extended and my mechanical knee was locked when my heel made contact. By swinging my right leg so high in back, I was taking a fraction of a second too long to bring the heel back safely underneath me during the moment of ground impact. That repair was fairly simple. In the back of my knee, there was a knob called an "extension promoter" that looked like an eraser head. Harsch just had to dial it down so that my heel rise was limited to something less than 60 degrees.

For the next ninety minutes, until the sky became too dark to continue, I happily repeated my sporadic dashes while Harsch occasionally fine-tuned the moving parts in my right leg. I had run. *I had run.* But I also had taken a giant leap toward my full revival. First I had survived the blast. Then I had learned how to walk. Now a series of sunset sprints had infused a massive jolt of confidence into a man who for so long had been unsure of his next steps. In that moment, with another obstacle hurdled, I felt that my momentum would carry me forward to conquer whatever bigger goals waited down the road. Once again, I felt the wind in my ears.

8

Big Lift

I was in trouble before I even walked in the front door.

After months of bugging the head coach of the U.S. power-lifting team about attending her exclusive camp in the Philadelphia suburbs, Mary Hodge had finally invited me. A warm-hearted coach with a New York accent who occasionally dropped f-bombs to pump up her lifters, Mary already had been forced to correct my language. In my previous e-mails and phone calls to her, I had repeatedly referred to her as "Miss Hodge." My Southern roots and army training were showing. She had politely corrected me each time, advising me that she ran an informal shop, adding: "Just call me Mary." Three times she had reminded me of this. Now, hurrying to the gym where she was holding her clinic, I called her from my rental car. And I slipped up again.

"I'm going to be a little late, Miss Hodge," I said.

"Kortney, what is your problem?" she asked. "Dude, just call me Mary!"

She had devoted her life to the cause of disabled sports. In 1988, she had launched the Nassau Thunderbolts, an award-winning sports team composed of adults with physical challenges, including cerebral palsy. They competed at national and international disabled sports festivals in events like shot put, powerlifting, and boccia—an official Paralympic sport similar to the Italian lawn game bocce. Powerlifting, "a real man's world," as she called it, had not allowed women to compete at world championships until 1998. But within that male-dominated climate, Mary had earned respect as a local powerlifting coach in Upstate New York. Just two years after women broke the gender barrier, she became the first female coach ever to lead a U.S. powerlifting team at a Paralympics—Sydney in 2000. By 2004, she was the U.S. team's head coach.

She was tough and a taskmaster, yet also upbeat and compassionate, willing to let big-muscled people cry on her shoulder after bad days on the bench. She also was strong enough to pick up and hand off a 600-pound bar while spotting for her lifters. Once you signed up with Mary, she demanded full investment.

"Somedays at five A.M. you don't feel like getting up. That's life. You're either committed or not," she would say. "This is a lifestyle—what you eat, what you drink. If you're willing to live this lifestyle, I'm willing to push you as far as you can get. Whatever you have deep down in there, we're going to get it out."

As I slipped in late that day through the front door of Northeast Fitness just outside Philly, I'm sure I had a slightly sheepish look on my face. The gym was actually a huge, refurbished warehouse with dark, cement-block walls, owned and operated by Paralympic shot-putter Michael McDevitt. Mary and Michael were leading the camp there. They had invited only five athletes from around the country—prospects for the national powerlifting team—to teach them the complexities and secrets of a little-known sport rooted in the bench press. The Olympics doesn't offer the bench press as a sport; the two Olympic weightlifting events require athletes to be standing.

Early on in that first session, the two coaches had read the faces in the room. On some, Mary saw a trace of skepticism. She thought she knew that look and was pretty sure she knew what they were thinking.

"This is not the Special Olympics or the Empire State Games for the Physically Challenged. No disrespect to those events, but they are held for disabled kids or for disabled young people who win awards and look pretty for their parents," Mary said. "The Paralympics? This is true competition, the most elite athletes in the world."

Some numbers: The bench-press world record for able-bodied lifters in the 52-kilogram (114-pound) weight class is 321.2 pounds, according to the World Powerlifting Congress. The Paralympic record for the same weight class: 418 pounds. The most an able-bodied lifter has ever benched in the 67.5-kilogram (148.5 pound) weight class is 464.2 pounds. The Paralympic record for the same weight class: 468.6 pounds. There were other examples, the coaches said.

They had our full attention, but before we could show our stuff on the bench, Mary walked us through the strict laws of the sport—the rules that make powerlifting actually harder than the traditional bench press. In any lift, an athlete must have full control of the bar on the way down, must pause it on his chest, and then show no wig-wags or wobbles in the arms—keeping the hands at even heights—while he or she is thrusting the bar back up into an elbow-locked position. The lifts were as much about perfect form as they were about hefty pounds.

Body weight, they told us, was a major piece of the sport's medal math. At tournaments, athletes are clumped by their body weights into ten classes. Within these individual groups, the lighter we were, the more points we earned with our lifts. If two guys hit the same high mark of, say, 500 pounds, the lighter athlete got the gold. At weigh-ins, we were taught not only to strip down before stepping on the scale but also to remove our prosthetic legs. Every ounce counted. The Paralympic officials then would add a fixed number of kilograms to our listed weight, depending on our level of amputation. For me, a single above-the-knee amputee, that was 2 extra kilograms (4.4 pounds). So if the scales showed me at 72.8 kilograms (160.2 pounds), I would be officially listed on the scorecard as weighing 74.8 kilograms (164.6 pounds). A double above-the-knee amputee received an extra 4 kilograms. An athlete missing his leg from the hip down received 3 extra kilograms, but 6 kilograms were added to his weight if both legs were gone from the hip down. That was weight-watching, Paralympic style.

At this point, we were just scratching the surface at Mary's clinic. After all, there were forty-one pages in the official rulebook put out by the International Paralympic Committee. Probably the biggest difference between our sport and normal bench-pressing was our positioning during the lift. Powerlifters were required to keep their legs extended and totally motionless on the bench. This took away the use of muscles in our butts, thighs, and lower back—key engines for a normal bench press. When I had powerlifted the first time in Oklahoma, my feet rolled off the bench as I reracked the bar. The Endeavor Games referee had said, "I'll give you that lift, but at a sanctioned meet that error would have disqualified you on the spot." To help keep our legs still and on the bench, Paralympic coaches were allowed to secure us with two straps—one wrapped below the groin and above the knees, the other looped above the ankles and below the knees. The coaches, Mary said, would supply the belts, which could be made of leather or vinyl. A sport involving leather straps? That was a first for me.

A final lesson of powerlifting school dealt with the muscles we would be using and training.

"What body parts do you think are most critical in powerlifting?" Mary asked.

"Chest?" someone answered.

"Biceps?" another person chimed in.

"That's what most people think, but both are auxiliaries to what you really use," Mary said. "At the end of the day, what will make you an elite athlete who finishes in the top three is your shoulders, your triceps, and your back. That's where your power comes from."

With our heads filled with muscle talk, we hit the benches and offered proof of our strength to Mary and Michael. That day, using the new techniques and following the new rules, I went up to about 290 pounds on my lifts—not as much as I had lifted in Iraq, but enough to show Mary I could play this game.

I scanned the room to watch some of the other lifters. There was a school teacher who was missing one leg below the knee. There were two people who had paralysis from the waist down. And there was a quiet young guy from Long Island with no legs but powerful arms—Rohan Murphy. At the age of four, a surgeon had amputated Rohan's legs due to severe birth defects. As a kid, his arms were his mobility. He built his upper body just by playing and getting around in the world. By the time he had reached the eighth grade, his gym teacher suggested that Rohan try wrestling. Like me, he would have preferred football. His idol was NFL Hall of Fame receiver Jerry Rice. He begged his dad for a football but when he got it, he only could toss the ball up in the air to himself. He couldn't play the game with other kids. Offered a chance to compete in the able-bodied sports world, he grabbed it. As a high school freshman wrestler, Rohan drew some stares but not a lot of wins, just two in thirteen matches. Over the next three years, though, he got stronger and savvier by attending summer wrestling camps. He finished his senior season with thirty wins in thirty-three matches.

Rohan enrolled at Penn State, added twenty-nine pounds of muscle in the weight room, and eventually convinced the head wrestling coach to give him a crack in the 125-pound weight class, the lightest in the NCAA. He would be remembered years later for scaling a local ski hill with his wrestling teammates, part of a traditional training drill. While the others ran or walked up the slope, Rohan used his arms to climb all the way to the top. By now, he was bench-pressing in the high 200-pound range. On the mat, Rohan often stood waist-high to the competition, using his hands to maneuver before spotting a weakness, then darting and grasping the opponent's legs. With his quickness and technique, he earned three wins in eight NCAA matches.

Until then, Rohan had never been a fan of disabled sports. To him, these events were "cheesy" because everyone went home with a medal. That was just feel-good play. In real sports, you either won or you didn't. So when Teri Jordan, Penn State's disability recreation programs coordinator, approached him with the idea of training for Paralympic sports, Rohan didn't exactly light up with enthusiasm. He wrestled, after all, for one of the top college programs in the nation. Rohan *was* an elite athlete, disabled or not. Then Jordan explained that, as a Paralympian, he could compete for his country. That hooked him. Jordan had ushered Rohan into rowing and wheelchair track, and she had driven him to the Philly suburbs so Rohan could try some powerlifting, cashing in on his bench-press prowess. I didn't know it at the time, but as I watched Rohan fire the bar above his head, I was watching my future teammate.

After the clinic wrapped up, Jordan, Rohan and I grabbed dinner at a pizzeria around the corner from Northeast Fitness. They talked about the rising disabled sports program at Penn State. I talked about my abbreviated college football career in Mississippi and about learning how to run after Iraq. Jordan already had proven her recruiting skills with Rohan. Next, she turned her saleswoman charms on me.

"We'd love to have you think about Penn State as your next school," Jordan said. "You could train in track and powerlifting there."

"Okay," I said, a little stunned.

"We'd love to have you come and check out the campus," she continued.

"Alright," I said, remaining fairly quiet.

After dinner, I called my folks in Mississippi. All they knew was that I had flown to Philly for a weight-lifting camp and that I still had a few weeks of rehab work left at BAMC. In their minds, that was all I saw on my horizon, so they weren't quite prepared for my news bulletin.

"You know what?" I said. "I just got an offer to go to Penn State."

That night, with a new excitement coursing through me, I could barely sleep. At the same time, though, this decision was not an easy one. To come to Penn State, I would have to leave my team, the U.S. Army, and face the secret doubts I held about an amputated man making it in an able-bodied world. Maybe this was the life mission for which I was destined. Or maybe this was too much, too soon. There would be more sleepless nights ahead.

After the lifting clinic ended, I flew back to San Antonio and began mulling the possibility of retiring from the army, of leaving my small-town, Southern roots and enrolling in a huge northern college as a disabled man at the ripe age of twenty-five. As lifestyle shifts go, this would be a doozy. I wouldn't be stepping away from my comfort zone, I'd be bailing out of it like a pilot jumping from a burning plane. I also was a little lost when it came to my direction in life. I still had a sharp vision of competing at the Beijing Paralympics, but no real road map for getting there. I had a fuzzy plan of someday attending physical therapy school to learn how to mend people like me, but no real plan as to where or when I would take up these studies. Maybe, I thought, a tour of the Penn State campus would help clarify things.

Two weeks later, I flew back to Pennsylvania for a college visit. How big is Penn State? Well, it has its own two-runway airfield, University Park Airport. Basically, it has taken over the surrounding town. The main campus is located in College Park, population thirty-eight-thousand, where 71 percent of the people are age twenty-four and under. But the school's influence spills so far into the surrounding townships, people have dubbed the entire Penn State region "Happy Valley." The university operates a $1.4 billion endowment, which is larger than the gross domestic product of twenty-nine nations, including Belize and St. Lucia. It is a massive place. Among its twenty-four total campuses in Pennsylvania, more than eighty thousand students are enrolled.

Coach Jordan picked me up from the airport and I got my first glimpse of life at Penn State. Old stone buildings with bells that rang in the spires. A canopy of tall trees that would grow green and lush in the late spring. High stairways and swooping hills. The sheer expanse of the main campus, the rolling slopes and all those steps, caught my eye. The scene was pretty, but it was a lot of ground to navigate in an artificial leg, I thought. One day of walking in a prosthetic leg was like one day of walking with another person riding on my back. We stopped by the gorgeous Multi-Sports Complex where I would be doing my indoor training. Earlier, I had checked out the new facility on my computer. In person, the place lived up to the hype. Under one roof, an oval-shaped, 200-yard track contained six 42-inch red running lanes divided by white stripes, surrounded by eight 60-yard sprint lanes. The track was special and rare. Its turns were built on hydraulic lifts, which meant the banked corners could be raised for distance runs and lowered for sprints. Only a few other indoor track complexes in the world had hydraulic banks. It didn't end there, though. On the building's south side, throwing and jumping events could take place on sixty-five yards of artificial turf. We walked past the long-jump runway, the triple-jump runway, and the two pole vault pits. We saw the weight room. I scanned the eight hundred empty seats that bordered the homestretch of the main track. This is where I could launch my running career, in a $16 million room so big that six varsity teams could share the space at the same time during rainstorms.

"If you run track and you die, you don't go to heaven," the father of one track athlete had told the Penn State *Daily Collegian.* "You come to this place."

We watched the track team work out, then I dropped off my college transcripts at the admissions office and checked out a Penn State basketball game and a volleyball game with Rohan. I was fairly quiet during that entire trip. As I absorbed the scene, I wondered how a wounded soldier who had seen so much blood and raw brutality might fit in with this mass of young people who were just starting to live. I returned to San Antonio still unsure about Penn State.

I sought advice from the people closest to me. My mom thought I was doing too much, too soon, that I needed some time off. My dad said he would support whatever decision I made. I had assumed I would retire from the military once I was officially discharged from BAMC—and that was just days away; my rehab work there had gone as far as it could. But before I cut ties with the army, I decided to call John Register. In his role with the U.S. Olympic Committee, he had talked to me before about the army's World Class Athlete Program, which could allow me to train for the Paralympics while still remaining a soldier.

"Let me give you two options to think about," Register said. "You can separate from service, get into the Veterans Affairs system, and go back to school. We have a Paralympic coach [Jordan] you can work with at Penn State. Or, you can stay in the army and we can probably get you into the World Class Athlete Program.

You can remain on active duty and train for the Beijing Games at the Olympic Training Center in Chula Vista, California. Either one is a good option.

"But *you* have to make the call as to which is best for you," Register said. "It's your life. And I'm not going to be holding the bag if later you feel like you made a wrong decision."

One of those scenarios seemed to carry some risk: if I stayed in the army, there was a chance I might get sent not to the Olympic Training Center but back to my infantry unit, although not back to Iraq. Without such a guarantee, I knew that I would officially retire from the army. That was certain. But school? I had to admit I was feeling a little overwhelmed.

I've been shaken up and I still have a slight brain injury, I thought. *Am I even cut out for college? Am I going to set myself up for failure?*

I decided I needed a little space and a little time, but I also knew Penn State was a good opportunity. Money would not be a major issue. I would get twelve hundred dollars a month in retirement pay from the army. The U.S. Department of Veterans Affairs would cover my tuition and books, and I could get a stipend for housing. I decided to enroll—but in the fall of 2006, not for the upcoming spring semester. I would give myself a little vacation and buy some more time to heal. I would also give myself an escape clause—if I didn't like it at Penn State, I would simply pack up and come home. But at least I would give it a try, and using my background as an army medic, I would major in therapeutic recreation so that someday I could help patch together people like me.

I called Coach Jordan to let her know my decision: I would be there by late summer.

And then, I changed my mind again.

Two days before Penn State's spring semester started in January 2006, as I began to think about all the students who were heading to campus to start their classes, I had one final revelation.

If I put school off until the fall, am I really going to go? Or am I going to go back home and drop into an emotional rut and spend the rest of my days on Davis Road? I asked myself. *I am not ready to go home yet.*

I didn't want to pass up this chance because I was scared, because I couldn't know how life was going to pan out at Penn State. That was the old me: control everything, make sure I can see the end game before I start something. In this scenario, I couldn't imagine the future and had no idea what I faced. This was a mysterious road, but one I knew I had to take.

"I'm coming! I'm coming!" I told Coach Jordan over the phone. "I'm going to be up there in a couple of days."

Like a person flipping on a light switch, I saw what I had to do and leaped into action. I signed my army retirement papers and said good-bye to everyone at BAMC. My SUV was now at my parents' house, so I packed my belongings into a bag and grabbed the first flight to Mississippi, leaving at about five thirty that morning. I landed, returned to Davis Road, and told my family that I was headed to Penn State. I napped from eleven until two. When I awoke, some of my family members helped me load my truck with clothes and a few knickknacks for my college dorm room. Then, at seven, Candy and I started our all-night drive to Happy Valley, hitting campus, bleary-eyed, at seven the next morning.

Coach Jordan let me settle in for a day. I attended my first classes, moved into a one-room apartment at a four-story, brick dorm that housed about eight hundred other students, and then I got to work at the track. In our early sessions—now three months after the first hard sprint with Peter Harsch—I didn't spend time analyzing or polishing my technique. The coaching orders were simple: "See how far you can run today." Or "See how fast you can run from here to there." I was just stretching things out, getting loose. In those early weeks on the indoor track, I also was limited by the running leg I had taken with me from BAMC. The Total Knee and Flex-Run setup was built for longer distances and slower paces, not the 100-meter bursts I aimed to someday run in Beijing. But a new sprinting leg would have to wait until I found a good local prosthetist.

As happy as I was to spend three days a week on the track, I was miles from where I needed to be when it came to competitive running. With stopwatch in hand, Coach Jordan measured some of my early 100-meter sprints at eighteen seconds, nineteen seconds, and some as high as twenty seconds. At the same time, I had started leafing through the 100-meter qualifying times for the Beijing Paralympics—as well as the world records for above-the-knee runners. Here's what my research showed: I had barely more than two years to carve six seconds off my time. In the 100-meter world, six seconds is an astounding margin, an eternity. It's a little like being in New York City and needing to make it by car to Los Angeles in twenty-four hours—you're going to have to find some extra zip to beat the clock.

As I worked to slice bits of seconds from my stride, I began to skid, trip, and fall more often on the track.

"Coach is pushing me a little hard," I told my mother in a phone call from Penn State. "But I'm going to hang in there."

"Well," Mom said, "you need to get back up and dust yourself off."

I understood that I would never find my old, smooth cadence or my old, blazing speed with the parts I now owned. But I also felt that I could do so much better than the clunky gallop I was now using to bounce down the track. I looked more like a little kid scooting around his backyard than a runner, like I was engaged in organized play, not an elite sport.

As brutal as these practices were, I eventually realized I needed to go through that ugly stage to someday get to the big stage.

I also needed hard-core training from someone who knew the sport from the starting gun to the finish-line tape—and every breath in between. Coach Jordan not only had a motivational flair, she had spent more than thirty years coaching track at the elite level. If I could tap just a fraction of her running expertise, I could find those extra six seconds.

In the early 1970s, as American track and field was cranking out a young pack of star distance runners that included Steve Prefontaine and Frank Shorter, Jordan was emerging as a force among the women in the sport. As a freshman at Kansas State University in 1972, she set an NCAA record in the mile (4 minutes, 45 seconds). That same year, she also finished sixth at the U.S. Olympic Trials, narrowly missing a spot on the team bound for Munich. In 1973, she set a world record in the 10-mile run and ran the fourth-fastest marathon in the world. She also held the American record in the 5,000 meters. At the 1976 U.S. Olympic Trials, she made the U.S. track team as an alternate. After the Summer Games in Montreal, she retired as a competitive runner so she could fully devote herself to coaching—her next passion, as she saw it. She figured she could be good at running and good at coaching, but only great at one. Later, I would have to follow that same blueprint.

She coached track at the University of Kansas for four years (three as head coach), at the University of Texas for four years, and in 1984 she was named the head women's track and cross-country coach at Penn State. Over the next fifteen years, her runners and throwers dubbed her "T. J." and said they were boosted by her powerful but supportive yells as they competed. Meanwhile, her Penn State teams filled the trophy cases. The cross-country squads won NCAA titles in 1984, 1985, and 1987. In 1989, the women's indoor track team took the ECAC championship. Her outdoor track teams were even more dominant, grabbing ECAC titles in 1985, 1986, 1987, 1989, and 1990. But you can tell the most about coaches, and their deeper inspiration, by tallying up how many of their athletes eventually go into coaching themselves. In her case, more than three hundred have coached track at the high school or college level. In 1999, she left her track and cross-country coaching jobs and took on new duties as Penn State's coordinator of disability programming—part of a push by the school to develop sports pursuits for students with amputations, paralysis, or other physical challenges. As the Iraq War bogged down, Coach Jordan saw that her fresh role would gain more importance as the casualty count mounted.

About sixteen months before I arrived at Penn State, one of Coach Jordan's athletes had reached the biggest dance of all in disabled sports—the Paralympics. Jeff Hantz, whose legs had been amputated due to birth defects, was a Penn State student and a trumpet player in the pep band that played at Nittany Lions' basketball games. Coach Jordan first spotted Jeff as she was driving through campus and he was pushing his wheelchair through a parking lot near his dorm. She saw such raw strength in his arm movements that she stopped her car and asked Jeff to join the school's wheelchair sports program. She soon was tutoring Jeff on throwing the discus, the javelin, and the shot put. He blossomed in the throwing sports, seizing the U.S. Paralympic record in discus and winning gold medals in the javelin and shot put at the 2003 World Wheelchair Championships. That earned Jeff a trip to Athens and the 2004 Paralympic Summer Games where he finished sixth in the discus with a toss of 100 feet, 7.5 inches. Remember, this was a man without legs.

Coach Jordan clearly had an eye for talent. It made me feel good that she had set her sights on me.

"I almost felt like all those years of coaching able-bodied athletes really prepared me for this job," she once said.

A centerpiece of her coaching philosophy was to train me like she would any two-legged runner or jumper, while understanding that the sheer physics of running in a prosthetic leg would affect my balance, my strides and, of course, my track times. But Coach Jordan prescribed some of the same drill work she been using for years with her track teams: I ran up small hills on campus, I dragged a weighted sled, and I began to sharpen the various phases of my dream race, the 100-meter sprint. The main task in those early weeks was to bring my hands tighter to my body as I ran. Again, this boiled down to basic physics—the constant interaction between matter, energy, motion, and force. As my right leg swung out with each step down the track, my hands and arms darted out to restore my equilibrium. That slowed me down.

"For every action, there's an opposite reaction," Coach Jordan said.

We soon understood that the arm-flying problem could only be fixed with fresh mechanics. I needed a new right leg and a new leg man to design it for me. My old pal, Peter Harsch, had the perfect person in mind.

Tim Rayer, a hard-charging former college basketball player with a Philly accent, had graduated from Penn State in 1994 with a bachelor of science degree in biomechanics—the study of how the body moves internally (its muscles) and how outside forces affect that movement. While in college, Rayer had volunteered at one of Pat Croce's Sports Physical Therapists centers—a forty-one-clinic empire that Croce had launched before buying the Philadelphia 76ers. While working at the clinic, Rayer saw how many grueling years it could take to help a person return to motion after a stroke. This Philly boy preferred to work at a much quicker pace.

Rayer also had played Division III basketball for one of the Penn State branch campuses. During practices one season, he had razzed a teammate for wearing a Neoprene knee wrap, teasing the guy for trying to mimic Michael Jordan's look. But the teammate had insisted that his knee truly ached. He was urged to see a doctor. In time, surgeons discovered that Rayer's buddy actually had bone cancer and amputated his leg above the knee.

When the same teammate visited him just weeks later while walking in a prosthetic leg, Rayer was impressed and surprised. Back at the physical therapy center, patient progress had seemed arduous and slow, measured in inches, but in prosthetics the impact seemed almost immediate. Rayer had found his calling. He completed his graduate studies at the University of Connecticut Medical School and Newington Children's Hospital. Later, Rayer cofounded Prosthetic Innovations, a Philadelphia clinic that offers advanced socket designs, bionics, gait training, and high-performance prosthetics for active amputees.

As spring 2006 loomed, Rayer drove to Penn State to check out my leg and my stride. As clinician and patient, we clicked right away. I learned to trust his instincts on running and his craftsmanship in sockets. He learned to understand my unique descriptions of pain or discomfort—kind of the way a great auto mechanic knows exactly what a customer means when he complains that his car is going "tick, tick, tick." When I complained about looseness in a knee or tightness in a socket, Rayer could open up the hood the pinpoint the problem.

"Prosthetist and patient, well, that's an intimate relationship," Rayer told me. "As an above-the-knee amputee, you now get your stability from your sit bone—the bone you sit on. In medical books, it's called the 'ischial tuberosity.' That's where I have to focus, and it's a pretty intimate place to be grabbing. So you'd better be comfortable with me, and I'd better be comfortable with you."

That was Rayer's human touch. On a cold, mechanical level, he aimed to create two things in my sprints: symmetry in my motion and rhythm in my steps. After watching me run, Rayer suggested that I change both my knee and my foot to bring me closer to a true sprinter's gait. He designed a new running leg that contained a hydraulically powered Mauch knee. With its aluminum framing, the Mauch gave me smoother motion and, according to the manufacturer, Ossur, it also could perceive changing terrain conditions and actively control its own stability. My new foot was another Ossur product called the Cheetah. Springy and made of light-weight carbon fiber, the Cheetah blade actually resembled the rear leg of a big cat. The fastest single-leg amputee in the world, San Diego sprinter Marlon Shirley, was known to wear a Cheetah foot.

I had a new leg, a new running coach, and a new place to train. In March, I got a running buddy. Several years earlier, Coach Jordan had worked with a double-leg amputee named Wardell Swann, a former electrical lineman from Maryland. Swann, who was in his early forties, had come down with a freak case of pneumococcal pneumonia in 2000. The pneumonia had roared through his body, coagulating the blood in his legs and hands like a case of bad frostbite. When the tissue in these areas eventually died, surgeons had amputated both legs below the knee plus nine of his fingers. Within six months of that operation, he ran his first race. At the 2005 Endeavor Games, while I had been getting my first taste of powerlifting, Wardell was winning four gold medals, including one in my favorite event, the 100 meters. Now, both of us had Beijing in our sights. Coach Jordan thought Wardell could teach me a few things about running and maybe about life.

"I'm nobody. I'm just this guy trying to survive, trying to run, man," Wardell said. "So we're just doing what we're capable of. When we run, we give other people hope."

Twice that spring, Wardell drove up from his home in Annapolis and we worked out together at Penn State's indoor track, running laps and sprints. We worked on how to explode out of the blocks, stand up, and reach top speed quickly. For both of us, each of those running phases was a metaphor for our journeys.

Somewhere ahead of us in this world was an outstretched tape at the finish line.

"Life is good," Wardell would often say.

But real life also required some real tests. In March 2006, Coach Jordan decided that I needed a little seasoning in front of a live crowd. At several Penn State varsity track meets, Coach Jordan set aside one heat for Wardell and me to run against some able-bodied runners. In truth, though, those first meets weren't filled with the thrill of competition or the adventure of just being out there. More than anything, I was terrified of looking like a fool.

As a football player, I had never been preoccupied with failure. As a cornerback, I was driven to be accountable to my teammates, motivated by being the last line of defense. But during those first track meets, I didn't run with the pure joy of the moment. I was worried about tripping, tumbling, and wiping out in front of the crowds in the bleachers and in front of all the young, able-bodied athletes who blazed down the lanes with such ease. I had a fear of flopping, and I didn't need any more dents in my dignity.

After all the personal triumphs of the past eight months, my arrival at Penn State had actually chipped away at my self-esteem. I suddenly was living amid a sea of young people who cherished, judged, and even glorified good looks. The social structure of that college—of most colleges—was built on physical appearance. Before I got wounded, I valued the way I looked, but as a one-legged guy, I felt as though I'd been thrown to the wolves. I wasn't just differ-ent, I felt like an oddity, an outcast. I wasn't just a minority, I was a double minority, so instead of embracing my amputation as a badge of sacrifice and bravery, I concealed it. Each time I went out in public at Penn State—to and from classes or to any place except the track—I wore long pants and an artificial limb with a plastic cover that matched my skin color. I never wore shorts.

Whenever you see amputees out in the world, it's safe to say that they feel unlike everyone else at the party, the office, the store, or the stadium. Sure, in time, many amputees get used to it or decide just not to care about the stares, but that feeling of being dissimilar from the group never completely fades, not totally. But take these same amputees and plunk them down at the Endeavor Games or at the Paralympics, and they will feel at home. No one is staring. Even Davis Road didn't feel completely like home when it came to me and my missing leg. When I rode between those Southern pine groves, I didn't see too many other amputees. At family gatherings, my little nieces and nephews sometimes shied away from me when they spotted the metallic knee and foot. In New York or Los Angeles, you might see guys like me, but not too often in the back country of Mississippi.

During my first semester at Penn State, I stayed way under the social radar. I would go to class, go train, and come back to my tiny apartment. I wanted to get out there and enjoy the college life, but I wouldn't let myself. On weekend nights, I sat and watched out my window as packs of tipsy college kids stumbled home from the bars and parties. Just below my place was a large set of steps. In what became a Friday and Saturday night ritual, they would weave up those stairs, teetering most of the way. Some needed to sit and rest during their climb. Some never made it to the top. I didn't judge them. When I was nineteen or twenty, I did lots of wacky things that made some adults shake their heads. But seeing those students just highlighted the vastly different worlds we were sharing right on the same campus. I couldn't fit in, and I really couldn't relate. With all I had seen and survived, I felt more like thirty-five than twenty-five. The differences in our experience, plus the amputation, caused me to wall myself off from them. Candy was going to college in Mississippi and was temporarily out of my life as a girlfriend. I had heard there was one other wounded Iraq vet attending Penn State at the time, and I talked with him on the phone, but I was never able to meet him personally.

Being alone so much only inflamed my PTSD symptoms. Whenever that anxiety disorder kicked in, I didn't want to be around people. I retreated even further, staying inside for longer stretches, once again trying to wrap my mind around what had happened to me, and what still might go down in my future. The rut of isolation deepened. I felt fatigued. I stayed in bed. I thought, *What's the worst thing that can happen to me if I don't get up today? Nothing worse can happen to me than what has already happened.* In time, though, I would pick up the mental pieces and venture back out.

During that first semester, I called my dad and floated the possibility of withdrawing from Penn State and coming home. My college visions had been drawn up with that exact escape plan in mind—if things didn't work out, at least I had tried, and I could just drive south to Mississippi. My father listened and pulled out an old speech he had used when I was in high school. At the time, my baseball coach wasn't playing me as much as I thought he should, so I told my dad I was going to walk away from the team. My father gave me two choices back then: stay on the team and finish the season with my mouth shut, or quit and give up the game for good.

"Once you quit, you're always going to be a quitter," he told me when I was a kid.

My dad didn't have to change the words this time around. I decided to stay.

That semester, I didn't see the truth about my war wound, but eventually I would accept my amputation with a simple thought: just because there is less of me doesn't mean I'm less than anyone else.

In addition to my Monday-Wednesday-Friday sessions on the track, I spent Tuesdays and Thursdays in the weight room, beefing up for my other Paralympic pursuit, powerlifting. But these two sports were tugging me in separate directions. In one, I honed my fast-twitch muscles and tried to stay light on my feet;

in the other, I fortified my shoulders, back, and arms, adding bulk to my upper body. Individually, they offered me separate paths to Beijing. Together, they were not a good mix. Track took away some of the gym time I needed to build my top bench-press lift from the current 315 pounds to somewhere above 400, to make me a true medal contender. Powerlifting, meanwhile, made me a bit top-heavy for the 100-meter dash and also stole some of the hours I needed to relearn running, to shave off some of those six extra seconds. That dilemma would dog me for another year. In time, I would face a tough choice.

While my heart was firmly in running, I knew that power-lifting offered me better odds on making the Paralympics. The American powerlifting squad was expected to take only three athletes to China. (Team USA's results at recent international meets had determined that roster size.) There were four lifters, including myself, who seemed to be in contention for those three spots. Meanwhile, in track and field, the U.S. Paralympic roster was expected to number about forty men and women, but I was one of about seventy athletes vying for a precious spot. I adored running, but the math told me to keep pumping iron.

After the powerlifting camp I attended in Philadelphia, Mary Hodge gave me a written training program to target my bench-press muscles, plus a "periodization chart" to slowly increase my personal-best lift. As I squeezed out my reps at the indoor track's weight room, Rohan Murphy continued doing his lifting with the Penn State wrestling team. That spring, both of our phones rang with the same blockbuster news: Mary had placed us on the American team bound for Busan, Korea, in May to compete at the 2006 World Powerlifting Championships. Our lifts at her small, invite-only clinic had convinced Mary that we belonged on the international powerlifting circuit. There was one catch: because I was so new to the sport, I had not qualified to receive funding from U.S. Paralympics, the umbrella organization that governs athletes and finances their travel. I would need five thousand dollars for airfare, meals, and a hotel room in Busan. I reached out to a friend I had met back in Texas, not long after I had first returned from Iraq. Donna Cranston, an army mom, ran a nonprofit called Defenders of Freedom that sends care packages to soldiers overseas. To help gather my travel money, Donna organized a motorcycle caravan across the Dallas–Forth Worth metroplex. They stopped at every Hooters restaurant along the route, collecting donations. Thanks to Donna and all those Harleys, I soon would be headed to Korea. Months earlier, Donna also had teamed up with Janis Roznowski, founder of a troop-support group called Operation Comfort, to pay for my trip to the powerlifting clinic in Philly. Now I would try to repay their kindness by making a big lift on the other side of the world.

On my South Korean hotel bed, thirteen time zones from home soil, I neatly laid out the contents of my lifting bag like a soldier preparing for inspection. Across the bedspread I placed my blue singlet with "USA" stitched to the front and back, my two white cotton undershirts, and my International Paralympic Committee passport.

When Mary Hodge stopped by my room that night for her eight o'clock curfew check, she stared at the tidy line of lifting accoutrements and immediately knew the score.

He is very nervous, the U.S. powerlifting coach thought as she took a seat.

Sure I was. After all, this was the night before my first international sports competition, the 2006 World Powerlifting Championship. As a wounded veteran, I would don the U.S. colors and once again represent my country. One big lift could propel me to the Beijing Paralympics, my dream. Making matters worse, I had missed the team flight to Korea, annoying Mary. This happened after I had stayed up all night at Penn State to study for my final exams and pack up my soon-to-be vacated dorm room. Exhausted, I had reached the tiny Penn State airport thirty minutes before departure. In fact, I saw Rohan sitting at the gate, beyond the small security checkpoint, but a ticket agent had told me it was too late to board. After a mad scramble and some phone calls, I had grabbed a second flight and then slumped, utterly drained, in my window seat: one groggy American powerlifter, now traveling overseas without my teammates—a retired soldier who had been warned by U.S. Olympic officials not to wear the red, white, and blue color combination during the flight for fear that I would attract any terrorist in Korea. A little edgy? Yes. I was.

Mary had seen it all before, of course. She had traveled with U.S. powerlifting teams to Athens, Greece; Sydney, Australia; and Saudi Arabia. It was why she made these curfew visits. She dubbed them "the calm-down time."

"You've trained. You've trained hard," Mary said. "You know where you're at with your lifts. You just have to get a good night's rest, show up tomorrow, and I'll take care of the rest."

Mary may be the most organized coach I've ever had. Every detail is ironed out and tucked away. Every weight-lifting strategy, contingency, and potential need is discussed, catalogued, and marked off her checklist. By instilling this climate of order and control, Mary tries to soothe and relax her athletes, to remove all unnecessary thoughts and worries from their heads—other than the sports task at hand.

During those curfew visits, she asked us to show her—piece by piece—our lifting gear. She asked us what we wanted to eat after the morning weigh-in, then would fetch it and put it in a Tupperware container. She told us what time to wake up. She told us where and what time to catch the bus to the venue. She asked if we wanted to ride the bus alone or ride with her. She reminded us to bring our iPods. And before saying good night, Mary always talked through and plotted the next day's lifts. In competition, you get three attempts.

"Okay, your opener tomorrow is going to be 147.5," she said. "Do you feel comfortable with that based on how you've been training?"

I did. Converting that from kilograms to pounds, I would start with a lift of 324.5 pounds. In practice I had nailed lifts of 330 pounds. The adrenaline of game day also would help. At powerlifting tournaments, you want to pick a first attempt that is aggressive yet tactically safe. Completing your opening lift is not just a psychological boost, it's also physically important. If I were to stall or really struggle on 147.5, forcing the two spotters to grab the bar off my chest or causing the referee to disallow the lift, I would immediately know that I wasn't strong enough on that day to go any higher. That would mean I'd have to shoot again for 147.5 in lift number two—only now I'd be a little more tired and under a bit more pressure to make it a clean lift.

After deciding 147.5 was a smart opener, we plotted my second and third lifts: 150 kilograms (330 pounds) and 152.5 kilograms (335.5 pounds). We'd have a chance to nudge those higher if I was feeling good energy, or if my competitors were pulling away from me on the scoreboard.

The next morning, Mary and I rode a bus to Kijang Gymnasium just three minutes from downtown Busan—also known as Pusan—a port city of almost 4 million people. Kijang Gymnasium reminded me of a small-college basketball arena. It had bleacher seating for five thousand spectators and exposed white ceiling beams that stretched above a lacquered hardwood floor. I already had been inside the venue several times for some light practice and to watch two of my four U.S. teammates compete. Just the day before my event, Anderson Wise, born with spina bifida, had finished sixth in his weight class. My roommate on the trip, Rohan, had actually led off the U.S. performances with a medal. A few days earlier, Rohan had boosted 269.5 pounds, good enough to win bronze among the junior division. Now it was my turn.

I walked into a three-room athletes' entry hall feeling both nervous and hungry, having skipped breakfast for the weigh-in. Mary would be waiting on the other side of the entry with my carb-heavy order of mini sausage links and Korean noodles. In the first room, I took off all my warm-up clothes and tossed them in a basket. In room two, only one athlete at a time is allowed to be present. I handed in my IPC passport, detached my leg, and hopped onto the scale: 164.5 pounds. I would quickly learn that this made me the second-heaviest guy among the twenty lifters in my weight class, a definite disadvantage. The reason for the single-athlete rule in room two was not about personal privacy but lifting tactics. It was where I wrote down my opening lift. I didn't want the other lifters to know where I planned to start, and they were just as protective of their planned first attempts. The game really started in room two. In the third room I put on my clothes and then walked out to the gym.

The place was packed with loud Korean fans. One South Korean was in my weight class, and I knew the crowd would erupt when he approached the bench. Also in my group were athletes from China, Croatia, Ecuador, England, Iran, Japan, Saudi Arabia, Kuwait, Malaysia, Mexico, Poland, South Africa, Turkey, and Iraq. That last one caught my eye. Fifteen months earlier, I had been fighting for my country in Iraq, never knowing who was friend or foe. Now I was representing my country and competing against an Iraqi citizen.

Feels good to wear the American colors. Feels real good, I thought. *I've come a long way in a short time.*

Before the event began, I didn't talk to anyone and kept my head down. I had borrowed Rohan's iPod and I was trying to stoke my inner fire by listening to rapper TI. Twenty minutes before the event began, each of our opening attempts was listed on the arena's electronic scoreboard. I saw that most of the guys were opening with heavier amounts than I was—some would start at more than 400 pounds. I reminded myself that my career was only a few minutes old and I just needed to stick to my plan. While most athletes preferred to remain in a private back room away from the main competition floor when they weren't lifting, I stood in the doorway of that room and watched each man enter the stage, slide onto the bench, and perform. The chief referee sat in a chair behind the bar, giving the commands. Not far from the left foot of each athlete, two more referees sat in folding chairs. The three would judge the lifts by pressing one of two buttons in front of them. A "good lift" would earn a white light from a referee. A "no lift" got a red light. In some cases, the reviews were mixed: two white lights and one red meant the lift was basically a thumbs-up, while two reds and a white meant thumbs down.

When I heard my name called on the overhead speakers, I stripped off my dark blue warm-up jacket and pants and walked briskly to the stage in my blue USA singlet and white T-shirt. I also wore my everyday walking leg: a Rheo microprocessor knee and a FlexFoot. At the end of each day, I would remove that leg and lean it against my bed. Now, as I neared the bench, the dark gray limb gleamed in the gym lights. Mary followed me, carrying the two leather straps. The loaders already had slipped the proper plates onto the bar: two red discs on each side, each weighing 25 kilos (55 pounds), and one green disc on each side, each weighing 10 kilos (22 pounds). The bar and collar-locks made up the rest of the weight. After I was announced, I had two minutes to reach the platform, settle in, and make the lift. Two minutes was a long time to think about the moment. I lay back on the padded bench as Mary buckled me in. She pulled hard on the belt above my knees to make me feel like I was melded with the bench. She secured the strap below my knees just snug enough to keep my feet still but not so tight that I would pop the artificial leg loose with all my straining.

"You have a minute forty," Mary said before stepping back.

There were no big thoughts, no major life assessments after I was alone, looking up at the bar. I had come to lift and that's what I did. I extended my arms to the ceiling, locked the elbows and waited for the spotters to place the bar in my hands. Once I felt the cold metal in my palms, I wrapped my fingers around the bar. The spotters let go. The weight felt good, manageable. With his Korean accent, the referee yelled, "Start!" Using my shoulders and triceps, I controlled the bar down. As Mary had taught me, I arched my back to push out my chest, reducing the length of the dip during the bar's descent. I held the bar on my chest, barely making a dent in my shirt, and counted "one Mississippi." Then, using my back, shoulders, biceps, triceps, and chest muscles, I powered the bar above me, hands even, arms steady, and elbows locked.

"Rack!" the referee yelled.

Yeah! I thought.

I sat up on the bench and looked at the horizontal light panel: three whites. I gave a small pump of my fist as Mary loosened the straps and we walked off together.

In the back room, Mary smiled. She could see that I was ecstatic and also that I had released some of my prelift tension. I had come halfway around the globe and put up 324.5 pounds. I felt proud and fulfilled, but I knew I had to get back to work in a matter of minutes. After the first round, I was ninth out of twenty. The three tops dogs—China, Mexico, and Poland—had each busted out opening lifts of 418 pounds. Based on that, I knew I was not going home with a medal. Still, I could add to my numbers with my next lift. That's all I really could control.

"How did that weight feel?" Mary asked.

"Good," I said.

"Okay. We're going up," she said.

We dumped our original plan for a second lift of 150 kilograms and entered a new weight with the referee: 152.5 kilograms or 335.5 pounds. This would be more weight than I had ever powerlifted in my life.

"Let's get out there," Mary said. "Let's kick some ass."

We repeated all those same steps for the second attempt. This time, though, with the extra ten pounds on board, the bar dropped a fraction of a second faster, my arms quivered slightly more and, after the dip, the bar pressed slightly into my chest. On the way up, my right hand was a just bit higher than the left and my head began to rise from the bench. I locked out my elbows, held the bar steady, and when the chief referee shouted "rack," I handed the bar to the spotters. In any gym in America I had just hoisted 335.5 pounds, but when I looked at the judging lights, two of them were red. Two refs had flagged me for technical violations.

For the final lift, we decided to stay with 152.5. I knew I could handle that weight. I just had to find more control in my muscles. I now stood in twelfth place, just behind Iran and just ahead of Kuwait. But on the third attempt, the bar felt much heavier and I stalled on the upswing. The spotters grabbed the bar and my competition was done. Officially, I finished thirteenth in the event.

Off the stage, Mary hugged me.

"You did great," she said, sounding like a proud mom.

But as she studied my face, she saw a look of sheer disappointment. I wasn't expecting to bring a medal home, but I had come all this way and missed on two out of three lifts. And standing now in thirteenth place, I sure didn't feel any closer to qualifying for Beijing. A top five would have put me in striking range, maybe even secured me a place on the U.S. Paralympic team. Not thirteenth. She saw tears well up in my eyes.

Mary grabbed my chin with her fingers and pulled my face toward hers.

"You did great," she said, now sounding like a mom trying to teach a lesson. "This is your first international competition and you are thirteenth. And if you take out the junior lifters in this weight class, you're in the top ten in the world. In the world!"

That clicked. I began to smile, and once I pulled my mind around everything—where I was, where I stood, and where I had come from—I began to see: I did great, just like Mary said.

After my lifts, the U.S. squad stayed in Korea for another week so we could cheer teammate Mary Stack's lifts. I continued training, going to Kijang Gym to use one of the ten practice benches there. While riding the athlete bus one day, I detected some Arabic words among the medley of international languages on board. It was weird—the last time I'd heard that language, I still owned both of my legs, was wearing sergeant's stripes on my arm, and had an M-16 on my back.

From my bus seat, I swiveled my head across the aisle and instantly realized that some of my fellow passengers were Iraqis. The first question that crossed my mind wasn't too friendly.

I wonder if any of these guys is the one, I thought, narrowing my eyes toward the pack next to me.

My hand brushed across the remains of my right thigh.

I wonder if one of them planted that bomb. Or maybe they know somebody who used to make IEDs.

In a flash, my suspicion vanished just as fast as it had arrived. I saw that these Iraqi weightlifters were also missing pieces of themselves, maybe from same hostilities that had taken my leg. Their country once had been full of athletes whose lives were immersed in sports, not just in war. Soccer is the national sport there, but Iraq's only medal-producing sport at the 2004 Paralympics was powerlifting. In Athens that same year, Thaair Hussin had earned a bronze for Iraq in the 82.5 kilogram (182 pound) division by raising 446 pounds. Even more impressive was the lift by heavyweight (220 pounds-plus) Faris Abed who had set a Paralympic mark by putting up 525 pounds for Iraq. His incredible effort was quickly topped, though, when an Iranian hoisted 551 pounds to grab gold. In my own weight class in Korea, I had faced a huge challenge from Jabbar Jabor, who attempted 408 pounds but missed.

Now Jabor and his teammates were riding the same bus to the venue, unaware that the guy next to them had been permanently changed on his last morning in their country. I wondered how Jabor had been maimed in his life.

You know what, man? I thought. *This is a person with disabilities just like me. He's here to compete just like me. He didn't give up when he got hurt, so he's almost in the same boat as me. I don't know what he had going on in Iraq, but here in Korea he's on the bench press with me.*

9

Precious Time

14.5

On a plain white notecard, I neatly printed those digits in blue pen. As the ink dried, I gazed hard at the number, imagining where it might carry me. Then I taped the card to the wall in my Penn State apartment, right next to my computer screen, where I would have to stare at it each day. 14.5. The little notation was not a world record. Not even close. But that was the goal I intended to eclipse in one month—when I would run the 100-meter dash at the 2006 U.S. Paralympics Track and Field National Championships in Atlanta.

14.5.

I had my reasons. If I snapped the wire in 14.5 seconds, that would place me near—or maybe within—the world's top-five times in 2006 for above-the-knee sprinters. Even better, it would qualify me to compete at the International Paralympic Committee's

2006 Track World Championships in Assen, Netherlands. That late-summer event, held every four years, invited only AK runners who had posted 100-meter times of 14.5 seconds or faster. Like Atlanta, Assen could be an important bridge to my dream, reaching the 2008 Paralympic Summer Games in Beijing. Each race on my 2006 schedule loomed as a big, blinking milepost toward China—individual strides toward completing my new mission in this life. But everything would begin in Atlanta, and it would all start with leaning into the tape there, looking up, and seeing the stadium clock flashing: "Clemons . . . 14:50." That was my hope.

No question, the number on my notecard was a bold target, but I felt it was realistic. In practice that spring, Coach Jordan had hand-timed me at 14.8 seconds on the indoor track. Although it was unofficial, seeing that mark on her stopwatch made us both grin. It was proof that five months of drills, sprints, sweat, and occasional falls had already shed five seconds off the 100-meter time I had clocked upon my Penn State arrival.

After returning from Korea, I immersed myself in summer school and training for the Atlanta nationals. On the track each morning before my classes, I ran some practice sprints and tinkered with two specific phases of my race. First, I concentrated on my starts—the bodily unfolding that takes place once I hear the crack of starter's pistol. Before every heat, I placed my curved Cheetah foot into the rear metal block, allowing me to extend my prosthetic leg behind me with the right knee slightly bent. Into the left block beneath me, I tucked my left running shoe, assuming a half-squatting position while waiting for the start. My back was flat and parallel to the ground. Both arms extended from my shoulders straight to the lane. My fingers lightly touched the track surface for balance. At the sound of the gun I twitched, surged up, and broke forward. Before the echo of that pistol blast even faded, I had pulled my prosthetic leg completely around me, toward the outside of my body, sweeping the bladed foot into the lane just to my right. I simultaneously drove my body ahead by pushing off with my left foot. In that same beat, my shoulders rose, my back tilted to a 45-degree angle, my eyes peered down the lane, and I planted the Cheetah foot firmly on the track—my first step in the race.

In a proper start—not always the case—I continued to stay low to the track while making my final thrust out of the left block and shifting my weight as my left foot hit the track. To improve my start, I needed to make sure I maintained that low, compact profile throughout my first strides, then pop into an upright position at the forty-meter mark.

My other practice task during those first days of June involved the main phase of the race, the final seventy meters. I needed to find a way to consistently stay over my knee as I ran, to avoid getting into what I called "the backseat." I noticed that other runners would start pulling away from me after the first three seconds, leaving me in the rear of the pack—the backseat—but by keeping my torso and hip straight above my right knee, I seemed to have better early speed. I tackled that flaw by trying to lean forward as I ran.

My 100-meter practice times were typically staying in the 15.5-second range, except for those rare, happy occasions when I touched the high 14s on Coach Jordan's stopwatch. One afternoon I sat at the computer in my Penn State apartment and looked again at that notecard taped to the wall. 14.5. With less than a month before the Atlanta nationals, did I have enough time left to slice a full second off my time? I tapped the keyboard and pulled up some Web pages—including Ossur.com—that contained background on the world's fastest above-the-knee runner, Canada's Earle Connor. Maybe a little computer surfing, I thought, could help me uncover some new hints on sprinting.

Connor's story was a mix of glorious world records and a sudden stumble from grace. Pushing thirty, he was considered the king of AK sprinters, a blur in white-framed sunglasses who had established the planet's fastest above-the-knee times in the 100-, 200-, and 400-meters all on the same day in 2003 at a meet in Levekursen, Germany. In the 100-meters, Connor had posted an electric 12.14 seconds. Three years earlier, at the Sydney Paralympics, he had bagged gold and silver medals.

Oh my God, I thought as I read the bio material. *I've got a long way to go.*

Connor was born without his left fibula, the bone that links the knee to the ankle. When he was three months old, doctors had amputated the leg above the knee. In the 1970s, that was the only medical option. But as a kid in the small western Canada city of Saskatoon, he was brought up as an athlete, playing both competitive hockey and high school basketball on his prosthetic leg. Eventually, he was drafted as a junior hockey goalie by the Lethbridge Hurricanes of the Western Hockey League. His career plan changed when Connor glimpsed some TV coverage of track events at the 1996 Atlanta Paralympics. He saw the finishing times and figured he already was fast enough to run with the best. Connor then moved to Calgary and began training to be a sprinter. World records soon followed.

Days before the 2004 Paralympics in Athens—where Connor had been nominated to carry his nation's flag during the opening ceremony—he learned that he had failed a drug test one month before, testing positive for an elevated level of testosterone as well as the presence of nandrolone, an anabolic steroid. He received a two-year ban from track and field that would expire in August 2006. Connor called the doping violation an honest mistake. In a statement he said he had been using a medically prescribed patch to normalize his testosterone following the removal of one testicle in 2001 due to a cancer scare. He also explained that he'd been taking prescribed and supplemental medications after being diagnosed in July 2004 with a severe gastrointestinal infection while competing in Germany. But the doping scandal killed his Nike endorsement deal and gutted his sports-related income, which at one point had topped six figures. He even had to get rid of two of his three cars. In Canada, a *National Post* columnist said the sprinter was "someplace between dirty and stupid." But I chose to give Connor the benefit of the doubt. I had only heard good things about Connor, and I believed his drug violation had been an honest error. It takes years of intense work for an amputee runner to emerge as an elite athlete. Connor had suffered from a medical condition, had taken steps to try to get his body back to normal, and now the antidoping authorities had stamped him as a cheater. Would he carry that label forever? To me, that wasn't fair.

I had investigated legal supplements through books and the Internet, had looked into the brands that were approved by the U.S. Anti-Doping Agency—the governing authority for drugs in American amateur sports. But I never had felt totally comfortable with the idea of drinking or popping a performance enhancer. Even if USADA had deemed a particular pill safe and legal, I worried that the manufacturer might still mess up and allow a banned ingredient to slip into its product. I had come so far doing it the right way, committed myself so fully to becoming a world-class runner, did I want to try a supplement and put everything I had accomplished at risk? Did I want to jeopardize my future and, like Connor, have people wonder about my ethics for the rest of my life? No.

Connor's violation had cost him a two-year ban in Paralympic track. He would be back later that summer. But all that history aside, he was the man I was chasing. He owned the records, and on the track, he was a role model. I wanted to beat his numbers.

"I'm not getting into this just to win," I had once told my dad about the sport of sprinting. "I'm getting into this to set records."

One of the most intriguing things I'd gleaned from my Internet research was that Connor wore a German brand of prosthetic knee—an Otto Bock. In my quest to cut that extra second from my time, an Otto Bock knee might be the solution, I thought. Training in my Mauch knee had frequently caused aches in my lower back due to the way it distributed the force from my pounding strides. Even worse, I felt like the Mauch knee was sometimes too slow to keep up with my natural pace, that it didn't always spring my right foot back below me fast enough to complete a proper stride. I called Tim Rayer, my Philly prosthetist, and told him my physical concerns—along with my wishes to switch to the same knee that Connor had worn during his record-setting spree. Rayer agreed to make the exchange, fitting me in Otto Bock's 3R46 knee—a compact, hydraulic machine made of titanium, weighing just 1.6 pounds and built for the rigors of running. The metallic gray 3R46 allowed users to increase or reduce the amount of resistance in both the knee's bend and its extension forward—whatever felt right to me. So, two weeks before the Atlanta nationals, I was bouncing down the track in my third prosthetic running knee. I now felt no residual back pain from my workouts. The last thing I had to do was learn how to fully control the new German knee by the time I ran my first race. Coach Jordan understood my decision to swap legs, but she wasn't thrilled with the timing. She worried that instead of cutting seconds in Atlanta, I might add a few extra tenths as I adjusted to my new parts.

"I understand that you want to try something if you think it's going to be the answer. You want to get everything as perfect as possible," she said. "But the change should not probably come within a week or two of the event."

As I prepared for the Atlanta meet, my 100-meter times stayed locked in the mid-15-second range. As it turned out, though, the new leg was not going to be the biggest headache I faced in Atlanta.

The 2006 U.S. Paralympics Track and Field National Championships took place between June 30 and July 2 at

Lakewood Stadium, a ten-thousand-seat sports venue in Atlanta's southeastern suburbs. The stadium's rose-colored track encircled a green artificial-turf field that was sometimes used for high school football games. Trees swayed in the hot summer breeze. I had two chances to try to hit that 14.5 mark. The first was a 100-meter dash against other above-the-knee runners. Then came an "all comers" 100-meter sprint that would pit a variety of disabled athletes against each other, including Vitalis Lanshima, a Nigerian man who at age twelve lost both his arms in an accident, and my old running buddy, Wardell Swann, a double-leg amputee.

The day before my first race had been earmarked for media interviews. Apparently, the details of my injury and recovery had started to grab interest among a few national news outlets, including CNN, *USA Today*, and the Versus Network. The tale of a wounded Iraq War vet returning home to run on one leg seemed to inspire some folks. I had been so wrapped up in my rehab, my internal battles, and my daily toils on the track, I hadn't noticed that people were starting to follow my progress. I was humbled but also motivated: if my story could move everyday Americans—especially other soldiers who had returned from Iraq and Afghanistan with catastrophic wounds—I felt obliged to share it. That was my duty. For so long I had lain in my hospital bed, staring at the ceiling, wondering if there was some greater reason for my injury and some larger meaning for my life. Maybe the reason and meaning could be found in telling my story, affecting other people. An energizing feeling of hope took root.

The media relations folks within U.S. Paralympics had scheduled interviews and videotaping time with CNN and Versus on one of my first mornings in Atlanta.

"One door closes, another one opens," Coach Jordan often said to me. "Sometimes you just have to know how to step through it."

Coach Jordan knew she had to walk a fine line—balancing my running preparation against a morning filled with interviews.

Her priority was my 100-meter time, but because the media sessions were scheduled for an off day, she had approved them. Camera people and journalists from CNN and Versus sat me down to talk about my life, then they asked to film me while I ran at the empty track. Wearing my dark blue Penn State uniform, I broke off a bunch of hard sprints and worked up a decent sweat over the course of a couple of hours. Around lunchtime, I took a shuttle bus back to my hotel room to rest up for the next day's race—the moment I had been working toward for months. The phone rang. It was Coach Jordan.

"Kortney, they've changed the entire schedule," she said. "You've got to run today!"

The event organizers had decided to combine several smaller groups of runners into a single, 100-meter heat, in part because there were only a few above-the-knee amputees participating in Atlanta. For my big race, I would be lined up with several visually impaired athletes plus an arm amputee. All of them would be much faster than me.

"Okay," I said, "I'm on my way."

Thankfully, the hotel was only a ten-minute ride from the track. I hustled back into my sweaty Penn State uniform, bolted out the door, and hopped a shuttle bus for Lakewood Stadium. As I rode, I wondered how all those morning sprints for the TV cameras would affect my 100-meter time when it really counted.

I sat in an athletes' corridor beneath the stands as Coach Jordan stood near a buffet spread and gave me her last-minute tips. Behind us, six track athletes in wheelchairs and prosthetic legs milled about and chatted quietly. What my coach laid down was not exactly a classic pep talk, just a critical reminder to help me meet my greater goal.

"There are other types of disabilities in your race. But remember, you are the only AK," she said calmly. "You won't win the race. Your time is now what's important."

My heat would include two legally blind runners who were ranked in top three in the world for their visually impaired classification, and two more who were in the top thirty globally for the same division. They could barely see the lane lines but their legs were strong and healthy. All of them could post 100-meter times in the 11-to-12-seconds range. Because they would all blow out of the blocks, kicking up grit from the track as they zoomed by me, I opted to wear a pair of black sunglasses for the race to shield my eyes.

I sucked in a few deep breaths of warm Georgia air as I walked to my lane in the center of the track. In the sun-splashed crowd along the main straightaway, my family had taken their seats. Dad, Mom, and my daughter had never watched me race before. And as I scanned all the faces, searching for my folks' bright eyes and big smiles, I felt an old sensation: the anxious flip-flop of butterflies in my stomach. Prerace jitters had overtaken me. And that was good. Because it was normal. That queasy feeling had nothing to do with amputations or limitations. It was how I used to feel before high school and college football games, back when I would sink my cleats into the high grass and search the school's stands for my excited parents. I would now try to transfer that raw, nervous energy into an all-out sprint. 14.5. That's what I wanted to see on the scoreboard after I hit that finish line.

I knelt onto the track, sticking my left foot into the closer of the two blocks and my curved Cheetah blade into the back foothold. The other runners were quiet.

What's going to happen in the next twenty seconds? I wondered.

Depending on my time that afternoon, my life could veer into an entirely new direction. I could be packing soon for the Netherlands and the World Championships. I gazed down the track and said a small prayer: "Just get me from point A to point B." That helped simplify the moment a little. It was out of my hands now. I would just run as fast as I could and let my racing life take its natural course.

At the gun, white smoke oozed from the starter's pistol and I jolted up and out of the blocks—a sharp, clean start although, once again, I had stood up too soon. Now into the meat of the race, I pumped my arms at my sides and felt the wind rush past my face. As expected, the other guys in my heat shot ahead of me early. At the back of the pack, I only thought about finishing strong. I kept my cadence tight—left-right-breathe, left-right-breathe, left-right-breathe. In the stands, there were shouts of: "Go! Go!" But about seventy meters into the race, I felt a small, momentary hitch in my sprinting tempo, barely more than a blip. That's all it took. In running, everything is about rhythm: one step builds on the next until your breathing and stride are in synch, your body is perfectly aligned, and you are moving at your maximum velocity. For me, it was much more complex: that natural cadence had to be meshed with all the whirling mechanics that went into operating a prosthetic leg. That little waggle threw off my timing just enough to make me a fraction of a second late for the very next step on my right side. During the next few strides, my stance spread a bit wider than normal as I gathered my balance. I recovered for the final twenty meters and cruised over the line, knowing I had been a hair slow. My time: 15.83.

"Not one of my best," I said out loud as the Versus camera picked up my words.

In our brief postrace conversation, Coach Jordan and I analyzed the day: I had probably cost myself a little time—maybe three to five tenths—as a result of the new knee and my earlier sprints for the TV cameras. I would have one final shot at the Atlanta nationals to hit my goal of 14.5 seconds. As I cooled down, I leaned against a shaded concrete wall that supported the bleachers. Above me, my dad leaned over a railing in the bottom row of the elevated stands and lowered his outstretched hand. I held up mine and he gave me a supportive slap on the palm.

"One more time," he said in his Mississippi drawl.

After arriving at the track the next day, I met once more with Coach Jordan to talk through some pointers. She boiled the race down to its basic elements.

"I want you to react to the gun, get out at the start, and run through the line," she said.

The "all comers" race would again include three runners who were faster than me. One of them was Swann, who had consistently posted 13-second times in the 100 meters. He also was aiming to make the U.S. team bound for Beijing. Before the race, he gave me a pat on the back and wished me good luck. I told him the same.

"Make sure you run hard through the finish line," Coach Jordan reminded me privately. "You're going to beat the other two AKs in this race but there will be some people who finish ahead of you. Your time, that's what's important. Not where you finish in this race. Run through the line."

She knew I had a tendency to slow up when I saw that the first runner had hit the tape. She wanted me to think about beating the clock, not the other people.

Before curling myself into the blocks, I stood, raised my face to the bright sky, and closed my eyes. The butterflies were back. I spread my arms in the air and focused on slowing my breathing.

Calm down, man, I thought. *You're going to blow up before you run.*

I crouched onto the track, got my feet set, flattened my back, said my prayer, and waited for the pistol shot.

Bang! I was up and out—another clean start. The scuffling feet of the guys to the right and left pelted my face and mouth with a fine spray of track dirt. They were literally dusting me. Some of those grains bounced off my sunglasses, but stride for stride, I felt smoother and stronger than I had the day before. This time I could actually hear runners behind me, puffing and scraping their feet on the track surface. At the finish line, I stretched forward and peeked at my time: 15.61. I had beaten the other two AKs in my heat, but I had not run fast enough to make the cut for the World Championships. Qualifying for the U.S. Paralympic track team—and China—would also have to wait for another day.

Coach Jordan told me that I had done well weathering the pressures of both the event and the Paralympic limelight.

"Any time you race at your first national meet, you're going to be scared and overwhelmed by the thing," she said. "On top of that, you had a massive amount of media attention. This was a great learning experience for you."

But I did privately wonder: *Am I going to do it? Am I ever going to be fast enough?*

I had been living by the clock since the morning that bomb went off in Baghdad. It was: How soon would I get to the hospital? How soon would I get home? When would I feel whole again? When would I walk again? When would I run? In each of those individual races of my life, I had eventually made it across the finish line, but in my head, that big clock was always ticking. Wherever I was going, I never seemed to get there fast enough. Fulfilling my sports dream was no different. I was still being ruled by the clock. All I could do was keep sprinting for the wire.

The national TV and print coverage from CNN, Versus, and *USA Today* generated a new wave of interest from even more networks and newspapers. Writers in Philadelphia, Atlanta, Washington, D.C., Pittsburgh, and London, England, carried my tale of recovery and racing. Wire services like Gannett, Cox, Knight Ridder, and the Associated Press picked up the story, too. I was invited to appear on a segment of the BET network show *Ballers*. ABC News named me its "Person of the Week."

I tried my best to stay grounded, and I think I remained the very same person. I appreciated the attention but I never believed that my story was somehow better or more worthy than the experiences of other American war vets who had left pieces of themselves in a foreign land. I didn't feel like I was anything special. I understood that the media outlets were using me as a symbol of hope during a bleak time for our country. I recognized that when I ran in front of a crowd or talked into a TV camera, I was representing other wounded soldiers. I took that responsibility to heart. Maybe by sharing a little of myself, I would help other Americans appreciate the deep sacrifices made by thousands of military men and women in Iraq and Afghanistan.

But on another level, my story became as just important to me as my dream to win gold in Beijing. In a way, the story and the running became intertwined. This was my mission—to strap on my leg and prove that we can accomplish whatever we want in this world so long as we keep moving forward, that barriers can be smashed, that excuses can be shed, that standing still is just moving backward. Every race was like a fourteen-second life lesson: have the guts to get to the starting line, have the willpower to run through the pain, have the fire to cross the finish line—no matter how you're running that day. There was grace in the effort. There was triumph in the chase. Of course, I also wanted to win, but the more I could help other people—maybe by encouraging them to keep trying on their worst days—the more energy I seemed to gain to continue my own quest. I fed off the sense that maybe I was inspiring someone.

As a person who had been disfigured, I found that the media coverage also became a kind of medicine for my soul. One magazine piece particularly soothed some of the inner doubts I had carried as a man since the explosion took my leg. In 2007, *Essence* named me as one of its "Do Right Men." I shared the honor with doctors, ministers, and millionaires as well as actor D. B. Woodside, NFL wide receiver Braylon Edwards, and singer Brian McKnight. They flew me to Puerto Rico for a photo shoot, and in their magazine they displayed me in midstride at an outdoor track, seemingly balanced on the toe of my running leg. My inclusion on that annual list helped change my perspective on my own appearance. It helped me feel more comfortable in my own skin. It reinforced the feeling that I shouldn't be ashamed of my body, that I could still be attractive to the opposite sex, and that there were many women out there who could look past an artificial limb and see the flesh and soul that lay within. In an online guestbook that accompanied the Web version of the *Essence* article, thirty-seven women left me notes, asking me to have dinner or inviting me on dates. They called me a "bionic man" and "an average Joe without all the glitz and glam."

"I was feeling down and I took up the *Essence* magazine and there you were, reminding me that life is full of challenges but we must keep moving forward," wrote Sharon from Barbados. "You have today encouraged me to be the best I can be."

Those were the perfect words, in my opinion. They summed up my new life. My self-image turned from "That's a guy who's missing his leg" to "Hey, you've got it going on." Folks saw the man beyond the disability. I had a new sense of purpose. I felt that I was reaching people, and some of them were in pretty high places.

A *USA Today* profile of my sports journey caught the attention of President Bush. In 2006, the man who chose to send me and thousands of other soldiers to Iraq took a few minutes to write me a letter, printed on White House stationery, that arrived at my parents' house:

Dear Kortney:

I recently learned about your accomplishments on the track. Your courage is an inspiration to us all, and your hard work to overcome adversity reflects on the strength and optimism of the American spirit. You are setting an outstanding example for generations to come, and you have made our country incredibly proud.

Thank you for your service. Laura and I send our best wishes for continued success.

Sincerely,

George W. Bush

President Bush signed the letter with a thick black marker, using broad, swooping strokes. I was amazed that he had been paying attention to my life and my dream to sprint for Paralympic gold. But he felt partially responsible for what had happened to me. I know, because he later told me so.

In time, I would get a chance to speak to the president face to face. We would stand near his large, natural wood desk in the Oval Office—the very room where his decision had changed my life—and we would talk about my missing limb.

Under a blazing blue sky, with the scent of the Pacific Ocean salting the August air, a small crowd of amputees waited to run. All of us were former military men. Some had been hurt in peacetime. Some had been hurt in war. One had inspired me to live my life in fast motion.

John Register had never seen me sprint. Now we were about to team up for a relay race. Dozens of other soldiers, seamen, marines, and airmen—participants in Register's latest military sports camp—stood at the edge of the track, clapping and yelling. We were gathered at the 32nd Street Naval Station just south of downtown San Diego. The huge complex served as the home port for more than fifty ships in the Pacific fleet. It also boasted a nice running track.

As always, the camp's atmosphere was poignant and play-ful, filled with inspirational Paralympic athletes as well as wide-eyed young soldiers who were fresh from Iraq—and even fresher from their hospital beds. There was laughter and lots of good-natured trash-talking, but I had arrived in San Diego carrying the frustration of a stalled 2006 sprinting season. Seven months after enrolling at Penn State, my 100-meter times remained stuck in the 15s—about three seconds too slow to reach Beijing. I had changed my running leg twice. I had studied my starts and streamlined the first steps after my takeoffs. I had learned to run through the finish. But I now had less than two years to qualify for the U.S. Paralympic track team. Where else could I look to trim three more seconds from a race that lasts barely longer than a pair of sneezes?

A relaxed race on a summer's day was a welcome distraction from the sprinter's math now jamming my head like a bad song, and a few minutes spent with Register would offer me some needed perspective on the long journey I had taken since our first meeting in San Antonio. The odd symmetry between us was unshakeable. He went to war but lost his leg while running track. I was using track to reclaim my life after losing my leg in war. We each were well acquainted with the subtleties of time—the bigger chunks needed for healing, the smaller pieces that com-prise life's goals, the tiny fragments that make up a 100-meter sprint. Register readied the cluster of runners. Each segment of the relay would cover 200 meters, and there would be four run-ners per squad.

Register and I comprised half of one relay team. One of the other guys in our foursome was Casey Tibbs, a navy officer who was my age. In 2001, he had lost his right foot in a motorcycle accident. Three years later, Tibbs had entered the Paralympic pentathlon in Athens—long jump, shot put, 100 meters, discus, and 400 meters—grabbing a silver medal. He also had won a gold medal there in the 100-meter relay. His best-ever 100-meter time—11.85 seconds—was clocked in Athens where, in addition to all those sparkling awards, he had become the first active-duty military person to compete at the Paralympics. Tibbs and I chatted about San Antonio, where he had once been stationed. Then we talked about his running the anchor leg in our relay.

We all took our spots at 200-meter intervals around the track. Every participant would sprint for half a lap—twice around the track per team. The gun sounded and the first group of runners burst from the blocks. By the time Register took the stick for the second leg, our team was trailing. When I grabbed the handoff from Register, we still had a lot of ground to make up. Even worse, the guy leading my heat was a below-knee amputee—a big edge for him over me. But I churned hard, raising my knees high and keeping my arms tight to my body. One of my weaknesses was my start, but I didn't have to worry about that in the relay. I actually caught that lead runner in the far curve of the first turn, and the two of us were even as we each handed off to our anchormen. Tibbs—the Paralympic double medalist whose personal best in the 100-meters was just two seconds off the able-bodied world record—stormed away from the pack and won the race for our foursome.

At the finish line, John smiled but didn't say a word. He had watched me glide in the California sun. I had been able to show him what I could do. He had been able to see the impact of his work. The moment was sweet, but a far more subtle highlight had come quietly in the middle of the relay race—when Register handed me the baton.

We had one other friendly race that day, a 100-meter dash. Register and I would now get a chance to sprint head-to-head as part of an eight-man field, but this little 100-meter grudge match would basically break down into two races. The six BKs in our heat would bounce out early and finish far ahead of us, leaving

Register and me—the only AKs—to do battle. He took the lane next to me and we each dug into the blocks.

"You know," he said, leaning my way with a smile, "I don't run the hundred meters anymore."

I just laughed, looked at the white lane lines in front of me, and waited to go. No excuses allowed.

At the gun, Register bounded slightly ahead of me, taking advantage of my sluggish start. But at the halfway point I pulled even with him. In the final thirty meters I cruised slightly ahead and, at the wire, I beat him by about three body lengths. Register, whose fastest-ever time in the event was a 13.7, finished in 17 seconds. I was clocked at about 15.5 seconds. The real boost came in our chat right after the race, as we were still breathing hard.

"You are so much farther along than I was at this stage," Register said. "Heck, after my injury, it took me four years to run competitively again. How long has it been for you?"

"Eighteen months," I said.

"You've got a chance to really do good things," he said. "Don't quit. Don't ever give up."

"I won't."

10

History and Headlights

We walked through the hallowed brick archways of Franklin Field, straight into a building full of ghosts and legends. From the darkness of the stadium tunnel, we could hear the low hum and occasional sharp roar of the huge crowd outside. Then we stepped outside, back into the daylight, ready to make track and field history.

On a soggy April day in downtown Philadelphia, I was scheduled to compete in the Penn Relays with Wardell Swann and five other men who had lost their legs as a result of grave illness, birth defects, or horrible accidents. Out of our dark times, each of us had rallied, recovered, and charged into brand-new lives. Three of the participants already had shined in past Paralympics, collecting a combined eleven medals, seven of them gold. Two of the guys owned seven world records between them. In the realm of U.S. Paralympic track, this was an exclusive field—the type of elite talent that the Penn Relays had been attracting since 1895. With just one year of competitive running under my belt, I was humbled to be part of the scene. At precisely 2:52 on that Friday afternoon, the seven of us would line up on those old red lanes, leap forward at the crack of the pistol, and begin the first amputee race in the 113-year annals of the famous Philly sports festival.

The idea for our breakthrough run had been hatched four months earlier during a casual conversation between Dave Johnson, the director of the Penn Relays, and Troy Engle, the new head coach of the U.S. Paralympic track and field team. During the annual meeting for the leaders of USA Track & Field—the sport's governing body—Engle had suggested that the time had come for an amputee race at Penn.

"Yeah," Johnson had agreed, "we can almost certainly do it. You can organize it, and I can carve out time on the schedule."

The night before our run—at a Motel 6 on the outskirts of Philly where Wardell and I were sharing a room—we sat and talked about history. As a rookie in the sport, I hadn't yet grasped the enormity of the Relays or the importance of our barrier-shattering moment. To me, this was another race, but Wardell simply beamed at the thought of our appearance on that track. For him, this run would be a major victory in our lives—and a big chance to offer an emotional boost to any people with disabilities who might watch or hear about our feat.

"We've already won, man. All we have to do is show up tomorrow," Wardell said. "You know, there's no rule book on living as an amputee, no direction or structure that you can follow or live by. You just have to use your God-given wisdom. It's the same for a high-profile athlete—it's living day-to-day.

"Every day we wake up and look at our limbs, but we have to see beyond them. We have to look at the things that happen in our lives. I have a family. You have a daughter. When I get up every morning, I do it for my kids. So we all need to look around and find those kinds of strongholds. But mainly, we have to be positive for each other, for other amputees, so we can lift each other up, day by day."

Running to inspire had become part of my identity, so those words truly spurred me. Wardell told me more about the Penn Relays, how the event held a sacred place in track and field lore, how men—and later women—had started racing on that same ground when Grover Cleveland was president, and before Utah, Oklahoma, Arizona, and New Mexico had even received statehood. During the century that followed, the Relays had often mirrored American history, reflecting the ravages of world wars and the advances of civil rights. The event's first seeds—really just a marketing ploy—were planted in 1893 when leaders of the University of Pennsylvania's track committee realized they needed to jazz up their annual spring meet. They cooked up the scheme of adding a relay race to their usual list of short- and long-distance events. They put together a four-man Penn team to run a relay comprised of successive quarter miles (440 yards), and then invited Princeton's track coach to assemble and bring a similar relay squad. In the first collegiate relay race, Princeton beat Penn with a time of 3 minutes, 34 seconds. Today, that event is better known as the 4×440, and the able-bodied world record is 2 minutes, 54.2 seconds. The relay—then made with just a touch of hands and not the passing of a baton—was an instant hit with fans.

In 1895, Penn's track committee decided to sponsor an all-relay meet to rekindle interest in the school's track program. They also used the event to dedicate their new track, Franklin Field, which boasted a single-tiered wooden grandstand. The new facility was both homespun and primitive. With permanent dressing rooms still a few years away, the organizers set up tents around the perimeter of the track. They gave the meet a circuslike atmosphere, leading attendees to dub it the "Penn Relays Carnival." The name stuck for more than a century. That first year, nine relay events were held for high school and college participants, including runners from Rutgers, Cornell, and Columbia. In 1898, organizers added the 100- and 200-yard sprints plus the pole vault, long jump and other field events. In 1920, after World War II had gutted the sports teams at Cambridge and Oxford Universities in England, the rival schools were invited to send a combined squad. That year, 30,000 people packed the expanded bleachers to watch the two foes compete together. Franklin Field became a hotbed of sports innovation, ushering in the first use of the scoreboard, the first radio broadcast of a football game (1922), and the first football telecast (1939). On that same football field inside those track lanes, Red Grange had set an NCAA record in 1925 by rushing 331 yards for the University of Illinois. By 1956, the Penn Relays was attracting 4,000 athletes. In 1962, organizers added women's events. In April 2007, the meet drew more than 109,000 spectators over its three-day run.

As I stretched and warmed up on that same field, almost 34,000 people ringed the track's grandstands. The game-day program contained the names of the seven amputee runners. Coach Jordan purchased a copy just to commemorate our first race.

"Regardless of how you run," she said, "you're helping to make history."

Wearing my dark blue Penn State uniform, I stepped onto the track, which was still damp from the day's rain, and we each took our assigned lanes. Mine was number seven, the outside lane. I was the only above-the-knee amputee in the event. Next to me was Wardell, a double below-knee amputee. In lane five stood Ryan Fann, who had lost his leg at age three after being hit by a car but later played high school football. In lane four was Danny Andrews. A broken leg he suffered while playing soccer had led to compartment syndrome—and an amputation—but Danny had gone on to win three Paralympic gold medals and set three world sprinting records. Jeremy Campbell manned lane three. A birth defect had led to the amputation of Jeremy's leg when he was a child. Now nineteen, he had been an all-district high school football player in Texas, starting as both linebacker and wide receiver. Jeremy also played baseball and basketball. Don Kosakowski, who was born without a right arm, would run in lane two. At the 2006 World Championships in the Netherlands, Don's 4 × 100-meter relay team had broken the world record. The assembled talent was probably the deepest I had ever faced. But there was one more athlete. Lane one contained a Paralympic legend.

Marlon Shirley was then known as "the fastest amputee in the world." (Double amputee Oscar Pistorius from South Africa was about to claim that title with a 100-meter time of 10.91 seconds.) But on that day no human being missing a portion of a leg had ever finished the 100-meter dash with a quicker official time: 11.08 seconds. And during a non-sanctioned 100-meter race in 2003 in Utah, Marlon had actually become the first amputee to bust the 11-second barrier, clocking in at 10.97. By comparison, Florence Griffith Joyner owned the women's world record in the 100 meters at 10.49 seconds. But Marlon's sports triumphs almost paled in contrast to his personal story. He had been abandoned by his mother at age three, then somehow survived with a group of other homeless kids on the streets of Las Vegas. He soon was placed into foster care, but while living at an orphanage he fell under a lawnmower and lost his left foot. He was five at the time. Four years later, he was adopted by a Utah family and eventually became a high school football player. But another gruesome injury in that sport forced surgeons to amputate the lower part of his left leg. He continued to run in an artificial leg and foot. Now Marlon was almost thirty years old, and his main events were the 100-meter dash, the 200-meter dash, the 4 × 100-meter relay, the 4 × 400-meter relay, and the long jump.

I watched Marlon as he did some last-minute stretches while waiting for the field announcer to introduce us. He would be a slam dunk to make the U.S. Paralympic track squad. But I also realized that every person in that heat could march together during the Beijing opening ceremonies on September 6, 2008. On that day in Philly we were competitors. Tomorrow in China, maybe we'd be teammates. The field announcer began reading the runners' names and lane assignments. I'm not sure it was true, but the Associated Press reported on that day: "The loudest cheers came for veteran Kortney Clemons." If so, I believe the fans were cheering for all the American military men and women who had been wounded in Iraq and Afghanistan. I knelt on the starting line and tucked my feet into the blocks. In that race, I had no thoughts of beating the other guys. My foe was the same indifferent adversary that had ruled my life and dictated my future since I had arrived at Penn State. As usual, I would be running against the clock.

In track, we all were just a number, hopefully an ever-falling number, but always a number. This was a sport that constantly identified, rated, and classified you by your best time, then decided where you could and couldn't run, like an exclusive club based on your level of income or your investment portfolio. As I entered the 2007 track season, my best 100-meter number—15.61 seconds—just wasn't good enough for me to be considered a sure-fire prospect for the Beijing Paralympics, and the days for proving that I belonged in China were growing short.

In the United States, the top amputee sprinters all have achieved a special number: in sanctioned 100-meter races they had eclipsed either 13.05 seconds (for above-the-knee amputees, officially classified as "T42") or 11.31 seconds (for below-knee athletes, classified as "T44"). As of January 2007, those were the formal U.S. Paralympic track standards, the measuring sticks for Beijing, and the benchmarks as to who received financial aid from the U.S. Olympic Committee. The thresholds were just an average of the current world records plus the top three times that had been run at the last three major meets: the 2002 International Paralympic Committee World Championships, the 2004 Summer Paralympics, and the 2006 IPC World Championships. Based on all these standards, the math was simple and clear: If any male above-the-knee amputee could clock a personal best of 13.05 seconds or lower, he would be deemed "elite" by U.S. Paralympic officials. Under that designation, he would receive two thousand dollars a year to cover his coaching costs, club fees, and training expenses. He also would get access to a health insurance plan, and his travel, lodging, and meals would all be covered when he was invited to selected meets and sports camps.

But there was another, less-stringent mark that U.S. Paralympics referred to as its "national standard." To reach that, a male above-knee runner had to finish a 100-meter race in 13.44 seconds, thereby earning him the same perks but one thousand dollars a year in aid (instead of the two thousand for "elite" athletes). Realistically, that was my goal, my magic line. My year would be a success if I could somehow hit 13.44 seconds in a race. That would open up my career and allow me to run in some exclusive meets, like the Parapan American Games in Brazil later that summer.

In the spring of 2007, running a 13.44 still seemed elusive to me. But I was not without hope. During my first two meets of the season, I had chopped my best 100-meter time by more than one full second, a testament to the sweat-soaked drills I was doing under Coach Jordan's supervision, the mechanical improvement made by my leg man, Tim Rayer, and the sheer patience I had learned to adopt as an amputee. My body would reach its optimum speed whenever it was ready. My waiting time was filled with training. I had launched my running career in January 2006 with a clunky form and a 100-meter time of almost

20 seconds. I had finished the 2006 season consistently clocking times in the mid-15 seconds. And I had begun the 2007 schedule with a bizarre blowout—followed by a race time so eye-popping, I figured it had to be a technical glitch.

First, the blowout: On March 16, 2007, I had been invited to an outdoor meet under sunny skies on the other side of the country. The San Diego State University Aztec Track & Field Classic, I had figured, would be a prime chance to gauge the condition of my legs and lungs following a long Pennsylvania winter. But unlike other track meets, I would have to run by myself in San Diego due to a scheduling mix-up. One of the reasons I preferred track over powerlifting was that I enjoyed sprinting head-to-head with other athletes, sharing the same air and the same space, maybe even rubbing elbows down the stretch. That reminded me of my football days. On the powerlifting bench, it was just me against the bar, a cold, impersonal rivalry. I preferred man against man. On that beautiful afternoon in San Diego, though, it would be just me, my lane, and the ticking clock.

The crowd had given me a warm cheer as I burst out of the blocks, but halfway down the track something seemed wrong. On my right-side backswings and my subsequent leg plants, my artificial knee felt loose and weak, like it was badly misfiring. Breaking my hard focus on the running lane ahead, I grabbed a quick peek at my right leg. What I saw was personally horrifying: clear hydraulic fluid was gushing out of the joint like when a car engine throws a rod and starts spewing oil. Obviously, one of the moving bars inside the knee had worked free and severed the fluid line. In the world of prosthetic parts, it was the equivalent of tearing my anterior cruciate ligament, or ACL. For a split second I hadn't been sure of what to do: keep chugging or stop dead and watch the rest of the fluid squirt out and form a pool on the track. I continued running, and the crowd continued roaring. Maybe some folks in the bleachers had spotted the shiny stream oozing from the knee, or maybe they had just been rooting for me to finish this lonely heat. I knew one thing—as long as they were going to clap and yell I was going to sprint. So I did—embarrassed but determined. Astoundingly, I hit the line at 15.16 seconds, at that point the best time in my career. Still, if there had been a hole in the ground, I would have crawled in and stayed until everybody went home.

One week later, I accompanied the Penn State track team to an outdoor meet at the Naval Academy in Annapolis, Maryland. Wardell also had been asked to take part, but since we were the only leg amputees in the competition, the meet's organizers had asked Coach Jordan if they could group Wardell and me with the women's 100-meter sprinters. She had come to me with their request.

"Hey, I don't care," I told her. "I want to run with the best."

At the gun, I had been slow to find my rhythm. But as Wardell and the women began pulling away, I dug hard to stay with them, stride for stride. I crossed the line just a few steps behind the winner, maybe the strongest final twenty meters I had ever turned in. Because my start had been fairly average, I was amazed when I first saw my time on the scoreboard: 14.14 seconds.

"Is that right?" I asked Coach Jordan. "Is the clock accurate?"
"Yes. That's a good time," she said with a smile. "Now if we can just get you in the thirteens!"

I still couldn't believe that time. I had never cracked the 14s in an official meet. Now I had almost busted into the 13s, truly rare air. The leap from my previous best time to a 14.14 almost seemed too much to fathom, like it had been a clock malfunction.

"Well I *was* chasing girls," I said afterward. "Maybe that's why I ran so good. You put me in there with girls and I go get it!"

Whether the time had felt real to me or not, it still counted, and I had carved a full second off my personal best. With the Penn Relays looming in one month, I stood just seven-tenths of a second from reaching the "national standard" and possibly earning a ticket to Beijing.

Seven-tenths: just a slice, just a fragment of a moment. Like the amount of time it takes a bomb to detonate.

As the race starter pointed his gun toward the gray skies above the Penn Relays crowd, a group of squatting photographers and cameramen aimed their lenses at the seven amputees. The press interest in my story seemed to be gaining steam. I had come to the track earlier that morning for a TV interview and I would hold my first news conference after the race. Both Wardell and Coach Jordan had been watching all this closely, making sure that the media requests were not stealing time from my training or my rest periods. I reassured them that I had it under control. I appreciated the attention, I said, but I would never let that hurt my sports dreams.

"They have a job to do, and I have a job to do—running from Point A to Point B," I said. "If I thought they would get in my way, I wouldn't bother with them at all."

As a kid, I had learned how to tackle distractions on the playing field—just one more lesson I'd received from my dad. During my Little League baseball games, members of my family would come and watch, and sometimes they would talk to me from the bleachers while I played the field. I would smile and chatter back to them between pitches. Finally, my father had seen enough.

"Son, you're participating in a game. Your coach and teammates are depending on you to do something," Dad said. "Whenever you're in the game, you don't need to worry about who's in the stands."

Two weeks later I was standing in the on-deck circle with a bat on my shoulder, waiting for my chance to hit. My dad had approached the chain-link fence next to the ball field.

"Kortney!" he yelled, trying to get my attention. "Kortney!!"

I refused to turn around. I had passed the test.

"That's how I am with the media," I told Wardell the night before the Penn Relays. "I let them know I'm ecstatic that they want to follow me, but I've got to do my thing first."

And my thing was about to take place.

"On your marks . . . ," the starter said into the track microphone.

"Set . . ."

The gun popped. History happened with our first steps. But so did something else—an early edge on Wardell who ran in the lane just to my left. He usually beat me head-to-head, and had posted a 100-meter time of 13.14 seconds compared to my 14.14 at the Naval Academy. Yet, in my side vision, I saw that I had him by a couple of strides. We all were running into a slight head wind, which can add a tenth of a second or two to your time.

I'm ahead of Wardell, I thought. *So I must be running okay.*

But by the fifty-meter mark, he had pulled even. At the sixty-meter mark, he had me by a half step. At seventy meters, he was fully past me.

Running okay? Take that thought back, Clemons, I told myself amid the arm pumps and leg plants. *You've still got a lot of work to do.*

I finished seventh out of seven men, pretty much what I had expected as the only AK in the field. My time: 14.88. Wardell hit the wire at 14.11 seconds and Marlon Shirley won the sprint with a time of 11.41.

"You didn't run through the line," Coach Jordan said later.

It's possible that I had let up at the end when I realized everyone else had already finished. This much I knew: I still had not put together a perfect race—a great start, a blazing middle, and a strong finish. I had accomplished those individually within different races, but never together on the same day, so I knew I still had a faster time inside me. I knew that I hadn't maxed out my ability in any single, 100-meter burst. Somehow, I had to pull all those elements together before the biggest day of my summer. On June 30, I would sprint again in Atlanta at the 2007 U.S. Paralympics Track and Field National Championships—the qualifier for the 2007 Parapan American Games in Rio De Janeiro, Brazil, and a possible springboard to China.

The Parapan American Games were a regional version of the Paralympics, where fifty-five hundred athletes from North, Central, and South America competed in thirty-eight sports. Thanks to my 147.5-kilogram lift in Korea the year before, I already had qualified for the Parapans as a powerlifter, so the Brazil trip was locked in. Powerlifting, I knew, might ultimately be my ticket to China, but deep down I ached to compete in the 100-meter race in Rio. That was my true ambition. Any strong man with two arms could lift a weighted bar. I didn't think I would inspire anyone by doing that. What I really longed to do was show the world that losing a leg in war would never slow me down in life. Running was my love. But to run in Rio, I had to soar in Atlanta. That's where I needed to nail that 13.44-second national standard to secure a spot on the U.S Paralympic track squad.

Each meet on my 2007 track schedule was a small stepping stone to Beijing, another opportunity to test my speed, to better understand my mechanics, and to somehow hack a little more time off my stride. But after the Penn Relays, only two races remained before the Atlanta nationals. During those two 100-meter dashes I desperately needed to nudge my time into the 13-second range. A very tall order.

My first chance came in England at the 2007 Visa Paralympics World Cup. Based on my recent progress, I had been invited to compete there with the U.S. Paralympic team. The American roster also included April Holmes, the women's record holder at 100-, 200-, and 400-meters, and Casey Tibbs, who had anchored our friendly relay at John Register's sports camp in San Diego.

The races were all held at Manchester Regional Arena, a six-thousand-seat outdoor bowl. Clad in a red-white-and-blue jersey with an American flag on the front, I lined up against above-the-knee amputees from France, Germany, South Africa, Bulgaria, Japan, and Ukraine. Earle Connor, the Canadian world record holder, was not in the field that day, but British runner John McFall would be feeding off the home crowd in lane two.

McFall, whose personal best stood at 12.87 seconds, had lost his leg in a motorcycle accident. Then, the year before our race, someone had stolen his car along with his artificial running leg, which had been stored in the car's trunk. He had to temporarily stop training. McFall had made a public plea for the leg's return—"I just hope someone's got the grace out there to realize what they've done, 'fess up, or hand it in to the authorities." One week later, two men surrendered the leg to McFall.

The Visa World Cup was my first international 100-meter race, and the colorful scene gave me a small taste of what might await me in China. In a slight mist, fans sat trackside beneath a white metal overhang and banged together plastic noisemakers. On the back of the straightaway, a large electronic scoreboard blazed with our names and our times in bright yellow letters. A foot-high blue border separated the red track from the grassy green field. I soaked it all in. Just beyond the outside lane, rainwater collected in shallow puddles. The temperature was a crisp 53 degrees. At the gun, I roared out of the blocks in possibly my most powerful start ever. But one of the other runners was whistled for flinching too early and we had to do it all over again. I still wonder what my heat time that day might have been had that original start been allowed. After the second gun, we cruised down the wet track to the home-fan chants of "Come on, John!" I finished sixth out of eight runners with a time of 14.57 seconds. Better than the Penn Relays, and a little closer to the 13s. But still a long way to go.

Less than a month later, I flew to Oklahoma to compete in my third Endeavor Games. But instead of continuing the slight momentum I had found in England, I actually lost ground, clocking a 100-meter time of 14.99 seconds and finishing second in the heat.

During the race, my daughter, Daytriona, watched from the bleachers with my parents. She was in Oklahoma to spend some time with me. But this was a first: she had never seen me lose to another above-the-knee amputee. She understood that this had been a bad day at the track for her old man. Did she feel sorry for me? Cry for me? Hardly. She comforted me by making me laugh.

"Dad, you *lost!*" she said with a teasing grin.

She caught the smile that was slowly creeping across my face. That prompted her to keep busting my chops.

"Yeah, Daddy, you lost! You lost today!" she repeated as we walked together on the track afterward.

"Yeah, baby, your daddy lost today," I simply responded, shaking my head and laughing.

It was cute and warm. But this loss was also something good for Day to see. You don't win every race in this life. When you lose—especially when you lose—you have to show respect, class, and heart.

The Oklahoma trip also gave me a chance to just hang out with Day. During the school year, she lived with her mom in Mississippi while I took classes at Penn State. Summers were time to catch up. When I first got injured, she had seemed a little scared to cuddle with me in the hospital bed, but two years later, she was proud of me, begging me to come and speak to her school class where she could show me off. Now she wasn't shy about playfully taunting her dad. Later that summer, she got me again. During a return trip to Mississippi, I took Candy and Day with me to the outdoor track at Meridian Junior College where I liked to train while I was home. Once there, I challenged them to a little race. I stood in lane four and told Day to take lane three and Candy to run in lane five.

"You two even get a head start," I said.

We marked off the finish line and took our starting places, each one laughing. I gave the signal to run.

After some hard strides, I had pulled closer to each of them. Sensing this, Day quickly veered right, crossing into my lane with a giggle, purposely blocking my way, and forcing me to slow down. She crossed the finish just ahead of me, but we all were smiling wide. It felt like a family.

By late 2007, Candy and I would start to talk again about a future together. We realized that the injury had put a lot of stress on both of us, and that we didn't handle it in the best way possible. I was nearing the end of my undergraduate work at Penn State, and Candy was almost ready to get her college degree. Honestly, I can't think of anyone else with whom I'd rather spend my life. She has been a great friend to me. I can talk to her and tell her anything. I think we will be together for a long time.

The main problem with my running leg—and my poor time in the Oklahoma race—seemed to lie in the socket, which was held in place like a suction cup. At the Endeavor Games, the socket had felt too loose. My leg was all over the place. But in other meets and often in my practices, the socket felt incredibly tight, like it was squeezing my right thigh. Sometimes I was forced to take the socket off for an hour or two to let my residual leg breathe. That cut into my precious training schedule. In order to complete my recovery and make it all the way to China, I knew I needed a new running socket, one that felt snug but comfortable. When I sprinted, I wanted the artificial limb to actually feel like it was a part of me. If I could achieve that natural feel, I knew I would be able to run not just in the 13-seconds range but even lower. I had natural speed. I just needed the right equipment to properly tap into it.

When I got back to Penn State, I called my prosthetist in Philadelphia, Tim Rayer, and asked him if I could book an appointment at his shop, which was four hours east of the campus. The 2007 Atlanta nationals were on the horizon. This was urgent, I said.

"You know, every time I see you, it's just in spurts. Just quick visits," Rayer said. "Why don't you come down here and stay at my house? Stay with me and my family for four days. Then we can really get some work done."

I was in my car and headed to Philly the next morning.

After midnight but still hours from dawn, Tim Rayer drove his Jeep Liberty onto a high school track and stopped only when his headlights had bathed the straight gray lanes in a fluorescent glow. Wearing a plastic socket that Rayer had crafted in his shop just minutes before, I exited the Jeep and stepped into the cold glare. While most of Philadelphia slept around us, we had come to test a new leg. There would be no rest until we got this right.

As Rayer stood on the edge of the outside lane, I broke into an easy run down to the dark end of the track. Then I sprinted back toward the headlights, listening hard for any feedback from my right thigh. As I ran harder, the hamstring muscles demanded more blood, and, inside the socket, my limb swelled to accommodate that surge. It began to press hard against the plastic socket lining, squeezing the blood flow. This was what I had been feeling so often in practice.

After twenty minutes of jogging, I stopped. I wiggled my leg and pushed on the socket for relief.

"What's going on? What are you feeling?" Rayer asked.

"It's still clamping," I said. "I just feel like it's cutting off the circulation. It feels like a vice is on me."

That's all Rayer needed to hear. We drove back to his shop, Prosthetic Innovations, which was located right next door to the high school track. There was still time before dawn to make and test-run another socket. And then another. Sleep could wait for another night.

"We've just got to get this done," Rayer said as we walked through the front door of his business, a one-story building south of downtown Philadelphia. Near the entrance was the clinical area complete with treadmills, fitting rooms, and a TV that seemed always tuned to ESPN. In back was a manufacturing area where he and his staff cranked out precisely shaped sockets for their clients. That's where Rayer was spending most of his time and energy in those early morning hours, trying to build me the perfect running socket.

My case was especially tricky. I needed firm control and a snug feel within the suction cup pressure that held the socket on my stump. Yet I also needed a design that allowed my remaining right leg to naturally expand as I sprinted or jogged in practice. I wanted to be able to train in that leg for as many consecutive hours as I needed, without removing it to relieve pain. Rayer was searching for the fine line between skintight and constricting. For amputees who simply wanted to be mobile in life—taking strolls in the park or going shopping in the mall—their sockets didn't have to be so dynamic or complicated. But mine had to wrap around a thigh that grew and shrank dramatically each day.

"This work is so out of the box, there's no box to be out of," Rayer joked.

Everything started with stability. I needed to be able to maneuver my artificial leg without too much thought or effort. It also had to be secure enough to brace me and propel me forward at full speed.

"We're trying to control the femur inside the socket," Rayer said. "But you have to remember that our thigh is just soft tissue and fluid surrounding a femur. It's basically like having a cup of Jello with a Popsicle stick inside of it. Now, imagine trying to hold that Popsicle stick in place. That's what we're trying to do."

Of course in my case, the femur was a cut bone. God didn't mean for us to bear weight on cut bones. And there was still one more complication: along my remaining right femur I had a boney overgrowth that the doctors called heterotopic ossification (or HO). After surgeons had removed most of my leg, my body produced an uneven clump of new bone along the outside of the upper thigh. Rayer had studied the phenomenon and learned that amputees returning from Iraq and Afghanistan were showing high rates of HO. According to Rayer, military researchers suspected that wound vacuums—the kind of device I had worn at the hospital to help drain and heal my leg wounds—might be related to the problem. However the HO got there, my socket had to be shaped to fit around it, to hold firmly on all the contact points of my stump. Rayer had witnessed the terrifying results of sockets that didn't fit right.

"I've seen video of a Paralympic race in which an AK was running and his leg just came flying off," Rayer said. "I remember when it happened. That is the biggest nightmare in the back of my mind."

But Rayer had to balance his worries against my complaints. I also needed a socket that was flexible enough to allow fresh blood to be pumped into my hamstring muscles as I ran. They were the power source on my right side. After a couple of trips to the track next door—where I ran those test sprints under the illumination of the Jeep's headlights—Rayer retreated to his shop with a new idea.

His manufacturing style reminded me of the craftsmanship that John Fergason brought to his job at BAMC. Rayer took a plaster-of-Paris impression of my residual limb. He then filled that mold with plaster and let it dry. Next, he used sculpting tools to allow extra space for the HO and to lessen the force on sensitive areas, or to add a bit more pressure to certain weight-tolerant areas. Rayer then melted some thermoplastic material onto that plaster model to create the flexible inner socket for my prosthesis. That was fairly standard stuff. The new wrinkle was to create tiny cutouts or grooves in the socket where the various hamstring muscles stretched beneath my skin. These small openings wouldn't loosen the socket's overall fit, but they would allow the leg to expand when I ran. At many prosthetic clinics, it can take a few days to build a new socket. That night, Rayer manufactured four sockets for me as we bolted back and forth to the dark track.

One final breakthrough remained before we locked up and went home. As I sat in Rayer's shop at about three in the morning, I noticed a pile of Otto Bock knees lying on the table. I had first worn the Otto Bock brand at the 2006 U.S. Paralympics Track and Field National Championships in Atlanta. After that meet, I decided to return to Ossur's Mauch knee because it seemed to give me a better running cadence. But Rayer had been trying to convince me to stick with the Otto Bock knee because he believed it offered a faster kick. The Otto Bock was billed as a "polycentric" knee, meaning it had multiple points of movement—up and down, back and forth—that were more like a natural knee. It also was hydraulically powered and allowed for a bumper to be installed in the back to make it, as Rayer said, "like having a trampoline right next to your butt." During a running stride, as the artificial right foot completed its backswing and approached the butt, the Otto Bock knee would snap the lower part of the leg forward again.

"Yo, Tim," I said, grabbing an Otto Bock knee joint from the stack, "what do you think about this?"

Rayer smiled. He took the Otto Bock, fastened it to my socket, and realigned the entire leg from hip to foot. Then we hopped in his Jeep and drove to the dark track for a final middle-of-the-night sprinting session. The new socket allowed my leg to expand and breathe. The new knee fired me forward.

"You're right there. You're right where you need to be," Rayer said, watching my form from the edge of the track. "You've got the right prosthesis. Now you just need to run. And when you run through that wall, I'll be right there with you."

I looked down at the track and saw the runner's shadow I was casting in the headlights. To me, it looked so natural.

Being a Mississippi guy, to me the Atlanta heat felt like home. The late June temperatures helped relax my muscles as I prepared to run in the 2007 U.S. Paralympics Track and Field National Championships. At the same time, though, the Georgia swelter added a dash of danger: Inside the socket, my thigh perspired, and as the sweat dripped away, the residual leg actually shrank a bit. That, in turn, loosened the fit. The goal of those early-morning sprints had been to dial in my socket's feel and its seal for those painful moments when my leg muscles expanded. We never took into account a smaller thigh. But that's just what I had when I stepped onto the track at Marietta High School, needing to run the race of my life.

To qualify for the 100-meter race at the Parapan American Games in Brazil—a potential springboard to the Beijing Paralympics—I needed to finish the Atlanta heat in 13.44 seconds. That was the American "national standard," and hitting that time would earn me a roster spot on the U.S. Paralympic track team. Two other above-the-knee amputees shared the track with me that day: Nick Sgarlato, whose right leg had been amputated as a result of a birth defect, and another newcomer to the sport, Lee Randles. Nick's personal best at that distance was 15.90 seconds, Lee's was 16.20. Mine was that 14.14-second effort that I had notched at the Naval Academy in my second race of the season—a time that seemed farther and farther away as each month passed.

I had the middle lane, with Nick to my right and Lee on my left. We took our marks, raised our backs when the starter gave his "set" command, and broke cleanly at the gun. Inside my socket, the suction seemed to be slipping with my first step. At the twenty-yard mark, I had the lead but I was losing even more contact with the socket. By the halfway point, my lead was two full body lengths but the socket was so loose, I stubbed my artificial running toe. I had a quick decision to make: continue to run hard and try to nail that 13.44 time, or run carefully and make sure I finished the race with two legs beneath me. Dropping a leg would be like taking a step off a six-foot cliff in the dark—you expect the ground to be there but instead you tumble onto your face.

If this leg comes off, it's going to get ugly, I thought. *I'll be going down hard.*

I chose to reduce my speed one gear and make sure that my right leg was fully under me on each stride, basically keeping the socket locked in place by putting extra weight on it. Still, I finished the race going away from Nick and Lee, winning by more than one second. My time: 14.57.

I felt good about the performance. Running at maybe 80 percent of my best, I had equaled the time I had posted in England. Obviously, the new knee and the late-night socket work that Tim and I had done weeks earlier had combined to make me faster. How fast? I still didn't know.

Coach Jordan hoped that my decisive victory in the only AK race at the Atlanta nationals would convince the U.S. Paralympic track coaches to let me run in Brazil. But they stuck to the rules—only a 13.44 would have sufficed, they said.

"I could have run harder," I told Coach Jordan.

"Yeah, I know. But finishing was important," she said.

The race symbolized the long road I had wandered since the day the bomb went off. My journey had been jammed with unexpected twists and challenges—depression and doubts, falls and disappointments. But I would never stop running. I would always keep moving. And in the end, I would break the tape no matter how long it took me to get there. I would complete the mission. I would finish the race.

I reminded myself that I still would participate at the Parapan American Games in August as a powerlifter. Maybe hoisting a barbell wasn't my true passion. Maybe it wouldn't be as moving as watching a one-legged man flying down a 100-meter track. Powerlifting could get me to China, though, and in that moment, I believed that was the only thing that truly mattered.

But as I loaded my bags for Brazil, I also packed my running leg. Just in case.

11

Heavy Lessons

My worst days came on a slab of Baghdad asphalt where I crawled through my own blood, and in a lonely hospital room where I searched for reasons but felt only sadness.

What eventually happened to me in Brazil didn't even compare to those bad times.

And yet it changed so much.

On a Sunday afternoon in August, I marched into Rio de Janeiro's Olympic Arena with 123 other members of Team USA. Some of us rode in chairs. Others walked on artificial limbs. Waving the American flag, we had come for the opening ceremony of the Parapan American Games, a regional athletic gala that has mirrored the global rise of elite disabled sports. In 1999, Mexico City hosted the first Parapan American Games, which brought together nineteen countries and a thousand athletes from North, Central, and South America to compete in track, swimming, table tennis, and wheelchair basketball. Four years later, when the event was hosted by Mar del Plata, Argentina, twenty-two countries participated and nine sports were staged, including sitting volleyball, cycling, and wheelchair tennis. In 2007, twenty-five nations and 1,132 athletes battled in ten sports, including powerlifting. The Parapan American Games contained all the pageantry and patriotic pride of the Paralympics and the Olympics. A Brazilian athlete lit the Games' flame by raising a torch from his wheelchair. We all lived together in an athletes' village, where the entrances and rooms were made handicap-accessible. Golds, silvers, and bronzes were fiercely contested. Medal counts mattered.

This was the life I had imagined when I first saw John Register breeze past me on a Texas track, when I heard his tales of swimming and running in foreign lands while wearing the stars and stripes. The Games spoke to everything I had worked to attain: displaying American grit while simultaneously proving that we all were just as fast and strong and willing as top athletes with four perfect limbs. In many cases, we were better. This was a brotherhood and sisterhood of the gifted and the gutsy, 1,132 people with an array of physical flaws who refused to sit in the corner and let only the able-bodied play. Yet the Parapan American Games were also just a miniature version of the massive and looming Paralympic stage. The Paralympics would be a true world gathering, packing arenas and stadiums, drawing at least four thousand athletes to China from more then 135 countries. And for the second time in my life, if I pulled off a big lift in Brazil, it could propel me all the way to Beijing and the 2008 Summer Paralympics.

Three days before my competition, U.S. powerlifting coach Mary Hodge led me through a practice session at the powerlifting venue, a dark pavilion with a raised stage, rows of lights that dangled from a tall ceiling, and slanted sections of blue folding seats, all housed inside the sprawling Riocentro Convention

Center. We worked on one of the ten warm-up benches that were grouped together behind the main competition floor. I loaded a bar with 135 pounds and reeled off ten quick reps, just enough to get the blood streaming in my arms, back, and chest. I added more plates to bring the bar to 225 pounds and chugged out eight reps, continuing that cycle until I closed in on 300 pounds. For that I would just do a single rep to make sure I didn't break down my muscles. I felt strong. My form seemed perfect.

For my last practice reps, Mary stood behind me and helped me get the bar into position. I guided it down to my chest, paused, and began to push it back toward Mary's hands. It seemed to burn my shoulders. My right hand was bit higher than the left, and my arms quivered. That was strange, I thought. My high lift in a competition had been 335 pounds or 152.5 kilograms. I had knocked that down at a powerlifting meet earlier that year in Oklahoma. It's also the amount I had planned to open with at the Parapan American Games. I was 35 pounds below that now. Even with all my prior reps that day, 300 shouldn't have tested me like that. Mary grabbed the bar and dropped it in the metal rack. She had a concerned look on her face.

"You okay?" she asked.

"Yeah, I'm fine," I said.

But we both thought otherwise. In Mary's mind, she wondered whether my dual training for track and powerlifting was hurting my efforts in each sport. I was trying to be light on my feet for the track while, at the same time, I was adding muscle mass for the bench. Physically, they were pulling me in opposite directions, requiring conflicting demands. In my mind, suddenly there was doubt about opening with a lift of 152.5 kilograms. That brief strain with 300 pounds had shaken me up. Lifting was such a mental game.

"I think I should go down in weight for my opener," I said.

"No, I don't think that's a good idea," Mary said.

She preferred to stay with the plan and, hopefully, I would increase from there, maybe competing for the gold medal. With the Parapan American Games being a regional meet, I had an excellent shot at winning my weight class.

"Okay, I'll stick with 152.5," I said.

I was not particularly nervous the night before the meet. Back in Korea, when Mary made her eight o'clock curfew check, I had carefully laid out my lifting gear on my hotel bed. When she came knocking this time, my stuff was scattered under my hotel bed, and I had to dig around to collect it while Mary laughed and shook her head.

"Dude, are you kidding?" Mary asked with a smile. She saw the difference in my anxiety level between Busan and Rio. She thought that was a good thing.

On the day of my competition, a number of U.S. Paralympic officials came to watch along with my powerlifting teammates and several other American athletes, including track star April Holmes. She was a world record holder at three sprinting distances, and we had become friends. But I didn't feel any extra pressure with their presence. In a sport like powerlifting, I used every small mental edge to help me dig down for some extra force.

Including myself, there were seven guys in my group, but my competition would boil down to three other men. Brazil's Rodrigo Marques was clearly the favorite. With the small crowd already in his corner, Marques planned to start with a lift of 170 kilograms or 374 pounds. His career best was 172 kilos. Fredy Pena of Venezuela had plotted a first lift of 135 kilograms or 297 pounds, but his career best was just a shade under mine at 145 kilos. And another Brazilian, Claudemir Santin, would begin at 145 kilos or 319 pounds. He had never recorded a sanctioned lift. Once again, I was the heaviest man in my group at 165 pounds, a disadvantage in the scoring. But if I completed my opener, 152.5 kilos, I would instantly hold second place and have a clear crack at grabbing a gold medal and, maybe, my ticket to China.

Pena was the first man up. I watched from a TV monitor in the athletes' room away from the stage. He strapped in, took the bar, and handled his 135 kilos without any problem. Next was Marques. With some scattered Brazilian fans yelling and clapping, he easily brought his 170 kilos down to his chest, then pushed the bar cleanly back above him. Three white lights beamed from the approving referees. The lead had been set. After a Peruvian lifter missed at 120 kilos (264 pounds), it was my turn.

In my blue USA singlet, I walked toward the spotlighted stage wearing my artificial leg. On both my natural foot and my prosthetic foot, I wore red and black Nike sneakers. Mary followed me carrying the two leather straps. A *New York Times* photographer who was chronicling my day swooped in close to snap some shots. Mary was clearly upset by this. She was trying to toe that same fine line Coach Jordan had walked: at what point did the press attention become a distraction for me? She knew that telling my story was important to me, but she also decided that this was the time to step in and shield me.

"They're in his face. Get them out of his face," she told a U.S. Paralympic media relations staffer. "When he's done lifting, it's fine."

I lay back on the bench, pulling my legs up with me. The loaders already had jammed and clipped the colored plates in place: two red discs per side at 25 kilos each, one green disc per side at 10 kilos each, and a pair of black 2.5-kilo discs at the ends. The bar and locking collars added the remainder of the 152.5 kilos. Mary looped the leather belts around my legs and buckled them tight. In a quiet voice she told me I had less than two minutes to complete the lift, then she stepped off the stage. With the warm spotlight shining in my face, small worries about my chosen weight drifted into the back of my mind. I had been rattled by my practice struggle. Still, I knew everything was up to me now, and maybe that made me a little anxious to get started.

I held my hands above me to receive the bar. It felt massive but manageable. The spotters placed it in my palms. I had just started to flex my elbows and dip the weight when I remembered something—the command. The referee had not yet yelled "Start!" I thrust the bar up a few inches, back to the starting position, and held it steady. My arms already were taxed.

"Start!" the referee finally hollered.

Once again I began to lower the weight to my chest. I paused at the bottom and began the heavy return push. Halfway up, my momentum slowed. I winced and threw everything I had against the bar. But the muscles were spent. There was nothing left. I stalled. The spotters grabbed the bar and racked it with a loud clang. Mary returned to the stage, unstrapped my legs, and we walked together back toward the athletes' room. She could see the emotional deflation in my demeanor; my body language showed defeat. When the photographer pointed his camera at me, Mary held up her palm as if to say, "Not now."

I walked quickly into the private back room with my head down. I unclipped my prosthetic leg, placed it to the side, and felt the frustration bubble to the surface.

"Shit," I said.

I rarely curse. But with that one word, Mary knew exactly where my head was. Not in a good place.

"That one's over," she said. "That lift is done. You're moving on. You have the weight. It's a piece of cake."

I looked at the floor. It was time for Mary to spice up her language to inject some adrenaline into the subdued moment.

"What the fuck? Let's go! Get the fuck in it!" she yelled.

I searched for some confidence. I *had* lifted this weight before. I just needed to be patient out there, to wait for the start command

and perform like I had in the past. Still, those doubts wouldn't shake loose.

Man, I can't go down in weight, I thought. *What can I do to get it done? It's going to be the same amount of weight the next time I'm out there.*

Adding to my misery, I knew that so many people believed in me—my coaches, my family, the other American lifters, teammates from the other sports, the U.S. Paralympic honchos. They had high expectations of me. I did, too. I felt that I was letting myself down but, even worse, I was letting them all down.

I had ten minutes between my lifts. I watched on the monitor as Pena nailed his second attempt, 142.5 kilos. Marques took the bench, trying to push the lead to 175 kilos or 385 pounds. He dipped the bar, paused properly on his chest, and returned to the locked position. It seemed like a solid lift, but the referees red-lighted him. After the Peruvian lifter missed his second attempt, it came time for me to try and find some redemption up on the stage. I could jump to second place if I did my job.

With my legs strapped in and the clock ticking, I talked myself into boosting that bar.

I've seen other elite lifters go out and miss on their lifts in Korea, I thought. *I can do this.*

"Start!"

The bar came down much faster on the second attempt—a bad sign. I paused for one beat and started my return lift. I knew immediately I was in trouble. So did Mary, watching from the side. My strength had abandoned me, almost like I had left everything on the bench during my botched opener. Again the spotters grabbed the bar after I hit the sticking point on the way up.

Off the bench, I stormed into the athletes' room.

"Fuck!" I screamed, flinging my USA warm-up jacket across the room—an even more urgent signal to Mary that my emotions had run away from me. I don't think she's ever heard me swear again since that day.

"I'm so sorry," I said to Mary.

Assistant U.S. powerlifting coach Kim Brownfield (a Paralympic lifter himself) rushed over to try to calm me and mentally prepare me for the final lift.

"Come on, man! You've got to get this. Let's go! Are you ready for this?" Kim asked.

Was I ready? No. For a second, I even contemplated scratching for my third lift and just staying in the athletes' room.

Oh my God, I thought with a mix of fear, anxiety, and disappointment. I felt like there was no good way out of the situation. People had come to see me, and I had let them down. I had flown all the way to Brazil, and I had bombed so far. *What's going to change between now and those first two attempts? It's not going to happen. I am not going to get this weight up. What am I going to do?*

"Come on, let's go! You can fucking do this!" Mary shouted. "Let's go! Let's go! Let's go!"

I glanced at the TV monitor when I heard a distant cheer from the small group of fans outside. The other Brazilian in the group, Santin, had just lifted 145 kilos to close round two. In his third lift, Marques missed again at 175. Then Pena set a new career best at 147.5 kilos to retake second place. The standings before my final lift: Marques was in the lead at 170 kilos, Pena held second at 147.5 and Santin stood in third at 145. I was in dead last. On my worst day on the bench, I thought, I should at least be in line for the silver medal with numbers like these. Then I corrected myself: in powerlifting, this *was* my worst day.

As I sat flanked by my concerned coaches, IPC Powerlifting Chairman Pol Wautermartens—a former able-bodied weightlifter—stuck his head in the athlete's room and tried to lighten the mood.

"Come on, you strong like bull!" Wautermartens said with a smile.

I sat on the floor and dropped my head. I waited to hear my name called, still not sure if I was going to walk back out there. What was the point? In weightlifting, either you are on or you're not. You can't change the blood flow or the amount of life in your muscles.

What do I stand for? I thought. *I stand for not giving up. That's what got me walking again. That's what got me running again. That's what made me an athlete again. I don't surrender when things get tough. I am going back out there. I need to push through this and just see what happens.*

As Mary strapped me in, she gave me one last pep talk: "It's a piece of cake. Nothing. Let's do it."

But this time I couldn't even get the bar off my chest.

Why? I asked myself. *Why on this day?*

I always hunted for reasons to explain the bad things that had happened to me. In the awful hours after I had lost my leg, I asked God if I had done something in my life to deserve this. I looked so hard for some sort of explanation. But instead of discovering a clear reason or something to blame, I had always found something much better in their place—a purpose, a motivation to keep moving ahead in this world. And this time was no different.

Instead of returning to the athletes' room, I walked alone down a hallway. Mary watched me disappear around a corner, trying to put some space on the moment. Back in the competition area, a small group of journalists was waiting to interview me. I had to compose myself and my thoughts. Over the years, I had watched postgame interviews on ESPN and seen famous athletes melt down after a loss, spewing blame and anger, pointing fingers at coaches and teammates, even venting at the reporters. That wasn't me. Sports had started to make me feel a little like a role model, like my personal story could make a difference in other people's lives. I wasn't going to inspire by losing and fuming. But I *could* move people by showing them that in loss, there are new lessons to be grasped. In defeat, we can learn so much more about our true character, the values for which we stand. On our hardest days, we can truly shine.

Please let me represent my country well, I thought. *Even though this may look like a setback today to most people, maybe this is a step forward for me in a bigger way.*

Before my interviews, I returned to the athletes' room and saw Mary. She spotted the tears in my eyes and wrapped me in a hug for two minutes.

"I'm so sorry. I know I disappointed you and Kim," I said.

"It's not about us," Mary said. "Don't worry about it. This is just one tournament. You're going to be okay."

A U.S. Paralympics official stuck his head in the door to remind me of the waiting sports writers.

"You don't have to do this," Mary said.

"I'll be all right," I told her.

I walked back into the gym and stood with the journalists as they placed their tape recorders and microphones near my mouth. A funny thing happened—as I spoke, I began to think of those three dead Minnesota soldiers and of the precious life and all the opportunities I still had—everything they had sacrificed.

"We lost three guys on that day, and those guys would do whatever they could to be in my shoes. I just want to take advantage of life because I know they would take advantage of life as well," I said.

My responsibility was to live well and compete hard for Jesse Lhotka, Jason Timmerman, and Dave Day, plus two of my fellow medics who never made it home, Taylor Burk and Charles Odums. If I got to Beijing, I would think of them. If I won a gold medal, I would honor them as well as all the guys who had helped me on that hostile, bombed-out road: Dan Perseke and Chad Turner from the Minnesota platoon and Matthew Bittenbender,

Bryce Rigby, and John Shatto from my squad. I owed them my life.

"Powerlifting provides me a way to put my energies toward something as opposed to just being home doing nothing," I told the journalists. "I feel like I still have something to offer to society, so this is a way I can offer myself back. It's like a win-win situation; it's good for me and it's good for other people to see a person bounce back from an injury. It's also good for myself just to sometimes look back at where I've come from and look to where I can go. For those guys in Iraq, I know they're rooting for me and I'm rooting for them."

As I spoke, I could hear my dad's voice coloring some of my words. I was repeating, in my way, some of the lessons and some of the tough love that he had imparted to me after rough child-hood days on the baseball diamond or the football field when bad games seemed so tragic, on sad evenings when I had threatened to quit my teams. I could hear my mom's advice too—all those times she had told me to get up off the ground, dust myself, and keep running. Wherever I went, my parents' wisdom always came along to guide me.

"This is one of the small steps before Beijing and it kind of helped me get ready," I said into the microphones. "This is kind of the smaller stage before the big stage. I look forward to going to Beijing, but today is one of those days that I will have to go back and reevaluate and move forward. Hopefully, next time I can put things together and come back with the gold."

The old Kortney, the guy before the injury, had tried to control his world. Even in the middle of a war, I thought I could manage and manipulate all the pieces of my life. Detours were not allowed. Obstacles were to be avoided at all costs.

The new Kortney, the man who had learned volumes after losing so much, saw the bigger picture in Brazil. Something good would come from this terrible day. I had to go down this bumpy road, because at the end of that rough little side journey, I would find something I needed.

Given the choice, there was one place I'd rather have spent my time in Rio: the João Havelange Olympic Stadium, home to the track and field events. One day after my powerlifting disaster, that's exactly where I headed. I needed to run.

Built for the 2007 Pan American Games—the able-bodied version of our Parapan sports festival, and held weeks earlier at the same venues—the Olympic Stadium was located twenty-five minutes northwest of the athlete's village. To get there, I rode a bus that followed the "Yellow Line" expressway through the city. Just outside the stadium walls sat a blue-painted warm-up track that surrounded a grass practice field. As I arrived, I saw American athletes preparing for some of that afternoon's events, including the men's and women's visually impaired 100-meter finals and the men's wheelchair shot put finals. That's also where I spotted Peter Harsch, the man who had helped me sprint for the very first time. He had been working with some of the runners, but as I walked up he was standing by himself. He had heard about my three missed lifts and saw the somber look on my face.

"Hi, Peter. I've got my running leg with me. Would you mind taking some time to work with me on my running?" I asked.

"Absolutely, Kortney," Harsch said without hesitation. "Get it on."

He wanted to recheck my alignment. He first asked me to run in place on the track, lifting each knee as high as I could. Then I did some hard sprints up and down the blue track as the other Americans worked up a sweat across the field. Harsch analyzed my stride and suggested that the spring in my prosthetic foot was set too soft and needed to be tightened to give me better bounce and energy. He examined my gait and pointed out that my artificial knee was set a bit too low. When I got home, I would report those observations to Tim Rayer. Those small changes alone could snip a few more tenths of a second from my time, I thought. Maybe push me down into the 13s.

Harsch also read my body language that afternoon. I was down. He knew I was now torn about my sports career—specifically, which road would offer the best and smartest route to China: powerlifting or sprinting? After those bungled lifts, I started to see that it was time to make an incredibly hard choice.

My decision was split between cold tactics and burning personal passions. If I stuck with powerlifting and devoted my time toward inflating my maximum lift, the odds were in my favor for making the U.S. team and competing in Beijing. Four U.S. powerlifters would go to China, and there were only five of us vying for those spots. But I also understood that it would be nearly impossible to add 200 pounds to my top lift by the time the Summer Paralympics were held in September 2008. To be in medal contention, I would have to raise and control between 490 and 539 pounds. In my weight class, that's how much the top guys from China, Iran, and Egypt could do.

If I chose to abandon powerlifting and immerse myself in sprinting, simply making the U.S. team could be my most difficult task. Among all the runners, jumpers, and throwers, the American Paralympic track and field roster would number about forty slots. But there were roughly seventy athletes trying to squeeze onto that team. On the flip side, if I made it to Beijing and lined up on the track, I had a strong belief that I would medal or maybe win gold. I felt that in my gut. I had faith.

For almost two years I had tried to hold tight to both sports, aiming to boost my chances by dividing my time. That wasn't working. Now I just had to figure out which sport to surrender. I had committed so much of myself to both.

Harsch recognized that the moment had come for some brotherly advice.

"What did you tell me when I first met you at BAMC?" he asked me.

"I told you that I wanted to be a gold-medal sprinter," I said.

"Then what are you doing powerlifting?"

"Well, that will get me to Beijing and running may not."

"Right now, you're young enough to run. Go for it now. Get the coaching. Get your time down. Screw the powerlifting. Focus on running and pursue the dream you've always had. Because I've never heard you say you wanted to be a powerlifter, Kortney."

Having worked with so many new amputees, Harsch understood our psychology. Confidence had become such a fleeting commodity for so many of these men and women fresh from the battlefield. They had suffered so many setbacks in their recoveries—so many small defeats and natural frustrations—that they had become scared to death of failure. For me, and for those wounded soldiers, a little slice of something warm and positive was better than a cold plate of nothing.

"What are you doing, Kortney? You don't care as deeply about powerlifting as you do about running," Harsch said.

I was silent. While I was in Rio, and during my training in the gym, I had committed everything to powerlifting. But he was right: it was not the sport that had become intertwined with my soul.

"You've got to get back to your passion," he said. "If you commit to this, you'll be lining up on the track for the 100-meter gold-medal race in Beijing."

But if I stuck to powerlifting, I would almost certainly be going to China, marching in with Team USA and savoring at least some of my dream. Follow my head or follow my heart? As I sprinted down that sunny track near the coast of Brazil, white lines guided my steps, but still I didn't know which way to turn.

12

Full Circle

igh in the night sky, the September moon looked so big, I felt like I could reach out and snatch it with my hand.

Against the back of my head, the hard ground was cold. But it also felt like home. At roughly half past two in the morning, I was lying face up on Penn State's outdoor track and staring at the stars. I had come to settle my stormy thoughts and quiet myself.

After studying for a psychology exam, I had been unable to relax and doze off in my basement-level room. I had tossed and turned for a couple of hours, then suddenly felt the urge to get out of my bed, get in my car, and drive. Restless and in need of space, I headed toward the campus about three miles away. I hadn't planned on going to the track, but somehow that's where I ended up.

For two years I had been trying to run away from a horrible moment on the battlefield. Sprinting had become my way to feel normal again, to challenge myself, to surprise anyone who happened to be watching. It had allowed me to live without football, to feel the butterflies of competition, to dream big. It had helped me put some distance on the day I almost died. But running with just one natural leg also had left me frustrated, anxious, and grappling with a single question that was now keeping me awake.

"What's going to happen?"

Not knowing the answer bothered me. It dogged my thoughts and sapped my energy. And it really broke down into four smaller questions: What was going to happen if I didn't succeed in sports? Would I ever be quick enough or strong enough? Where was I headed? And how would I get there? That was my first dilemma and my immediate worry. I needed to choose one sport and hurl myself into it.

What do I do? I thought, staring up at the moon. *The powerlifting? Or the track?*

For me, the tension really boiled down to expectations: mine and those belonging to anyone who was now following my story and pulling for me. As an athlete, I was in the public eye. People were expecting me to perform. If I didn't, what would happen? I knew that people were waiting for me to do great things. They believed in me. I believed in myself. But it was all taking so long.

If you're not doing so hot on the track, what are you going to offer people? I asked myself. *What can you tell them about yourself right now?*

I propped my elbows under me, raised my head, and looked across the empty parking lot. Over there, Beaver Stadium sat quiet, blanketed in darkness. It was home to Penn State's football team. How ironic that I was lying outside that place. In another version of my life, maybe that's where I would have played. Instead, I was trying to learn how to sprint in a hydraulic knee. I dropped my head back on the track.

I wanted to be able to run so much faster. I wanted to be further along in my progress as a sprinter. Part of that impatience came from my own muscle memory: I knew how it felt to zoom effortlessly down a football field. But my brand of running was different. I longed to get out there and fly, but physically I couldn't. I constantly needed to adjust my knee, tweak my socket fit, change my foot, or realign my prosthetic limb. My long history of mechanical repairs seemed to have no end in sight. The inability to find a running leg that felt natural had left me more and more frustrated. On top of that was the squeezing pain or burning sensation that I felt in my thigh after minutes of hard training and the falls I had taken.

Then my thoughts drifted from my leg, to the explosion that took it, and finally to the Minnesota guys. Slowly, I was able to refocus my head a little, concentrating on the good in my world, the next day ahead, everything I had done since coming back home, the fact that I was still alive.

I'm here. They're not, I thought. *You shouldn't be down on yourself. This is a good situation to be in. These are good problems. You've got a chance to move forward.*

In my hurry to make teams, increase lifts, cut times, and reach goals, I had never allowed myself to fully appreciate my accomplishments along the way. I had written off my achievements. Whereas most people might look at my life and say, "You're rolling along good," I had been so fixated on grabbing the ultimate prizes—making it to China and winning gold—I hadn't let myself feel satisfied with the smaller victories along the way. That had to stop, I thought. It was time to try and live in the moment.

I stood and walked to my car. It was three thirty in the morning. I drove back to my room, thinking about the day ahead and only that. I sat on the edge of my bed, removed my artificial leg, and leaned it against the mattress. Then I fell asleep.

I had two phone calls to make—one to my parents and the other to Jonathan Hart, my old buddy from BAMC. They knew me better than anyone on the planet. To make one of the hardest decisions of my life, I would need to hear their advice.

"I need to choose," I told my father. "I need to go after one sport and go after it hard."

In all my phone calls back to Mississippi, whenever I talked to my parents about my sports pursuits, I spent far more time on the topic of sprinting than powerlifting. That should have been a dead giveaway as to where my heart was when it came to this question. Of course, I was trying to wade through both the emotions and the cold calculations. What was in my heart wasn't necessarily the smartest option. My mom and dad also thought I had spread myself too thin while chasing both sports. They were happy to hear that I was about to narrow my focus. If nothing else, they believed that was a healthier, less stressful direction for me. My father gave me his view and two good reasons to back it up.

"I think it would be better for you to stay in track and field," he said without much hesitation. "For one, weightlifting can really tear a man's body down in the long run. For another thing, I can't watch you lift. The powerlifting is too far away for me to come see you do that. But I can watch you run."

In his mix of the logical and the sentimental, my dad had hit on a great point: much of what drove me in sports was to share those special moments, those game days, with my family. That always had been important with me, stretching back to high school and college football. When I traveled home to Little Rock, my dad would often drive me to Meridian Junior College and watch me run on the track there. My parents had been able to come to Atlanta twice for the nationals. My father's words moved me one step closer to a decision.

The real wear on my body may have been my constant attempt to build my lifting muscles while simultaneously trying to tone my running physique. I needed to be bulky on top for brute strength yet also lean for speed. Those two philosophies didn't mesh well, and in my separate workouts for both, I was doing just enough to get by because I could only devote limited time to each. But when it came to longevity, powerlifting did hold a distinct edge over track. In strength sports, people seemed to get better as they got older. Among the six lifters in my weight class in Brazil, one was thirty-four years old, one was thirty-eight, and one was fifty-one. Whereas my personal-best lift was 200 pounds away from being gold-medal caliber now, it could be 250 pounds higher ten years down the road. In track, meanwhile, there was a limited window to reach my peak speed. I would be faster at twenty-eight years old than I would be at thirty-eight. That nudged me ever closer to picking sprinting. Next, I called Hart.

"My heart's in track," I said. "What do you think I should do?"

"It's like this here, man," Hart told me. "No matter what, you've still got to get your satisfaction. If you're going to Beijing or if you're not going to Beijing, if you're more competitive in one or less competitive in the other, the only real question is: which one satisfies you the most? If you're going to China, don't just go to get there. At the end of it all, you have to have some personal satisfaction.

"You don't have to stick with powerlifting just because that's how all this started for you. I know you were really into lifting. I know because you and I drove up to Oklahoma so you could do the powerlifting. But I think that was something that helped keep your mind positive and competitive at a time when you had no idea that you were going to be running."

"I need to talk to my coaches," I said.

"It's not them," Hart said. "It's you. You're the one that has to figure this thing out. You're the one that has to be satisfied."

He was right. It was my choice. And the odds on getting to China had to be pushed to the back of the equation. The first thought had to be: what made me the happiest, the most fulfilled? What put the biggest smile on my face? Running. If you follow your passion, wherever it takes you is where you're supposed to be.

What was my best shot at glory? That also was running. Right now, I was a competitive powerlifter but not a great one. Maybe I wouldn't qualify for China as a sprinter. But if I did, on the day of the gold-medal race, I had a shot at winning. In my past life—and someplace still deep inside my body—I was a fast man. Someday that speed would return.

You have plenty of time to chase powerlifting, I told myself. *You have all the time in the world to get to the Paralympics. But if you do go to China, why not go for something that's in your soul? You are a runner.*

I called both Coach Jordan and Mary Hodge to let them know my decision. Coach Jordan thought it had been smart to continue both sports to boost my chances for making it to Beijing. Mary had believed that as a powerlifter, I would almost certainly be standing on the competition stage in China. But each one understood the path I had chosen.

As a full-time trackman, my first move was to try and shed 10 pounds, from 165 to 155, to lighten my stride. I tweaked my diet, swapping bacon and eggs for turkey strips and egg-white omelets. My training schedule changed, too. I continued to run and work on my sprinting technique on Mondays, Wednesdays, and Fridays, but Tuesdays and Thursdays were no longer dedicated to bench-pressing and triceps-pumping. In the weight room just off the indoor track at Penn State, I hit the leg machines to power up my hip flexors and reeled off numbing sets of leg presses, leg extensions, and leg curls. I noticed that with one sport in my head, my practices were more intense and my concentration was more fixed on the task at hand.

Coach Jordan watched and guided me. Then she came up with a brainstorm to build on my love for track and field—yet also boost the probability that I would reach Beijing with Team USA.

"Why don't we try the long jump?" she asked one day at the track.

She had prodded me to try long jumping in the spring of 2007, figuring that my speed and potent leg muscles would make me a natural. What's more, adding a field event that uses lower-body power wouldn't conflict with my sprinting training, and scheduling would be a breeze as well—as opposed to trying to balance powerlifting and track. But when Coach Jordan first suggested jumping, I wasn't sure I wanted to go airborne. I had worried about my prosthetic leg flying off during a 100-meter race. Would a suction-fastened socket stay attached at the explosive end of a flying leap? Would the knee and foot stand up to the pressure of a hard landing? If I kicked up plumes of sand during my impact, would some of those grains find their way into my hydraulic joint?

"Ahh, I'm kind of scared of it," I told her back then.

In the fall of 2007, I was still nervous about making a jump, but maybe I had gained a little more confidence in my prosthetic parts and in myself. When Coach Jordan asked this time, I recognized it as a pretty good idea.

"Why not?" I said.

My first jump was more like a swan dive: I sprinted down the runway on the indoor track, planted, leaped, and landed flat on my face. Sand from the pit covered me like a gritty blanket. Some of the Penn State jumpers had watched me and then glanced over at Coach Jordan.

"Yeah, I know," she said to them, "he's overrotating."

"Kortney, when you jump," she said to me as I dusted myself off, "you've got to look up. You do that and you'll land feet first. You have to trust yourself."

When long jumpers look at the ground or even at the pit as they sprint for the takeoff, they tend to reach out and lean forward once they hit the air. That causes the feet to fly up behind them. A belly landing usually follows. To stop the overrotation, Coach Jordan told me to keep my eyes and knees up during the jump. If I was long-jumping outside, I focused on the top of a nearby tree.

Inside, I looked at a metal barrier that was situated up and ahead me. Without worrying about hitting the takeoff board—a task we would tackle later—my early jumps measured 10 feet.

Next, we tried to stabilize my landings. I was worried about damaging my prosthetic leg by jamming my feet hard into the pit. But to jump properly, I had to drive with my natural left leg and then get both feet out in front of me before I made impact. It turned out that the prosthetic leg withstood the landing just fine, and Tim Rayer would build me a special cover to keep the sand from penetrating the knee's inner components. Still, there was one other flaw in my landing—my hands were tucked behind me. That created drag.

"Pull through and push forward with your arms," Coach Jordan advised.

Eventually, I began hitting 14 feet, and there was still a lot of room for technical improvement, and better distances. As I was a beginning jumper, we weren't too concerned with where I took my last step. I was trying to land as close to the takeoff board as possible—ideally the toes are just a fraction of an inch behind the back edge. I was usually starting my jumps before the board.

"I can work with a junior high kid and within an afternoon have him pretty close on the board," Coach Jordan said. "I'm not worried at all about getting you on the board yet. Let's just learn what it feels like to jump correctly."

The other piece of the takeoff involved my jumping foot, the dominant one that I pushed with at the end of my sprint. I had a choice—use the leg that felt normal or use my springy prosthetic foot, a possible advantage. I chose to stick with my natural foot because that's how I had always jumped. But Jeff Skiba, a below-knee amputee who holds the American and world disabled records in the high jump (6 feet, 10 2/3 inches), leaps off his prosthetic leg.

The final decision centered on my approach—how far back from the board and pit should I stand before breaking into my sprint? Most track coaches liked to say that a shorter approach was better than a longer one. The idea was to be at maximum acceleration when you leaped. You didn't want to be slowing down. Some of the best long-jumpers in the world used a 100-foot approach. Olympian Carl Lewis used a 171-foot approach—remarkably long—but he was still gaining speed at 100 feet. Mine, we figured, was about 80 feet.

With my technique fully assembled, it only took a week or two to see that long-jumping offered me an immediate chance at medaling in Beijing. I was consistently landing at 15 feet, 7 inches, or 4.75 meters. Among above-the-knee amputees in the sport, that would have ranked me fourth in the world in 2007 if I hit that mark at a sanctioned meet. The king of AK long jumping was a Polish-born German athlete, Wojtek Czyz. Born the same year as me, Czyz had been about to sign a contract with the Fortuna Cologne Football (soccer) Club when, during a game, he collided with the opposing goalie as they each chased a loose ball. The impact shattered his knee and ripped major blood vessels in his leg. He should have been rushed into surgery to restore the blood flow, but due to a delay in his treatment Czyz developed compartment syndrome and surgeons soon were forced to amputate his leg. Three years later, he represented Germany at the Summer Paralympics where he snared three gold medals in the 100- and 200-meter dashes and the long jump—an event where he set the world record at 6.23 meters, or 20 feet, 5 inches. Whether it was in sprinting or long-jumping, I knew someday I would come up against Czyz.

"Don't think about what you were, but about what you are—and what you long to be," was his motto, according to the Ossur Web site.

Smart words. And a hard lesson that all new amputees had to learn and embrace.

I always liked to know who I was chasing and what numbers I needed to attain. That information drove me toward my goal.

I asked for an orange cone to be put in the sand to mark an 18-foot jump, but Coach Jordan figured that my looking at the goal would cause me to overrotate and belly flop. She figured it would take a jump of 17.5 feet to qualify me for the U.S. Paralympic track team. Not that I was leaving sprinting behind. Obviously, Czyz excelled in each sport. But shortly after Coach Jordan planted that number in my head, I burst down the approach toward the pit, sprang off the board, got good air, and slammed my feet just a little deeper into the sand. Nearby, some Penn State long jumpers cheered not only my distance but my form.

"Wow, he looks like us," one of the long jumpers told Coach Jordan.

"That's because I trained him just like I would train an able-bodied athlete," she said. "I wanted to do as little variation as possible from how you train. We're working to make his form vary as little as possible from yours."

She clipped one end of the tape measure to the takeoff board, walked to the spot where my feet had slapped the sand, and placed the tape on the ground. She smiled.

"Close to eighteen feet!" she said.

Had that been an official track meet, my jump (5.47 meters) would have been the third-longest in the world that year for above-knee amputees.

"If you jump with a little wind behind you on a nice warm day, you could easily hit nineteen feet," Coach Jordan said. "You could be in the hunt for a medal right away."

Maybe it was the stress of school, or the challenge of balancing term papers and wind sprints. Or maybe it was what I had learned in school, specifically in one of my classes—Abnormal Psychology 270. Either way, as the cold weather settled in at Penn State, I fell into a funk. As it often does, the post-traumatic stress disorder returned without notice or reason, quietly tugging at my doubts and stealing my energy. This was a private battle waged by so many veterans of the wars in Iraq and Afghanistan. I needed to talk, but I didn't want to. I needed to share my feelings, but I wasn't close to anyone at Penn State who I thought would understand.

Strangely, as I was wrestling with the symptoms, I was also studying the disorder. In my psych class, we were looking into the high rate of PTSD among soldiers, watching footage of people who suffered from it. My classmates and I were learning about the very ailment that had been plaguing me since I returned to the United States. Pretty coincidental, when you think about it.

But while examining PTSD on an academic level, I realized that I had never really dealt with it on a personal level. I had asked a few questions about it while at BAMC. I had been prescribed antidepressant pills. But that's about as far as I had taken the battle. My classroom attention on the disorder may even have triggered the relapse. Then my phone rang. It was Jonathan Hart, and he was checking up on me. Two years earlier, his no-nonsense advice and patient listening skills had been my way out of the previous PTSD rut.

"You sure know when to call," I said. "I'm down. I can't put my finger on why. I'm surviving instead of thriving. Right now, I'm not living."

"Kortney, you know I have both legs so I can't sit here and say I know what you're going through," Hart said, talking to me as he drove through Birmingham. "But I can give you some of my thoughts if you want."

"Just speak," I said. "I need it."

His theory was that I had been running from reality ever since I got home.

"You know, you took on a lot, man. I mean, like going to Korea and the sprinting. You just jumped out there and you never really took the time to realize that you don't have a right leg. For the rest of your life, when the day ends, you've got to sit down and push off that leg."

I was listening.

"Sooner or later, you've got to accept the fact that after all the excitement of the day, you're still a man without his right leg and you will be for the rest of your life. All the running and weightlifting can take its place, but that's just temporary. When you get up in the morning, you have to be satisfied with yourself."

He was talking about acceptance. I had been slowly finding my way to a level of inner comfort. When I arrived at Penn State, I hid my prosthetic limb behind long pants. Then I wore an artificial leg with artificial skin. Then I wore the mechanical leg while in shorts. Semester by semester, I felt more at ease. But there also was a burden that came with being an amputee, the feeling of always being on display. There were the little eye-contact games. Some people stared. Most people would look at the leg from a distance but avert their eyes up close. I felt them watching me. That was never going to stop.

"Hey, the bottom line is, you have to accept yourself," Hart said. "People are just going to be people."

But maybe I hadn't really slowed down enough to grieve the loss of my right leg. There had been some tears at BAMC. Maybe there hadn't been enough. Maybe I really needed to sit with this reality.

"You can song-and-dance it all day long but still, when the sun is going down, this is what it looks like: a man without a leg. When you wake up in the morning, you're still a man without a leg," he said. "You have to allow yourself to mourn, allow yourself to get over it."

"Sometimes I revisit the things I went through back there," I said. "But once you get past the present, it doesn't mean it's gone forever. Once you get past the 'why me?' stage, someday you're going to want to know, 'Why me?' Maybe now is that time."

Chatting with Hart felt good, like I was able to let go of some tension. These weren't topics I wanted to share with anybody except maybe Hart and my parents. If I hung out with other friends, I didn't want to introduce these dark anxieties to them, to sit them down and say, "Okay, this is what I'm going through." They hadn't been in Iraq, but Hart had been there. He knew what it was like and went through it, too.

"You're a young man. This is going to come up with you again. But you are realizing that you can ask questions and you can figure it out," Hart said. "Pushing it off to the side and overlooking it? That just allows the disease to grow and hurt you.

"I guess it was about one year ago that we were talking about this same thing," he added.

"Yeah," I said. "Maybe we can make it two years before the next one comes along."

I decided it was time for me to talk to somebody on campus. I found a social worker and began unloading some of these thoughts. I realized that by keeping them buried, I was harming myself. I would always be a one-legged man sprinting toward a dream. But as I ran, I could also chase away some of those demons.

One afternoon after classes, I was riding my Segway across the hilly pathways of the Penn State campus. The upright, two-wheeled transporter was basically a high-tech scooter and probably best known for being favored by computer programmers in the Silicon Valley. My Segway had been donated in the fall of 2006 by a nonprofit group that was buying and distributing them to wounded military personnel. Walking from class to class in an artificial leg made me sweat and tired me out, but by navigating through Happy Valley on my Segway, I saved most of my energy for track practice later in the day. Once, when the Segway batteries died—forcing me to walk all day—I suffered muscle cramps in my legs during practice and actually fell on the track. For me, the Segway was an important sports tool. As I rolled along under an orange, red, and yellow canopy of autumn colors, my cell phone rang. But when I glanced at the screen to check the incoming number, it mysteriously only read: "202." I answered.

"Hi, Kortney," said the voice on the other end. "This is Dan Gade. I work at the White House."

The White House?

"How do you feel about the president?" he asked.

The White House wanted to know my opinion on the president? What was this all leading up to? I suddenly had a feeling the phone call was being tape recorded. I didn't have any problem with the president. I didn't hold a grudge for what had happened to me in Iraq. I knew when I enlisted in the army that there were risks, and that I might even die. President Bush had made a decision to go war. I had been asked to serve. I had done my duty. He had done his job as commander in chief.

"I'm not mad at him," I said. "I know he's doing the best he can."

"How would you like to come to the White House next Tuesday?" Gade asked. "You'll be riding a Segway there and you'll be riding with someone really important."

"I'll be there," I said.

Gade, it turned out, was a lot like me. While he was serving as an army major in Iraq, his infantry company was assigned to find and destroy insurgent-placed IEDs. On January 10, 2005—seven weeks before my injury—Gade's Humvee was rocked by one of those bombs, costing him his leg. After he recovered, President Bush appointed him as an associate director of the White House Domestic Policy Council, making Gade responsible for disability and health-care issues, including matters relating to active military personnel and veterans. He used a Segway, too. And he's been part of President Bush's work to overhaul the veteran's health-care system—which was shown to be overwhelmed and outdated in a 2007 *Washington Post* exposé on Walter Reed Army Medical Center. Bush had assembled a panel to study and write those health-care reforms. Gade, meanwhile, had been looking for two veterans to attend an important meeting of that presidential commission, and in his search he had turned to the man who had given me my Segway. Jerry Kerr ran a nonprofit called Disability Rights Advocates for Technology, or DRAFT, and he had dropped my name to Gade.

Kerr's group had donated eighty Segways to wounded vets, at a cost of about $5,300 apiece. I had been among the first recipients of a free, 12-mph scooter after submitting an application on the DRAFT Web site. Kerr said he had selected me because I had been an army medic and was hurt while saving another man. Kerr was a Segway user, too. He broke his neck while diving into a shallow lake in 1998 at the age of forty-four. The former real estate developer and home builder in St. Louis and Dallas was told he would be paralyzed from the neck down. But three hours of physical therapy each day helped Kerr relearn how to stand for limited stretches. The Segway gave him better mobility in his home and in his travels for the nonprofit, spelling him from constant wheelchair use.

"What was," Kerr liked to say, "is irrelevant. That's gone. You've got to remake yourself. I was a great golfer before this happened. I had a great life. I have a great life now but I've had to remake that life."

Kerr's undying belief in his "Segs4Vets" program was rooted in both function and psychology. People who lived in wheelchairs also lived below the eye level of the rest of the world. Conversations go on over their heads. Some folks feel awkward bending down to talk to them. Often, they are just overlooked. But when you ride a Segway, you are standing. And in Kerr's case, he used a seated Segway that raised him to about a 5-foot, 5-inch eye level. When he spoke, he looked people straight in the eye.

"I'll fly you to Washington and have someone pick you up at the airport," Kerr said. "They'll take you to get a Segway to use while you're at the White House."

On the day of my visit, I arrived at the northwest gate of the White House—off Pennsylvania Avenue—at about two thirty. I was accompanied by the other wounded vet that Kerr had recommended: Ryan Groves, who had served as a marine in Iraq and who had lost his left leg when a rocket-propelled grenade exploded near him in October 2004. Groves now was studying law at Georgetown University. After making our way through security, we each drove our Segways right into the West Wing of the White House. We rolled through a long lobby, took a left into a hallway, and then an immediate right into the Roosevelt Room. On top of a long wooden conference table, beneath a large skylight, I saw a name card: "Kortney Clemons." That was my seat.

The windowless Roosevelt Room, just across the hall from the Oval Office, served as the daily meeting spot for White House staff. Originally, it had been the president's office when the West Wing was built in 1902. Teddy Roosevelt had been the first president to work in that space. Now, a painting of Roosevelt on horseback, depicting his Rough Rider days, hung on a wall above the white-painted fireplace. I took my place. Also seated at the table were Secretary of Defense Robert Gates, several more wounded vets, some doctors, and the commission cochairs—former senator Bob Dole and former Clinton administration health secretary Donna Shalala. Then the president entered. He shook several hands and patted several backs. He made eye contact with me and squeezed my outstretched hand.

"Hey, Kortney, how's it going?" he asked. Apparently he remembered me from the *USA Today* article.

"Good, Mr. President," I said, still not believing the moment.

I hadn't expected to be part of an official White House meeting. I had envisioned maybe riding a Segway with the president, chatting a little. I had even brought along a gift—a blue and white Penn State tie—plus a thank-you card for the letter he had sent me. The front of the card read: "You're probably the kind of person who wakes up wondering, How can I make someone happy today?" On the inside, it read: "I'm so glad I was one of those people." Then, I added a note of my own: "Thank you for taking time out of your busy schedule to think of this little country boy from Mississippi. The letter I received from you guys really lifted my spirits and showed me what great people you are." I added a P.S.: "I'll be on the lookout for this tie!"

I had not anticipated attending a working meeting with President Bush. But there I was, sharing the table with the most powerful man in the world. He started by saying that later in the day he would be urging Congress to pass the series of reforms written by the commission. Their plan was to streamline the system under which military disabilities are evaluated and compensated, give retired soldiers financial incentives to go back to school, improve the treatment for soldiers with PTSD, and offer more help to the families of traumatically wounded veterans. That hit home with me. When my mother came to BAMC, she wasn't getting paid during those two months she spent in Texas, but she was eventually able to return to her job. Other patients' parents or spouses had lost their jobs while sitting next to those hospital beds for long stretches. The commission wanted to give parents and spouses the chance to take up to six months of unpaid leave without losing their jobs when their loved ones were seriously hurt in combat. Unlike other injured soldiers, I had not become tangled in the bureaucratic red tape of the current system. But as the president and the commission members each spoke about the issues, I was happy to see them hammering out a solution. Every U.S. military member in Iraq and Afghanistan had risked their life for the United States, now the government needed to show its support for those men and women who would never be the same.

At the table that day, I was glad to hear Bush say to Dole: "Whatever it takes."

Then the president looked at me with a smirk on his face.

"So, Kortney, when have you been up to?" he asked.

I wasn't expecting a personal question.

"Aw, nothing," I began, almost with a wince, knowing I had to come up with a much better answer. "Training for the Paralympics and going to school at Penn State right now."

"Where are the Games going to be held?" Bush asked. "Shanghai?"

"No, Beijing," I said. "I hope to be running the 100-meter dash there."

"I hope you do."

Then it was my turn to talk about the topic for the meeting. I told the commission members that these reforms and these benefits would help get maimed and disfigured soldiers back into the community where they belonged, not hiding in their homes.

"What most vets need to know is that they still have something to offer," I said. "Once they feel they have something to offer, they can be engaged in the community and just be productive in society."

After the forty-minute meeting, our group headed to the White House Rose Garden to meet the press. The president's speaking podium was flanked by beds of small yellow and red flowers. Journalists sat in chairs on the grass lawn. Six American flags hung along the sides of a walkway that led back to the West Wing. Dole and Shalala sat in chairs behind Bush. On the roof, a sniper watched the grounds with rifle in hand. Wearing a gray suit and a yellow tie, I stood off to the side on my Segway.

"Good afternoon," the president began. ". . . I just finished an inspiring meeting . . . with service members who are rebuilding their lives after being severely wounded in the service of our country. . . . I appreciate the fact that they are helping to define a culture that says we're going to judge people by their potential, not their disabilities. I appreciate the fact that they are demonstrating the great breakthroughs in technologies that are now available for the wounded. I don't know if you noticed, two of them came in on a Segway."

Bush then detailed the commission's work and explained its reform ideas. He had enacted the changes that he had the power to make, he said. He then called on Congress to put the rest of the recommendations into law. Dole and Shalala followed the president with short speeches. Then Dole looked my way.

"Come up here, Penn State," he said.

I liked Dole. He was a wounded vet, too. He had joined the army to fight in World War II and earned the rank of second lieutenant in the 10th Mountain Division. In April 1945, his unit had clashed with Nazis in the hills of northern Italy. When one of the platoon's radiomen was hit with gunfire, Dole crawled out of his foxhole to help him and was immediately strafed by a Nazi machine gunner, taking bullets in the upper right back and right arm, which was left almost unrecognizable. An army medic jabbed Dole with morphine to ease the pain and marked his forehead with an M in his own blood to alert other medics that he needed urgent treatment. After a nine-hour wait on the battlefield, Dole finally was taken to an evacuation hospital. His right arm was paralyzed. He earned a pair of Purple Hearts and the Bronze Medal Star for trying to save the radioman. He was tough. He was smart. He was funny. But now he wanted me to speak into a massive bank of microphones.

"Penn State, say something," Dole told me.

Oh, my God, I thought, *Senator Dole just put me in the hot seat. Whatever comes out of my mouth, let it be good.*

"We're taking a step in the right direction," I told the reporters. "We're providing our veterans with a chance to get back out in society. All of the vets who have come back seriously injured are walking inspirations without having to say a word. So these new benefits will help get them back into the community. It will better them and also better the public."

That day, there was one other surprise.

"You guys want to go to the Oval Office?" the president asked Groves and me.

We rode our Segways through a West Wing hallway, onto the carpet of the president's office, and right to the edge of his desk. We tried to get the president to step on and drive one of the transporters, but he declined with a big smile.

"No, I ain't getting on anymore," he said, referring to the day in 2003 he tried riding one but tumbled over the handlebars. "Somebody had a long lens and shot me from afar and put me on the front of the *New York Times*. I fell like a fool that day."

The mood was light. But the president understood that we were missing our legs because of a decision he had made four years earlier. He looked right at me and took responsibility.

"No matter what people's views are, if I should or shouldn't have gone over there, what we need to be doing now is getting behind you guys," he said. "This is not a publicity thing, having you here today. I'm going to do all I can do to make sure you guys are taken care of.

"You were injured because of my actions. The least I can do is to make sure you are taken care of when you get back home."

I had never held any bad feelings toward the president or his decision to send troops to Iraq. I saw my injury as a noble sacrifice. I believed that the morning the bomb exploded beneath me, I had been put in that spot for a reason. After returning to the United States, I had met one Iraq vet who had flown home physically intact only to lose his leg in a car accident. I was in therapy with a soldier who, on his way to Iraq, fell off a transport boat, got clipped by the propeller, and lost his leg. As awful as it was, my leg amputation had happened, I felt, in the best way possible—while in battle, working as a medic, helping another person. My wounds were sustained while I was serving a higher purpose. I could live with that. I had no anger about the circumstances of the injury. I held no blame toward anyone, except the person who made and placed the bomb.

The night President Bush had announced his launching of the war in Iraq—March 17, 2003—I was lying on Sgt. Mario Rodas's couch at his home on the army base in Germany. I had just undergone hernia surgery and had asked him if I could recuperate there. I'll never forget watching that moment: Bush sitting at his desk and speaking into the camera, to his right, an American flag, and to his left, a flag containing the presidential seal—carefully draped to show just the eagle's claw tightly clutching thirteen arrows.

"I know that the families of our military are praying that all those who serve will return safely and soon," he said that night. "Millions of Americans are praying with you for the safety of your loved ones and for the protection of the innocent. For your sacrifice, you have the gratitude and respect of the American people and you can know that our forces will be coming home as soon as their work is done."

Now I was talking with that same man. I was standing in front of that same desk—a 127-year-old piece of furniture made from the timbers of the British Royal Navy ship the HMS *Resolute*. My journey had come full circle.

This was the room where my life changed, I thought. *This was the place. I have become the man I am today because of the decision he made while sitting at that desk. I am standing here four years later. And I am not angry. I am proud.*

At my first big run of 2008, there were no clock and no lane lines, not even a starter's gun. But my heart was thumping hard enough to tell me that those were some of the most crucial strides of my life.

On April 9, five months before I hoped to run beneath the Paralympic caldron in China, I jogged with the Olympic flame in hand through the streets of San Francisco. I had been selected as one of the eighty torchbearers for the flame's only stop in the United States before it was flown to South America and Africa and ultimately delivered to the Olympic stadium in Beijing. I was humbled by the honor, yet also just a little bit nervous.

After the flame had arrived via jet from Paris, it was taken to the breezy shores of San Francisco Bay to begin what was supposed to be a six-mile relay—a "Journey of Harmony"—through the waterfront area. But thousands of protesters had vowed to disrupt the torch run to increase awareness of China's human rights policies in Tibet, throwing the afternoon into a chaotic blend of supersecrecy and police protection. First, city organizers decided to slash the planned route in half to bulk up security. That meant that we each had to share the torch with another runner. And at the last minute, the torchbearers were whisked around town in buses, unsure where we would be dropped off or where we would tote the flame. We weren't even allowed to bring cell phones, to ensure that the location of the torch wouldn't slip out to the protesters. The threats and the precautions were a shame, really. Politics had bled into sports. Even more, the flame is supposed to be a symbol of unity and peace, representing the Olympic ideal that feuding nations can lay down their arms and compete peacefully on the playing field. But I also understood that I had gone to war, in part, to protect the sacred American right to protest perceived wrongs and to speak our minds freely. I had risked my life for days like this.

In the back of one bus, I rode with NBA commissioner David Stern—that day just another torchbearer and not the boss of Kobe Bryant and LeBron James. Like the other runners, I wore a white, long-sleeve sweatshirt with the right shoulder and arm dyed red and adorned with the Olympic rings. I also sported white shorts and my artificial running leg. Stern noticed the hardware.

"Do you think I could play in the NBA on this prosthesis?" I asked with a grin.

"Actually," Stern said without missing a beat, "I was thinking of putting you in the slam-dunk contest."

Eventually, our group was deposited at different spots along Bay Street and told to wait for the relay. I stood with one other runner, a sixty-four-year-old Franciscan nun named Patricia Rayburn. Together we clutched our unlit torch, which was fueled by propane. My chest pounded with excitement. Our moment neared. Seconds later, we saw the wavy flame approaching in the hands of Stern and a young female athlete. They were engulfed by dozens of police officers on foot and on motorcycles. Stern and his running partner stopped and touched the cone of their torch to ours. The fire was transferred with the hiss of natural gas. I instantly felt the heat above my head. Then, Patricia and I were off and jogging, moving past hundreds of cheering people on the curbs and sidewalks.

Mom was squeezed into the happy pack that day. She had flown with me to San Francisco. Her presence there was fitting. How could I ever forget that day three years earlier when Mom had leaned close to my bed in a Texas hospital and told me I was going to conquer this thing? That afternoon in San Francisco, she represented all the people who once helped a broken man stand and then pushed him forward again.

This torch is a sign, a bright signal that the enemy didn't beat me and that the injury didn't beat me, I thought. *I'm still moving ahead in this life. Mom was right: I have defeated the wound; I have outrun the doubts.*

Not that I had made it all the way home. Not yet. My golden goal still pulled me forward like a distant, shining light on a dark horizon. It would all come down to a single meet in Atlanta in the summer of 2008. Run fast and jump far on that day, and I would be packing for China in September. I hoped to hit a qualifying time. I hoped to finally put together a perfect race, from start to middle to finish. I hoped to someday be the first above-knee amputee to officially cover 100 meters in less than 12 seconds. But my long trip—from two legs to one, from schoolboy to medic to man on a mission—had taught me to live in the moment. And on that April day, with the salty scent of the wharf wafting through the air, I was just enjoying a nice, slow jog, barely more than 100 yards in length. It gave me enough time to reflect on my tour of life and death.

Before my injury, if you had asked me to describe myself, I would have rattled off my sports accomplishments as if my trophy shelf made up the very best parts of me. For so many years, I thought that what I did made me who I am. Now, I see things a little differently. Who is Kortney? He's a guy who loves family. He's a guy who realizes that our true purpose for living is far bigger than just serving ourselves. It is to be there for each other. He's a guy who is happy as long as he's cutting through the sunshine, and not buried six feet below. Another few seconds on that Baghdad highway, and maybe that's where I would be today. But there was a reason why I have remained here. And I believed that reason was to run, to overcome, to inspire.

In the end, I have found my way. I have been permanently wounded, yes. But it hasn't ruined my life. I once had fallen. But I have never quit.

I slapped Bay Street with my artificial foot and then with my natural foot. As we moved closer to the next torchbearers, ready to make the handoff, the Olympic flame danced just above my head. I was running in the moment but headed to somewhere. And in my ears, I felt the wind.

Index

Printed in the USA
CPSIA information can be obtained
at www.ICGtesting.com
JSHW082154140824
68134JS00014B/227

9 781630 260422